HEALING POINT OF WORLD
INTER- RACIAL HOPE
WHO AND WHAT WILL CHANGE AMERICA 2016 ONWARDS?

BERNIE SANDERS – INSPIRES HEALTH & EDUCATION

HILLARY – FIGHTING FOR YOU

TRUMP – MAKE AMERICA GREAT AGAIN?- HOW?

WHAT AFRICANS ARE MISSING

PREVENTING THE THIRD WORLD WAR – PUTIN OR OBAMA

Is Russia-China making Love with Africa- for a New World Order? HOW CAN
AMERICA LEAD AGAIN? ESTABLISHMENT VS DEMOCRACY

HOW TRUE DEMOCRACIES WILL PREVENT 3RD WORLD WARS

OBAMACARE CIVIL WAR - LEADING TO NEW WORLD ORDER

INTERNET-NEWEST WEAPON TO NEW WORLD ORDER

CLIVEN BUNDY SLAVERY POLITICS OF GLOBALIZATION

MENTAL HEALTH –BERNIE SANDERS' CALL

Emeagwali – Super Computer internet Discover y

Clinton to Barack–Apology to Slavery great

Baraka, Peace, Netanyahu

Tribal - Blind Formula

Collin Powell Turning

AUTHOR – DR. UHURU NYABUTO MANGERERE (FORMER CEO - RITAR PHARMA)

Healing Point Of Inter- Racial Hope

Uhuru Nyabuto Mangerere

authorHOUSE®

AuthorHouse™
1663 Liberty Drive
Bloomington, IN 47403
www.authorhouse.com
Phone: 1 (800) 839-8640

Published by AuthorHouse 04/08/2016

ISBN: 978-1-5049-8417-1 (sc)
ISBN: 978-1-5049-8418-8 (e)

Library of Congress Control Number: 2016904129

Print information available on the last page.

CHAPTER I

NEW WORLD ORDER -BY AMERICA OR RUSSIA?

HOW TO PREVENT 3ᴿᴰ WORLD WAR

MIS-EDUCATION - THE ROOT CAUSE OF THIRD WORLD WAR

INTERNET DISCOVERY, ONLINE EDUCATION CRISES MAY TRIGGER WORLD ORDER – (Obama vs Netanyahu on Israel vs Iran) who should order who? Who has the right to order the world?

GLOBAL IDENTITY AND WORLD ORDER POLICY ROOTS OF WAR

It is America's time of elections in the 2016 year when racial issues have been so intensely highlighted than any other electioneering period in more than half a century of American history. It is important to differentiate the three major candidates that include Bernie Sanders, Hillary Clinton, and Donald Trump to determine what and who can real influence a new world order based on an American orderly politics. In an American electioneering, it is usually either a political substance or a race-based choice that influences voters. While Bernie Sanders seems to be the most inspiring and as a former civil rights activist in the 1960s at the times of Dr. Martin L. King, Hillary Clinton points out that she will keep fighting for us based on record. While that is happening, Donald Trump keeps saying he is running to win so as he can make America great again without actually substantiating on the process or method he will use in order to do the job. That is why it is very important to read this book in order to see who is best qualified for the job of a US president that can influence the development of a new and workable world order for the healing of inter-racial tensions in the United States to make America great again.

For the past several years and decades many people and particularly leaders have shied away from discussing the real issues in America that have resulted in the current inter-racial tensions in the country and around the world that sometimes include terrorism. As a consequence, the United States racial protests have displayed a wrong picture to the world so as to look like a disorderly country where a world order cannot be cultivated or originated from. In that respect, many people and particularly democrats have accused Republican presidential front-runner candidate, Donald Trump for being the patron of such tensions from which protests have originated even though he denies it all. While many people do question what and why there should be a one world order for the planet we call Earth and how or whether it can ever be valid, the majority don't seek the real answers to determine the root causes of the current world disorders or wars for that matter. Whether we accept it or not a valid new world order is strictly going to depend on plain respect between one another in terms of people and countries counting on equal opportunity in education and employment from a global perspective. The number one priority on the race to determine the inventor and owner of the new world order is a totally dependent on a diversified educational program and a united power base among the few superpower countries of the world with guaranteed respect between them and other nations. Whoever will be more united at home will actually determine the future of the new world order abroad especially when we look back 500 years in human history in many references including the ones in the back of this book. The current wars that are both holy and physical are still based on anti-colonial sentiments of the past centuries. Among the two superpowers, Russia seems to be more united at their homes than outside while America is getting more and more divided on the issues of race and equal opportunity such as on employment and universal healthcare. China remains the economic superpower which can decide to play a role as to who sways the new world order while Africa remains the pillar of the same new spirit in scramble. It is extremely crucial to determine the causes of the extreme deterioration on unity in America that still claims to be the wealthiest in the world. That is why the second chapter in this book is dedicated to the issues of mental health in the current world and especially among our own leaders in America as pointed out by the inspiring Bernie Sanders in 2016.

According to the most recent news online by **Epoch Times, House of Commons,** some media sources claimed that a major nuclear war may be on the edge of exploding due to continued tensions between Russia and the United States nations on which account they quoted the West as the likely loser by the view of things. Globalization which controls the world order seems to be in bad tune and should be well understood to prevent that possibility of the third world war. Globalization is the ability of many people, literacy, ideas, culture and technology to move from country to country to interact under various diverse lines or identities and educational backgrounds for the better even though the current indications are worsening. America has been the best for most of the last century and described as the land of opportunities and freedom for all. However, America is terribly being weakened in that leadership by the escalating internal civil wars based on reduced opportunity and diversity and hence utilized as a weapon of destruction by foreign superpowers like Russia and China. The author of this book is mainly focusing on how the audacity of hope can still be reclaimed by whoever will envision the dangers behind its dishonest opposition both at home and abroad. In that respect, it is good to start at the very basis of the current conditions which are strictly confounded on global identity and culture as implicated by networking and online education.

The term culture is the strongest phrase that has recently come from president Putin that scares most of the western world and its true allies. Russian President Putin's strongest words came from one of his bloggers as follows: Leonid Kaganov, one of Russia's most influential bloggers, recently posted what he labeled the "Ten Commandments of the New Russian State." It opens, in pitch-perfect parody of the regime's latest line, with the statement: "Russia is the country that is the world's biggest in size" Well, that is true, but other mentioned things might not be necessarily true including population, level of development, culture, intelligence, modesty, honesty and justice. Under the same article, Russia went on to lament those others by saying they are completely surrounded by Gayropa and its whores are visible on all sides. Those people who falsely worship a notion of liberty deeply alien to them and are actually likely to cause a cultural problem. While that may be true under the terms of culture and intellectual illiteracy, America has stood as the leader of the new world order for most of the last century strengthened by an economic powerhouse that was only second to none. However, with China having overtaken America just two months before the end of the year 2014, there are fears that a new world order might be heading on to a new course that will leave America more struggling than ever before. Culture and literacy seems to be the determining factors for America, Russia or China and whoever will come up with the fairest strategic formula will determine the implementation of the new world order in that perspective.

According to Carolyn Howard in the Forbes magazine, it was generally agreed with some heat last year that world power had been swayed from America when they named the Russian President, Vladimir Putin as the most powerful man in the universe. That was quoted following one year after president Putin annexed Crimea and staged a proxy war in the Ukraine while still concluding a deal to build a more than $70 billion gas pipeline with China that became the planet's largest construction project in history. Within that perspective our choice simply became prescient without concrete remedies to such a development. As a consequence, Russia currently looks more and more like an energy-rich, nuclear-tipped rogue state that is equipped with an undisputed, unpredictable and unaccountable head of the world as much as it continues to stand in favor with unconstrained world survey opinions in the pursuit of its superiority ideals and goals to be achieved.

The more the spread of the above information especially on the terms of the human culture and civil rights through the discovery of the super-computer, the more the fresher and critical the new world order gets affected and probably into place with unstoppable speed. There are only three words which would determine the future of the new world order and those include banking, money and equality for a healthier world. Those are the same words that have shaped the previous world orders and particularly from the beginning of the industrial revolution and even currently so by the discovery of the supercomputer and the internet communication. The internet communication has actually led into the current distribution of banking rights and skills all over the world so that any underlying disparities and inequalities are easily detectable by everybody at the touch of a button on the internet. The consequence is that everybody or whoever understands it will stand to the base of the shaping of the new world order. That is the same basic cause that is currently determining the crisis between President Obama's internal civil war in health care and other unaccomplished opportunities for all Americans. Similarly, there is an eminent war between him and Putin on a possible route to a third world war that is leading to the fight between the dollar and other financial currencies and to what the real money identity should be for the world trading systems with freedom and wisdom. The real cause of the current world order crisis seems to be based on the questions rooted in the financial wisdom of the prevailing systems and the attached constitutional foundational histories. While many including United States Former Secretary of State to President Richard Nixon, Henry Kissinger has recently asked some similar tough questions in his book, he did not really offer specific and workable answers that can lead to a fair new world order especially for the for the Middle East or Russia and China as Super powers. According to him the U.S. must be prepared to answer a number of questions for itself as: What it would do or seek to prevent, no matter how it happens, and if necessary alone? What it would seek to achieve, even if not supported by any multilateral effort? What it would seek to achieve, or prevent, only if supported by an alliance? What it should not engage in, even if urged on by a multilateral group or an alliance? What is the nature of the values that it seeks to advance? And how much does the application of these values depend on circumstance? Some of these questions are real tough and so costly that former very intelligent General Collin Powell could call a turning point to them as he did when he was the United States Secretary of State before self-resignation on the basis that the resulting profits are next to nothing.

One of the above statements is just like quoting the words of former South African Nelson Mandela's book of "on no easy walk to freedom" where he said that no particular force will stop a determined group of human beings from achieving their freedom rights and which I think is the basic determination of the future of the new world order to be. However, since the world is so large, the determining factor has to be cultivated from the root causes among the major players of America and Russia as charity begins at home. Is the America leadership able to see that as well as its voters? That is where the points of healthcare remain the greatest blessings if a unifying agent could be formulated and implemented. If America cannot unite on healthcare to cover all races fairly in the given context of proper vision, then anything contrary could only be the weapon of self-destruction and a source of happiness to its major rival nation of Russia and its allies like China.

Globalization either stands behind educational achievements or an expansion of the status quo in terms of the classical pursuits of various opportunities in businesses. The former seems to be true because as recently as in the year 2011, an African, Maurice Johnson, with a doctorate in engineering physics was standing out as a homeless person in the township of Boston in the United States of America. World history confirms that globalization has always been basically induced by monetary factors or related interests like healthcare insurance disparities that have created the greatest internal civil war in the United States. That can lead to a global or more precisely a Third World War because such domestic wars accompanied with unemployment discrimination add up to display a weakening factor that can be utilized by several competitors or enemies towards any downfall of America and hence a disordered world in cultivation. It is basically true that such kinds of policy differences and interests caused the United States president Baraka Obama to accuse Russia for not inviting or allowing any immigrants into their country while his own republican opponents are against all that he administers as their president including the current immigration bill in dilemma and confusion.

As Presidents Obama for United States and Russia's Putin keep on sparring, the world has to remember that when elephants fight, it is the grass that suffers and much the same way as when they make love. While that was happening, Obama was being sued for trying to solve a century old healthcare insurance problem among minorities or African Americans even when he satisfied billionaire Donald Trump with a birth certificate to prove he was born in America. It seemed to some that both the impeachment suit by his Republican Party opponents and Putin's sparring tactics are based on the mental health of wealth wellness along the lines of cultural competency and literacy. The scramble for money will never end as the process aims at how and when to accumulate wealth in banks and other institutions indefinitely without any foreseeable satisfaction. Consequently, the world is experiencing many new turning points as the scramble for wealth deposit interest escalates all over the world. It is time for a real healing strategy to be implemented as the concern of this publication will indicate in all forthcoming chapters.

Education and identity has exploded as recently as this year of 2014 with new analyzes that may be recognized in the case of Russia and the United State scrambling for Ukraine as well as Cliven Bundy who was broadcasted as a rancher from the Southern states of America talking about African slavery. In ages past people, ideas and technology have interacted with one another in crucial ways, but none has been more emphasized than those related to identity and territorial land reclamations around the world particularly in Africa, Middle East, and Russia. While many may try to overlook on the effects of identity in globalization, certain experiences are very substantial in explaining the source of several disparities that are often a universal challenge beginning with educational propagandists in some institutions. The basic cause of war in any place in world history whether in the past present or in the future is always construed in behavioral injustices and disparities among human beings across various groups, races or tribes. It should be a serious mental health issue for anyone or any leader not to be able to focus and understand such an element that is so obvious in life. Justice has to be clear and transparent especially in educational opportunities if we expect to gain a healing point and declare victory to claim the new world order leadership once again. Since it seems to be getting hotter in that perspective, the current Obama administration needs to assign more funding into the healthcare research that is strongly focusing on mental health developments as stated in the second chapter of this book and as called upon by the 2016 democratic presidential candidate, Bernie Snaders. It is either Universal Healthcare or free education as we see in Germany or the struggle continues.

CHAPTER II

WORLD ORDER BY MENTAL
HEALTH LITERACY

CORPORATE POLITICS (IDENTITY AND CULTURAL)

As stated, a mind is terrible thing to waste. Mental health depends on the state of the mind which dictates the nature of the world order or otherwise disorder is inevitable. A peaceful mind would always be based on good mental health that can trigger proper judgment on small domestic matters as well as big ones like the foreign policies in development. Among the three 2016 presidential candidates mentioned earlier, Bernie Sanders has apparently a high score based on his judgment against the Iraq war in 2003. Thus, he recently called for the establishment of more mental clinics in America because of what he saw going on the immediate previous night within the Republican party debate where Donald Trump is the front-runner. When we see such a reaction from a strongly principled and inspiring presidential candidate presenting such criticism for and for the whole world watching on CNN news then the conclusion is that I have a valid case to analyze in this chapter as well as the forthcoming ones for especially the younger generation to read on.

It is commonly an indisputable fact that differences in ideologies and politics have resulted in the world viewing the proper definition of mental health in different ways as a complex issue. Consequently, the two major world ideologies of capitalism and communism have continued to shape up politics so as to expand or reduce the exploration of education, colonialism and slavery whenever it doesn't benefit the majority. While we tend to think that we could be mentally the best group in the way we live in United States, there are a lot of people out there who think China or Russia are still better thinkers in terms of what mental health should be for the pursuit of happiness. Who is really mentally sick or mentally illiterate? Is it a capitalist, communist, socialist, all or none of those elements? As early as during the writing of this book, we have cited the previously mentioned and former Cuban President Fidel Castro accusing former presidential candidate John McCain on the basis of justice in the Middle East between Israel and Palestine statehood. Castro went on to compare North Atlantic Treaty Organization to Nazis and while blasting out at the United States of America under the famous justice, Henry Kissinger was talking about world order elsewhere in a new book in publication process. As much as it may concern some of us, it looks like the melting point of world justice starts from an inclusively justified world order measurable by one yardstick that allows the pursuit of happiness by all humans inhabiting the earth.

Fidel Castro became popular when he offered full and tremendous support towards South Africa's Freedom when former President Nelson Mandela was serving the 27-year prison term in Roden Island. For the past half a century, Fidel Castro has emerged as a public eye for the oppressed without realizing that he had always been regarded by America as a dictator ruling without a democratic principle of free will and power-sharing strategy. According to some related comparisons that could include pictures online, the Cuban leader and former president Fidel Castro were spotted sitting next to his brother and current president, Raul, in Havana in the year 2013. At that event which took place in Havana, the former Cuban ex-president Fidel Castro criticized the United States and Europe as the main instigators of the current misunderstandings on racing upon superiority military contests.

Under the same circumstances that appeared in a humiliating article that was actually published in Cuban state media, the father of the island's communist revolution added more fuel to the issue when he went ahead to attack the United State Senator John McCain on other issues. In that respect, he expressed a lot of negativity on the forefront runners of world justice who he claimed were simply political pointers who lacked instrumental implementation of equality in that perspective. Later, the senator advised President Obama against the establishment of independent States in Eastern Asia or Middle East that could support justice development and transparency in that region of the world. That could have been before visiting Kenya as the first Kenyan African American President of the United States of America in the year that followed. However, President Obama avoided buying into that ideology. The condemnation was something that needed the world to deeply analyze to re-ignite a peaceful dialogue and lead a new healing on inter-racial hope in justice. In that point of reference, he did reveal that the world has seen no sign of justice or equality in recent years within the given superiority contest based on the military powers. During that session they found it quite necessary to reiterate that time had come to impose factors that demand world equality by settling scores with what was left of two great nations of Russia and China in order to begin a new healing process on inter-racial development. In the given circumstances the 88-year-old former leader or dictator as some could describe him reiterated that the two great nations had carried out the most justifiable economic and political events that many considered extraordinarily popular deeds by putting an end to the imperialist military or colonially influenced universal order that only history could analyze. That speech is still under scrutiny even though widely popular in some areas or regional centers.

The above speech while sounding so spectacularly peculiar continued on to accuse the West of practicing biases while talking peace and democracy and said the vestigial related structures had become a signal of imperialist policy explorations that is still being defended in various educational and political strategies. The former leader singled out McCain, who was the 2008 Republican presidential candidate by saying that as contrary as he was he had supported Israel's Mossad intelligence agency and participated together with that political development in the creation of the Islamic State and other regional spies in the region. Consequently, at the writing of this book that agency was quoted as the controller of a considerable and vital portion of Iraq and reportedly one-third of Syria as well when assessing the whole region in the same political or military context.

Inter-racial healing cannot be achieved without raising all the past related issues openly and peacefully without fear. In that respect, many commentators and politicians have stayed calm on Germany in the past because truth might be too bitter to take as the common saying states. Thus, in one of the most tortuous speeches in recent years, Castro reminded the world more about Germany's role on inter-racial healing when he said that Adolf Hitler's greed-based empire went down in history with no more glory than fire with the encouragement provided to NATO's aggressive operations and influences. The warriors' influences to other national and international governments, exposes the real interests that implicates them as the laughing stock of the whole world.

The above article could definitely anger a lot of people, but there are always workable elements on both sides of the coin who find themselves in one or two tunes of alignment. The above writing comes only after a serious racial incident in Ferguson city in Saint Loius of the Missouri State. Racism is based on mental health and extrapolated by those who are mentally handicapped and who were recently described by some researchers as idiots in terms of the intelligent quotient analysis. As previously mentioned above, the current poverty in the world and especially among Africans goes back to the consequences of slavery for which the remedy is still on and developing. However, as of the writing of this book, racism is the main cause of poverty and inequality as more and more billionaires continue to be created and the gap between the poor and the rich gets larger and larger. In the same respect the greed, selfishness and ignorance are founded on the vestiges of education, colonialism and slavery. Before the end of that sentence someone somewhere could have already submitted a conscious reaction of an underlying case of a mental health issue. Thus, it is important to examine some analytical points in mental health research itself in the world of diverse backgrounds and the related impacts in various cultures in legislation programs on globalization development.

Another awarding winning author, Andy Schmookler stressed that the spirit that drove America to civil wars is back in 2014 with the conflicts that prevailed through the year which were mainly centralized on equality and health insurance. Some of the statements that were displayed in various news lines seemed to depict that the works of literature parables which reflect examples of identifying by match-ups if the features match up. When such features are displayed then one concludes that it is almost certain it is the same guy being identified in the given politically driven circumstances. Consequently, it seems quite conceivable that it is with the match between the force that drove us to Civil War more than a century and a half ago, and the force that has taken over the Republican Party in our times that is in operation. One can question whether there a genetic match or simply a political miscalculation coincidence. While many may not be able to see through the analysis, it certainly seems to be true with some visible similarities because in both cases, we see an ignorant group of people and probably within the middle and the class levels insisting on monopolizing their so called liberty. In that they hold strong feelings by which they mean the freedom to dominate whenever their tactics are convincing and purely undetected on any flaws or loopholes that there may exist. In many perspectives the so called elite have declared that their "freedom of speech" gives them the right to buy our elections. That means that if one is not able to be part of the buying team, the person is excluded and locked out without any rights accessibility to see, be heard or involved in any participation.

On the issue of freedom and participation rights, it is fair and interesting to look back into the 1850s, when the slaveholders insisted that their liberty had a specific implication that they had given them the right to take their human property to any place they so wished in the continental American territory. Many of the enslaved culture and community citizens were struggling to survive in the opposite side of the freedom lines of development. However, in both cases of the aisle, the use of the structures of American democracy was combined with contempt for the democratic values that inspired many people and particularly several fore-founders of the current systems.

In what is considered an initiative to destroy democracy as an institution, the Republicans have made a national effort to pass voter identity laws to address a non-existent problem of voter fraud. In many perspectives the idea may just be a plunder which is a campaign that is in itself a fraud whose transparent intent is to dismantle the democratic followers. Such strategies usually backfire within a short scope of time. That is because they are all backed by the current conflicts of racism as instituted in various sectors and in natural human behaviors as depicted in a variety of writings. However, back in the years leading up to the Civil War, the slaveholders banned the distribution of anti-slavery writings, and sometimes suppressed anti-slavery talk by violent retaliations as it can be witnessed current situations in unemployment and inequality on opportunity.

While various protests could be initiated in the above struggle in the given cases, the elites driving the polarization of the country surrounded by racial tensions and conflicts justified their dominance by truth distortion, in degrading methods, the humanity of those they sought to exploit in undernourished political atmospheres. That is still happening in large operations as of the writing of this book.

In another recent political explosion, republicans talked about a 47 percent or about the half of the country by characterizing them as "takers," even though many of those 47 percent work multiple jobs just to make ends meet. They continued on to expand the exploitation by voting to strip them of unemployment benefits, at a time of massive joblessness, in the mistaken belief that only desperation will get these lazy people to work. That happens when they talk about aiding other countries they so call allies.

Something that could cause laughter to many progressive groups in the world is to commend slavery as it is understood from the past centuries. During those dark times of the past in the time of the Slave Power, the slaveholding class declared they were doing their black slaves a favor to discipline them into an ethic of work as they claimed there was an element of laziness detected among Africans. Along with that claim, they reiterated that freeing the slaves would be cruel, because those blacks were inherently too lazy and incompetent to survive on their own. That was very controversial and irrational untruthfulness because it was the slaves who stood as the main workers as they did so without pay.

At the turning point of world history in events that may lead to the third world war, the United States party of republicans does not seek to negotiate or compromise. According to any such initiatives the dynamics of the party are such that anyone who works toward compromise is condemned and demonized so much as to quit or run out of office by a challenger from the more extreme, uncompromising wing of the party or the base lobbyists. However, back in the years under which slavery caused the terrible American Civil War, the South's insisted on the unfettered expansion of their domain for the survival of the insane political goals in what could later be called political blindness on the basis of long term achievements. That same structure of the circumstances led to the overturning of the great Missouri Compromise, which had held the nation together for more than thirty years. The final consequence was the encountered fracture of the peace that instigated the return to the political arena of Abraham Lincoln, and set the nation on course to a bloody civil war that should be a good lesson in today's political events.

One of the major lessons in recent democracy is that for the first time in the world or American history, a minority was elected president contrary to the belief that the majority must always rule no matter what the case may be. According to the above events in both cases, the powerful elite in the grip of that destructive force refused to accept that in a democracy sometimes you win and sometimes you lose, and sometimes you have to accept being governed by a duly-elected president you don't like to avoid dictatorship. However, the current republicans have tried to nullify the presidency of Barack Obama, whom the American people duly elected twice regardless of his minority status. Like no other opposition party in American history, they have refused to accept the temporary minority status to which American voters have consigned them. Blocking the president from performing the function for which the people hired him has been their top priority even when they openly know the feelings and consequences of the backfiring that is always inevitable.

On the basis of the historical collections, it was noted that around the eve of the Civil War, most of the conservative Southerners who had displayed political inequality dominated the upper structures of the national governing councils from the time of its foundation roots. One may then ask the question of whether the same truth could be emerging again in the current political differences and how solutions can be initiated. Those conservatives actually considered the election of Abraham Lincoln as president an unbearable frustration. Consequently, they decided to move promptly with an intention to break apart from the Union that made up the United States in a unilateral way. Thus, they then formed an army to defend the unilateral decision to invalidate the democratic process if they could not win the election. It seemed therefore that democracy was only favorable when the conservatives won the election and the final outcome was aligned to their interests instead of waiting to try their luck in the next election.

As much as the author recommends, the answer to the above question of indifference resides on both cultural education and environmental influences as many things keep spreading continually without any appropriate filtrations. That is because as with facial recognition, the configuration of the features that start from such high places as Washington and Moscow, it is quite conceivable that the same ugly thing is or has just come back again with the gun laws that differ from state to state. It is the same reasons that I will be expanding on the educational base expressions in my upcoming publication series of this book. In those series, I will try to expand on the ways in which some of the most disturbing patterns of educational or political conflicts match up to shape the future of the world order both politically and militarily. Respectively, I will also be explaining how inheritance counts more than any other factors in shaping history and as to how such patterns can dictate and re-emerge in a cultural system over the course of generations unless it is well marked.

Whether we accept it or not the current racial conflicts in America are proving some facts of interest to the world that may result in several conditions towards the creation of the real turning point in human history. The consequence of such conflicts is that in its re-emerged form, the magnitude of pattern or force or spirit has retained its destructive nature without reasonable and long term remedy measures because in our times, it is damaging everything in American civilization that it can reach in every capacity.

According to the current mongering about the Third World War, it is virtually true that diversity is an important agent of treatment or rehabilitation in the development of a new world order. There is no way a new world order can prevail with recognizing the importance of one another in co-existence. It is important for the United States Health Insurance policy reform systems as well as the whole world to prevent the possibility of a Third World War or more precisely a nuclear war. Consequently, Russia had the following message from last week's news by the publishing of this book which is one of the most important and intelligent actions to take in preventing the looming third world war:

As recently as last year around September 16, 2014, Russia's Lavrov pronounced

Africa as the future pinnacle of new world order without too much shyness or any reservations. Lavrov was in a situation where he had to tell the truth about Africa because of the repeatedly wrong images that had always been displayed about the great continent. According to his statement and mired in a conflict in Ukraine and isolated by the West,

Russia sought to woo African allies on various political dialogues, with foreign minister Sergei Lavrov hailing the continent's role in a new world order despite its long term description as a dark continent. Russia and China seem to have learned the greatest lesson in world history of recognizing the least of this or the most disrespected of all human beings. "Africa is one of the pillars of the evolving world system," Lavrov said during a visit to Zimbabwe, where he signed co-operation deals and won diplomatic backing for the fight against Western sanctions.

Russian Foreign Minister Sergei Lavrov (L) and Zimbabwean President Robert Mugabe (R) shake hands in Zvimba on September 16, 2014 (AFP Photo/Jekesai Njikizana)
Darwendale (Zimbabwe) (AFP) –

During that speech, Lavrov delivered some of the strongest and positive words about Africa for a long time. While describing his sanction-hit host President Robert Mugabe as a "legend" and "historic figure", Lavrov slammed the West's increasingly tough response to Russia's actions in Ukraine. The most recent wave of Western measures targeted Russia's banking, energy and defense sectors which resulted on the ruble's crashing to record lows after long term stability. In same special words, Lavrov said that all were convinced that those unilateral coercive policies have no future," Lavrov said. "What is important these days is to recognize the pluralism in the international community and respect for one another with equality."

Over the last century, a notably main world feature was that during the Cold War the Soviet Union and the West scrambled for influence in Africa particularly on installing puppet leaders and igniting proxy wars that killed millions from Angola to Mozambique. Within the given perspective Russia hopes to once again enlist allies on the continent, where rapid economic growth is predicted in the coming years, as a counterweight to the Western or American influence. As carefully laid down, there is no coming back to a unipolar or a bi-polar world in the current transformation of the new world order. The future of the world order would only be multiple; otherwise the whole system would not be sustainable. From a point of accomplishments based on political neutrality, Lavrov won support from Zimbabwean President Robert Mugabe who hosted him even though he has long been thorn in the side of Africa's former colonizers inflicting a lot of suffering for more than a decade all based on sanctions imposed to counter the events of rights records. In response to such sanctions, President Mugabe said that the Western sanctions against Russia were groundless an illegal because they had not been approved by the United Nations. President Mugabe said delivered that statement after sealing a $3 billion or an equivalency of 2.3 billion-euro investment for Russian business to tap Zimbabwe's platinum resources. In the same respect, president Mugabe said the sanctions are so lawless that displays part of our international community seeking to dominate the rest of the world and the answer should be no. He noted that there are proper rules that should be followed and such a reaction must never be allowed to go on if a new world order is ever going to be dreamed about with acceptable mental health standards in that approach.

In this chapter and the underlying analysis, the focus is to evaluate the extent to which a new world order in terms of diversity and cultural competence affects the law of mental health in organizational development in progressive institutions. Mental health is one of the most complex human subjects in modern science especially when superiority and civilization get to a crushing point as witnessed between Russia and the United States. The global tensions that hold the most heat are rooted in the diversity of cultural superiority between the European and Russian civilization or more precisely between the West and the East under the political terms of description. The so called cold war is and was nothing but an expansion of the East or the Western civilization which resulted in the development of nuclear weapons that can destroy the whole world in a matter of days. It is definitely a mental disorder to think along the lines of expanding self-interests from one's home area to the rest of the world claiming to be superior to others and vowing to crush any resistance to that superiority. Mental disorders and their care present unusual problems within biomedical ethics as defined by culture and diversity. The disorders themselves invite an ethical critique, as does society's attitude to them while researching the diagnosis and treatment of mental disorders also presents special ethical issues. The current high profile of mental disorder ethics, emphasized by recent political and legal developments, makes this a field of research that is not only important but also highly topical for the betterment of health care law and administration. The big question is that of determining the best state and site to tackle the problem.

As quoted earlier, the most important site is the development of a law that can overhaul the root causing agents of the diversity injustice on the basis of education, colonialism and slavery from a universal perspective. When people hear that there is a body of United Nations Organizations in the world, there develops an immediate reaction with an excitement of actually improving good, positive and honest intentions of bringing all human beings to a universal family. However, as rare as it has been always and as feasibly postulated there is an extremely slim number of leaders or professionals who have tried to identify the corrective mechanical site or root cause at which a non-working law can be repaired. Just like any other overhauls in development, any law can be overhauled or amended much the same way as was the case on segregation during the civil Rights Movements. For an industrial world that keeps on inventing and formulating new innovative technologies too much love for money seems to be the root cause of all bad laws and wars that lead to mental health issues such as those related to racism and discrimination on education and employment.

An important area that can serve as a high resolution site is an overhaul of the law of elementary education or the irrational non-cultural developmental law with respect to the proposed theory of permittivity mentioned earlier. That site could be quite appropriate for the corrective applications for the resultant mental health repercussions or consequences related to international conflicts around the world. Many people could politicize such an idea with the claim that it is unlikely to function if democracy has not taken root in some countries even though they are part of the United Nations workforce. While that may be true, it is also true and reasonable to recognize how the world's former largest nation and Super-power could come to a point of accepting democracy as an imperfect system of government, but still stand as the fairest option that is second to none in administration. Any system has its own disadvantages especially when it comes to corruption mental disorders unless early therapeutic overhauls are implemented at the highlighted specific site in development. However, the law of educational growth and development is still the most controversial from a universal and cultural perspective. Consequently, the worldwide nations can never be at war if a diverse equality law is devised so that all human beings see one another as equals in terms of freedom and independent self-productive as opposed to slavery through colonialism and globalization in education. The question is how far has the world been transformed in the last one hundred years to correct the mistakes that led to the last world wars.

Part of the answer to the above question on mental disorders is to examine something like the case of Germany when it invaded France and became part of the triggering inspiration to the Second World War. What was the really motive behind that and how could intelligent people get into that kind of a deal or plunder? The points of such an invasion can be debated for a reasonable length of time, but many could agree that the root cause of the conflict was a mental incapacity of one or a few of the presiding leaders of that time and mainly headed by President Hitler. In retrospect, such a mental health problem must have been caused by the inability to lead an economic crisis towards a brighter status for his country or corruption within the system. While that stands to account for a strong answer to the invasion, it is also true that the cause might have been simply due to super-greed, ignorance and selfishness. Contrary to the concept of going to war when an economy of any country doesn't progress as well as expected, many developed countries find it hard to avoid the consequences even when casualties are in large numbers. The United States is one of the examples even though it did not go for war during or after the great depression of 1930s, but stood against Germany to rescue France and the Jews in the famous holocaust. What did France learn from that and has it demonstrated any lessons to the world? In actuality, France proved that it learned a lot from that experience because it stood almost sparingly alone on opposing the United States invasion of Iraq in the year 2001. That was partially due to the suspect of hoarding the terrorists that contributed to the bombing of the world trade center in New York's Manhattan Island in the commonly known as the 911 operation. There are several establishments that disapprove worldwide invasions of one country by another, but the Iraq case was the most unpopular in human history that most professionals described as primitive and idiotic or more precisely a mental disorder inspiration after killing the Superpower's economic image both at home and all over the world. It was an outrageous regret for a former president George Bush for having followed his vice president blindly to present a fake case to the American people and the world and lead to the conditions that many described as the great depression or worse. That was actually what made China the number one and world economic leader while still a communist state of government after lending money to the United States.

The above collection of facts is a big indication that a belief on wars and invasions is a mental disease that could be genetically inborn or simply infectious through learning and teaching. One thing that has been proven is that energy resources are as abundant as the sun's rays so long as the lightening continues to strike and shine on the world as good as ever before. If that is a case that can be truly learned and understood, then the idea of world hunger and poverty could as well be forgotten as a once upon a time era or event of history.

Currently, the world is undergoing a lot of change and through one of the most challenging times of economic crises. This is very evident from the view of the sanctions being imposed by the Western World against the Eastern World along the various products including the financial systems of operation. Whether it is based on mental disorders or not there is always over-production while greed remains the driving agent that builds the gap between the consumers and their own sanction crises and the related miseries.

One of the best examples that represent the misery in the above given contexts includes the Madoff case that defrauded the registered bank members out of $165 billion dollars in the most and worst corruptive scandal in the United States or world history. The Madoff discovery should be renamed the Madoff Depression of the New Millennium. After the discovery of the Madoff Depression, there should be no further question about some of the answers given to mentally disordered case above and as to who is actually responsible for holding the world back as we know it. The Madoff case resulted in a jail term of more than 150 years in prison or more precisely life in prison. The timing of the Madoff great depression scandal of the year 2008 was a clear indication that there is no lie that can last forever no matter how much the truth is concealed below that same lie. That was definitely a clear mental disorder which led to the belief that many similar corrupt operations are actually happening both domestically and internationally. The big question then is whether that was a real fraud or a great conspiracy in the making of that sandal.

Part of the answer to the above question resides on the law of developmental banking. The banking systems have actually been founded to benefit a few who claim to be fortunate on the basis of the accumulated wealth right from times of slavery and slave trade which based on mental disorders in that perspective. There is no way Africans can own a bank after only claiming their rights of citizenship less than 50 years ago today by the writing of this book. The banking industry is supposed to be the most honest and straight forward among all institutions because it defines the medium of exchange between every kind of commodity that the world produces or ever produce. Thus, without proper mental health, trustworthiness, accountability, and transparency on such an extremely important tool, corruption, depressions, recessions and collapsing systems of European civilization could become the order of the day for generations. At the time of the writing of this book, the news reveal that Russia's president Putin is seriously resisting any penetration or expansion of the European civilization into their culture or the former Soviet Union. Is he the one with a mental disorder or his acts are out to prevent the spread of mental disorders into his territory and culture? Is money and banking the root causes of all such conflicts?

According to the theory of money and wealth, the answer to the above question resides on the full understanding of the root bases of the foundations at which the development of the current banking institutions is based. Is the theory of permittivity a big factor on the making of a slave according to William Lynch or it is simply education, slavery and colonialism in action? Is Zimbabwean President Robert Mugabe factoring such bases into his current behaviors within his administration before he can assume or claim to be a poor or one of the greatest leaders of the world? Could the recent predatory banking or lending behaviors a result of mental disorders in that perspective? Without all these questions answered properly then the overall faith is an empty assumption whether it is focused on the International Monetary Fund (IMF), World Bank, or the newest BRICCS that was just formed to counter the underlying status quo in the loaning practices.

As more and more human beings interact with one another through various world explorations, diversity continues to impact on different patterns of cultural developments which may imply new definitions and standardizations of mental health capacities? The various ways by which mental healthcare is affected by diversity and cultural competence is a subject that has attracted a lot of attention to many professionals. For the past few years the issues of mental healthcare have displayed several types of challenges that have created various controversies within the prevailing compliance standards of the human rights and ethical developments. The most common one is based on decision making rights within the mental illness situations and the related treatment consequences. Deciding whether someone is legally competent to make decisions regarding their own treatment requires an assessment of their mental capacity through a universal standardization method which rarely exists in the diversified workplaces. The assessed capacity required for legal competence increases with the seriousness of what is at stake. While there is no validated standard that can fit all, the usual explanation is that patient is being balanced against best interests. An alternative explanation, that we require greater room for error when the consequences are serious, implies a change to clinical practice and in the evidence doctors' offer in a presiding court that may be dealing with the mental illnesses.

The historical background of the human rights related to mental illness can be traced back to the World Healthcare Organization (WHO) regulations. That is described in the WHO Mental Health Policy and Service Guidance Package in Mental Health Legislation and Human Rights. In the regulation of involuntary treatment, a balance must be found between duties of care and protection and the right to self-determination among the diverse cultural groups in existence. However, in spite of its shared common roots, the mental legislation of the diverse Commonwealth countries approaches such a balance in different ways. When reform is planned, lessons can be learned from the experiences of other countries to generate fair and legal requirements of compliance. In retrospect, criteria for involuntary treatment used in a sample of 32 Commonwealth Mental Health Acts were compared using a framework developed from standards derived from the Universal Declaration of Human Rights. Reasons for non-compliance were considered and examples of good practice were noted. Changes in the criteria used over time and across areas with differing levels of economic development were analyzed to determine the legal compliance requirements to be generated. Some of those included; the widespread deviation from standards that was demonstrated, suggesting that some current legislation may be inadequate for the protection of the human rights of people with mental disorders around the world; and that the current trends in Commonwealth mental health law reform would include a move towards broad diagnostic criteria, the use of capacity and treatability tests, treatment in the interests of health rather than safety, and regular reviews of treatment orders.

Explanations for deviation from the standards include differing value perspectives underpinning approaches to balancing conflicting principles, failure to keep pace with changing attitudes to mental, and variations in the resources available for providing treatment and undertaking law reform. Current good practice provides examples of ways of dealing with some of these difficulties. Some of those practices are based on the respective laws that serve as the fundamental background in the given perspective.

In any level, a respective analytical evaluation supports the underlying legal issues raised in the past about the human rights. Beginning with the Universal Declaration of Human Rights (UDHR) efforts have been made to codify such moral rights. The Universal Declaration of Human Rights has since been operationalized in the form of enforceable instruments such as the European Convention on Human Rights, the American Convention on Human Rights, and the African (Banjul) Charter on Human and Peoples' Rights.

However, in reality, mental health legislation may not fully reflect either coherent philosophical arguments or the various Conventions and Declarations, since legislation is influenced by the specific historical, social, political, and cultural context in which it is enacted. Arguably, mental health legislation in general pays insufficient attention to the human rights of people with mental disorders. Such inattention may reflect a wide variety of factors, from shortage of the necessary economic resources in the context of the enormity of other problems. Thus, in the given analytical view, it is indicated that in many capacities new legislation should be devised to raise the moral standards of professional and personal lives for the future of human rights development in order to deal with serious ethical problems in the existing mental health equality legal issues. It seems quite conceivable that the impact of diversity and cultural competency would offer some green light towards the realization of such an achievement. Such a vision would become spectacular on account of the prospective studies based on the previous literature findings accordingly.

The past few years have shown that the development of diversity has been a major issue in mental health law and the related general healthcare delivery. As a consequence, professional people moved on and it was witnessed in the year 2007 when the world marked the 15th Anniversary of Day. That was a remarkable day when medical and non-medical organizations around the world put on events to raise public and professional awareness of a specific mental health issue. According to the immigration movements and political conflicts around the world more people than ever before are living in a country other than the one that they were born or raised in. A major impact is encountered with dramatically different languages, religions, family relationships and values, as well as views on health care and treatment along different destination localities.

Diverse immigration movements can cause or affect mental healthcare and hence the respective laws in one or several ways. For instance, living outside the country one was born in may not always be due to personal choice. However, as the worldwide information pack highlights, some people may have been displaced for reasons beyond their control such as civil war or natural disasters. They now find themselves in a culture that they do not fully understand or that does not fully understand them. It can be difficult enough to cope with the challenges that these situations produce without the added complication of mental illness.

According to the world Human Rights diversity records, the potential for the political equality depends on the proper use or misuse of mental health legislations around the world. Respectively, it has occurred in the recent USSR and its surroundings, in South Africa during the apartheid era, and is reported to be occurring in present day China in one way or another. In such circumstances it requires that such legislation is underpinned by clear ethical and legal principles that are acceptable internationally. That idea has not been well structured for better mental health law enforcement especially in the areas of research that utilizes human subjects without the informed consent legislation in all countries. The requirement for informed consent is an expression of an important principle in moral philosophy, namely "respect autonomy". Autonomy has been defined in many different ways, but fundamentally it means having the freedom to be self-governing. The bases of the respect autonomy principle and its justifiable limitations have been the subjects of extensive philosophical debate.

According to several studies it is argued that the above principle gives rise to a strong moral claim or right to autonomy. That may be derived from a reasoned claim to equal respect for dignity alongside other members of the moral community or from the necessity of respecting people's interest in self-determination, in order that they may promote their own best interests.

On the other hand, the mental health justifications for limiting autonomy rights include the prevention of harm to the person in question (paternalism) or of harm to others. Many authors have argued that paternalism is only justifiable if decision-making capacity is significantly impaired such that the choice being overridden is essentially non-voluntary. Interference to prevent harm to others is justified because interference with an assailant's autonomy preserves both the autonomy and the physical integrity of any potential victims.

On the given perspective, mental health legislation seems to vary widely across the world going beyond the tribal or ethnic lines to simple differences in faith. This picture is reflected in the Commonwealth of Nations, an association of 53 countries with nearly 2 billion citizens representing a broad range of religious faiths, ethnic groups, cultures and traditions, which share the same common-law basis for legal systems. Within this association, there is a variety of statutory mental health legislation, both recently enacted as well as the long-standing ones.

For the past few years, guidance has been developed to try to ensure that national mental health legislation, while reflecting the conditions of the specific country, complies with human rights instruments as derived from the Universal Declaration of Human Rights and the abiding world organizational health boards. Like many governing bodies in healthcare administration, respective guidance takes the form of legal principles that should be incorporated to deliver the expected services. Most mental health law collections in this analysis have been selectively undertaken in response to debates encountered within various health boards including Great Britain which implemented the operation reforms of the Mental Health Act of 1983. However, disagreements between government and the majority of the people were so explosive to the point where they resulted in stagnant levels of healthcare delivery services. To repair such a problem, it required an amendment of the above Act which was realized as a fresh implementation of the Mental Health Act of the year 2007.

In many perspectives, respect for autonomy is a key issue in any mental health systems, cases or any forms of the related laws. However, autonomy should stand hand in hand alongside the related concept of free choice in personal capacities. That is in addition to the role of the assessment of capacity in determining whether compulsory treatment can and should take place on any given individual suffering mental health disorders or in general mentally related healthcare diseases. It is not the general population which is familiar with such a theory or the related consequences, but the relevance of the concept of "decision-making capacity" to mental health law has become broadly expanded in many educative programs in various theoretical analyses supported by evidence from empirical research studies as well as the law cases themselves. In the given perspective, research suggests that the impairments of cognition can characterize serious mental disorders that often times may affect the ability to make decisions about the status of treatment or the capacity to be treated. Moreover, physical disorders have also been implicated in worsening the decision-making capacities of many mental health patients.

At these times of advanced technologies in health care, mental health still presents serious human issues which are far from being understood properly for better treatment directives in the diverse world ahead. That is motivated by lack of universal laws of validation to define the underlying issues across the spectrum as defined by the World Health Organization. Such issues include inequity and inequality of care, discrimination, and mental disability which seem to be neglected in various policies and procedures of many institutions.

While it remains to be seen how the world will react to an enactment of legislation where mental health qualifies to be considered the main factorial hope in the healing of inter-racial conflicts, it is good to summarize its linkages with the respective prevail able resistance. Collectively, a legal issue like mental disability is actually one characterized by multiple interlinked levels of injustice, inequality and discrimination within classes or groups in a society. In such characterizations efforts directed toward achieving formal equality should be inclusive of other groups to display diversity. Thus, they should display similar efforts in all operations so as to achieve substantive equality for persons with mental disabilities and other related disorders. On the basis of the recent inter-racial tensions experienced in America, it is true that the structural patterns of living such conditions as in unemployment, poverty, inequality, homelessness, and healthcare accessibility or health insurance discrimination contribute to several risks for mental disability and impact negatively on the course and outcome of such disabilities. Many do realize and understand the importance of a human rights approach to mental disability, but few try to take the initiative of walking the talk to implement such a reality. In many perspectives the significance of such an approach means affirming the full recognition and respect of those with mental disabilities by honoring their life contributions to community and inherent dignity, their individual autonomic capacity and independence, and their freedom to make their own health living choices for the desired terminal treatments. In a practically defined order and essentiality a rights-based approach one can expect that there should be a requirement that many or all of us get to examine and transform the language, terminology, and models of mental disability programs that have previously been sustained especially within the recent healthcare programs within a specific spectrum in order to offer new and hopeful inter-racial healing proposals. Such an approach also requires us to examine the multiple ways in which inequality and discrimination characterize the lives of persons with mental disabilities and to formulate a response based on a human rights framework that is fairly applicable all over the world.

In recent years, policy makers in high-income countries have placed an increasing emphasis on the value of maintaining good mental health, recognizing the contribution that this makes to quality of life and the hopeful inter-racial mobility. While that holds true in various streamlines as those calling for workplace diversity, it is more of the same case in many that are mindful of the socio-economic consequences of poor mental health. However, the given perspective as presented in many other parts of the world is much less encouraging because of the fact that policy attention and resources are still directed largely at communicable diseases as opposed to the life-threatening cases or chronic disorders without the hopes of healing.

With the healthcare laws and related legislation initiatives still under threat, it is inevitable that the past will keep shaping the future of universal insurance especially with the cases involving mental health. Respectively, for the past few years, it has been quoted as confirmed in certain project surveys that the burden of mental illness could be predicted to increase from its current level of 12% of global disease burden to approximately 15% by the year 2020 and probably beyond. Without the healing of the inter-racial conflicts to choose cooperation as opposed to mere competition, much of the additional burden could project to occur in the developing or low-income countries. The consequences of poor mental health in such countries may be even worse than in high-income ones, because of the absence of social protection safety measures like mosquito nets on specific diseases cases as in Malaria. That is true when motivated by the high levels of positive reputations and high hopes in the direct or daily institutional healthcare operations and governmental programs in administration. Mental health legislation programs are still under scrutiny as they involve many cycles some of which are not clearly defined and are in continuous research. However, the cycle between poor mental health and poverty in low-income countries has been observed in several studies. For instance, the poor maternal mental health which is mostly experienced by women from conception through delivery also has long-term adverse consequences for infants in all developed and developing countries, which disrupts their standards of living and their own lifetime opportunities. Low standards of living with such poor infrastructures as in many cases of sanitation are endowed with the majority of the communicable diseases. Such structures are the central foci of much health policies in poorer countries. In the reality of the matters in practice such structures or healthcare facilities are also conceivably linked and exhibited by lack of mental health programs or primary initiatives. In that respect, interventions to prevent and treat mental health problems are highly recommended as they could help in the management of those conditions, as for instance in the cases of HIV/AIDS and tuberculosis diseases that can affect all human beings without discrimination.

Inter-racial healing of hope can be well implemented by removing the financial difficulties and disparities that exist in healthcare legislation. According to financial literature, the economic costs of poor mental health are well documented in high-income countries like the United States. With respect to such documentation, it is revealed that they are conservatively estimated to account for between 3% and 4% of gross domestic product in the undersigned countries. That is relatively small an amount to reflect the expected changes in the whole health industry that determines the consequences of the mental health disorders. However, in comparison, only a few estimates of such analyses have been made outside the developed world. There were exceptions encountered because in one exception study in Kenya it was estimated that the total costs per patient for 5,678 individuals with mental health problems hospitalized in 1999 were about Kenya shillings Ksh 200,000 which is equivalent to US$ 2,351 and less of other co-pays. Collectively, those figures included out of pocket costs to family members of US $ 51 and productivity losses of US$ 453. Overall evaluation revealed that the total economic costs for this group alone were more than US$ 13.3 million. As low as expected, the total expenses were simply close or equivalent to 10% of the Ministry of Health's budget. From an economical perspective and taking into account the alternative medicine, these figures would have been substantially larger if costs had also been included for those individuals who were not institutionalized or were treated by traditional healers which are part of the roots designed to improve the healing process of inter-racial conflicts.

On the basis of the current perspectives on legislative programs, the development and implementation of the mental health care laws seem to follow the same system of regulations as the general healthcare rules. In the given scheme, the healthcare system is characterized by a short-term perspective. Consequently, the government is well endowed with a systematic election-to-election planning structure that is closely respected and followed even though not fully diverse as advocated politically. However, the vision of the enterprises is mostly focused on the short-term financial and profit objectives that can sometimes impact negatively on the overall result of the common goals and mission. However, from an economical perspective, a longer-term enterprise perspective should consider healthcare strategy and investment to be a socially responsible economic investment that can become part of the solution to the inter-racial healing process. That is true particularly when engulfed in the social, ethical, and corporate structures of healthcare administration.

On a verifiable ethical development, it is in the U.S. where the Health Insurance Portability and Accountability Act of 1996 (HIPAA) have created some new legislation on privacy and accountability. The new legislation came with a long-term perspective endowed with strict rules for the protection of individually identifiable health information and secures public safety. Consequently, HIPAA took major steps toward social responsibility by recognizing the rights of patients and forcing significant changes in the enterprise procedures, data management, and activities.

In another view, the Sarbane- Oxley Act, created by the U.S. Congress in 2002, was designed to initiate the financial healing structure to protect investors from corporate accounting fraud which takes place behind the curtains in healthcare and other institutions. The main support was constituted in various healthcare sectors to boost corporate responsibility and transparency to uproot institutionalized disparities. There are other validation certification agencies such as the International Financial Reporting Standards, which have been proven to be considerably effective in changing the long-term accounting and healthcare business operations. Such agencies have established, very transparent and more stable and secure markets for world inter-racial healing developments. Consequently, if the major government and enterprise players decide to strategize and adopt a new inheritance that can hold long-term healthcare perspectives together, they may be able to envision that improving population health is, in the long-run, the real winning economic scheme to adopt. Such an adoption will be a prove bestowed in the system that can pay back more than the short-term profit maximization approach currently used in evaluating Healthcare costs in most developed countries. The prevailing approaches are not clearly coordinated to sustain better patient services and public health outcomes. However, most of them are rather associated with service delivery configurations of the yesteryears. While the talk on the prevailing methods of inter-racial healing are still being initiated and implemented in certain parts of the United States, the above approach has resulted in actual large variations in healthcare availability and use, increased cost, reduced employer participation in health insurance programs, and reduced overall population health outcomes upon any healthcare interventions as applicable. Even though some other countries are still faced with similar healthcare issues, it is high time that the United States had better considered taking an advanced priority in the matter.

A major goal of healthcare is the establishment of a universally accessible inter-racial tool that can guarantee enhancement on patient health outcomes. This objective is not realized in many countries because of structured misalignments of financial budgets on the basis of disparities related to inter-racial conflicts in many environments and where incentives and structures are currently not standardized for maximizing population health. The misalignment occurs because of the competing interests between the representatives in healthcare administration. In a simplified model those are individuals motivated by their low income prejudiced banks without fair regards to enhance the public or their own healthcare needs and other enterprises for economic developments. Some of the examples of real cases in the current systems include organizations for profit and nonprofit, government providers, payers, and suppliers most of which are politically motivated under the governmental influences failing to address the issues of inter-racial conflicts. Failure to use effective preventive interventions in both private and governmental institutions is perhaps the best profound example of the implicated misalignment of the required incentives. A variety of actions are necessary for maximizing population health within the constraints of available resources and the current balance between the healthcare representatives with the indicated interests. Those actions include overall patient autonomy as mentioned earlier, improved and justified transparency of all aspects of medical treatment decisions, more patient participation in shared medical decision making cases as in the chronic or terminally ill, greater understanding of guideline development and coverage decisions, certified and acceptable directives to consumer advertising, and the need for an enhanced role of the government as the public health advocate on inter-racial healing developments.

The result of a healing inter-racial hope is a product of the healthcare system that can be unanimously supported by all parties. It should be the health of the population served by the system for the people and by the people of a given government. That is even though other objectives such as fairness, equity and responsiveness could be important considerations in the allocation of healthcare resources among all the diverse groups of people. While that remains to be the target case, it is usually found that the impact of healthcare on health is rarely measured, discussed, or effectively used for resource allocation. One purpose of this book and chapter is to argue that services and resources in healthcare should be directed toward maximizing the public health. We use the United States as an example because of its extreme consumption of healthcare resources, and because it is currently implementing a healthcare reform. Yet still, many if not all of the considerations herein are also virtually implementable to other healthcare systems in both the developed and developing countries.

In March, 2010, U.S. President Obama signed the newly voted and passed healthcare bill that was named the "Patient Protection and Affordable Care Act". With several difficulties surrounding the bill and exasperated by the explosive political atmospheres, the underlying complex set of regulations will be phased in over several years. According to the first phase of the bill that began in September 2010, insurance companies can no longer deny coverage to children who have preexisting medical conditions and insurance companies are required to provide coverage on the parents' policies for young adults up to age 26. Also, along with that the first phase was structured to include a creation of a temporary high-risk pool for those with pre-existing conditions. In the same respect and by the year 2014 most U.S. Citizens and qualified legal residents were required to have health insurance. Moreover, large employers were to be required to offer health insurance, or provide their employees with a tax credit for purchasing health insurance and all of which should have been implemented or are actually working in most institutions despite the opposing political climates. Thus, in order to give all citizens, the benefits of being under the wings of a large healthcare purchaser, the bill requires that the states be able to create health insurance exchanges that are accessible to all individuals and small groups regardless of the underlying healthcare or ancestral grounds. While the objective of healthcare is to produce a healthy population, much of the current focus is on the wrong metrics. According to medical research, a health outcome can be defined as a product of life expectancy and quality of life. In that respect there is wide agreement that healthcare systems of the modern times should maximize average healthy life expectancy under the most applicable parameters. However, instead of measuring health outcomes, healthcare systems often measure variables that may not directly affect the most desired health outcomes. In many applications productivity has been measured by quantity other than quality by counting the units of services delivered, and quality has been defined by number of units of service that comply with guidelines leading to the assigned destinations. The results of such a circumstance are that many resources end up being used in the support of services that have little impact on any interventions or patient outcomes. That happens because of failure to recognize that while that is operational other services may actually be in a position to have a substantial impact on health outcomes but are well underutilized.

An evaluation of the consequences of mental health diseases confirms that the laws governing the prevailing operations are inadequate both in the developing as well the developed world. While there are many factors that lead into that as in inter-racial conflicts, the physical inequalities in mental health exist, are pervasive and often ignored. The most profound example is illustrated by the oversight and complete neglect of a mental health focus in the Millennium Development Goals. According to the World Health Organization, health inequalities can be defined as 'differences in health status or in the distribution of health determinants between different population groups'. Healthcare inequality is by far the forefront of any political issues and particularly in the United States of America where inter-racial healing is currently needed more than ever before.

The consequences of mental health inequalities include escalated inter-racial violence and related conflicts, continued unnecessary suffering and premature deaths, increased stigma and marginalization, lack of investment in mental health workforce and infrastructure, and limited or lack of treatment for people suffering from these conditions.

In many developing nations with limited mental health policies, the issue is sometimes worsened by ethnic misunderstanding that are less equivalent to the universal inter-racial conflicts. Moreover, there is also a scarcity of modern healthcare financial resources and infrastructure, ineffective advocacy as well as the lack of political will which limits effective mental health legislations and interventions. The developing nations often lack effective mental health champions who can capitalize on cultivating communities and policy makers so as to address mental health needs on long-term perspectives. In retrospect, the experiential indicators show that families of people with mental health problems are often marginalized because of the inability to cope with the normal conditions. In many cases they are limited in their ability to champion for mental health issues due to the stigma associated with the underlying chronic disorders. Nevertheless, some progress, however, is being initiated for future implementation with the intention of addressing the challenges posed by mental health problems. Many healthcare conferences are fundraising for such activities, but the real physical efforts are few and need to be scaled up to adequately meet mental health needs.

In an effort to extend the initiatives of the inter-racial healing point of hope some healthcare laws are becoming more simplified for better understanding and utilization. Respectively and according to other studies, it is stated in the legislative literature that, except on a case in a court of protection order, a consequence of which is the deprivation of liberty is in place, the Mental Capacity Act cannot be used to give care involving deprivation of liberty. While such a language sounds straight forward, it is not necessarily correct because by following this advice it might make readers to believe that they may not be expected to give lifesaving treatment that could entail the deprivation of liberty for physical illness to a person without mental capacity and without an existing court order when it is lawful and circumstantially necessary to do so. In view of that, it is illustrated as in the Section 6.52 of the code of practice of the Mental Capacity Act 2005 here it explains the interpretation of "deprivation of liberty" derived from European Court of Human Rights judgments. In the same class of establishments Section 50 paragraphs (2) of part 2 chapter 2 of the Mental Act 2007 amends the Mental Capacity Act 2005 specifically to provide for situations where it is lawful and necessary for deprivation of liberty necessary for life sustaining treatment. All these legislative illustrations are quite protective and can contribute positively towards mental health development and hence the healing of the current inter-racial conflicts in the given perspective.

One of the most underdeveloped legal issues in mental health is inequality in housing and particularly for the elderly people in the United States and around the world. The issue is politically motivated and is getting more and more diversified in various departmental administrative structures as in healthcare administration. Consequently, some studies have confirmed that while physical and mental health is clearly interconnected, research on housing and mental health is particularly underdeveloped or overlooked for political ends meets. That is why I decided to deliver a mental research proposal to the former Boxing Heavyweight Champion or greatest Muhammad Ali to support the development and establishment of clinics to support mentally related studies as in his case on Parkinson's and Bernie Sanders' inspiration earlier in this chapter. A complex and inherited disorder is one that holds people from seeing or understanding that there is sufficient evidence to suggest that the type and quality of housing affects psychosocial processes. Such a factor is quite evident and actually contains elements which in turn can affect mental health that is the base of the inter-racial healing in a variety of ways that may include identity and self-esteem, anxiety about structural hazards, worry and lack of control over maintenance and fear of neighborhood crime. Consequently, a cross-sectional survey of adults in two electoral wards in one northern London borough was conducted to offer more supportive evidence and the results confirmed that structural problems in the housing disparities were commensurate with the mental health outcomes. Respectively, they found a significant increase in cases of depression in those living in newer housing where access was from a common balcony. That is an indicator of the consequences of mental health cases in the making of the new world order through the healing of the inter-racial tensions on the basis of housing disparities.

The housing factors as part of the mental health legal issues have been supported by other studies. In that respect, the finding that the quality of housing and financial security are more important explanatory factors in explaining the mental health of older people than housing tenure seems to be supported in that perspective. Respectively, in a supportive study, it was revealed that experiencing financial difficulties at baseline levels was a good predictor in the new episodes of depression in the General Psychiatric Morbidity Survey that determines the capacity of mental health in many situations. A similar case was also encountered in the British Household Panel Survey, which was conducted for the adjustment of more objective measures in the standards of living such as in the occupational levels in various communities affected in health outcomes. The indication is that the housing social underdevelopment gradually becomes a mental or biological issue that can translate into a legal matter in any environment and become a determinant point of inter-racial healing of hope.

While it is strongly stated that mental health is very broad term in definition that is still being studied and expanded for inter-racial healing, the explanation as to how "the social becomes biological" is likely to have many strands. Housing is part of the network of health resources that can either promote health over the life-course or increase susceptibility to illness and disease over time. However, the quality of housing is particularly important to health at older ages as we see in various nursing and assisted living facilities, because susceptibility to low temperature increases with age and older people are exposed more than other age groups to the indoor home environment. Moreover, data from the first five channels of the British Household Panel Survey, which studied by looking at residential mobility for those over 55, confirmed that, relatively few older people made any specific movements in the given perspective. However, in what might be another case of the inverse care law, older people on low incomes may also lack the funds to maintain and repair their homes as desired, or actually be able to afford the co-payments to take up public funds to improve their houses and health living standards?

Nevertheless, it may be highlighted that inequalities in housing quality together with a household's ability to deal with financial problems have a small, but significant effect on mental health. Housing quality and financial security, exemplified by the differential availability of pensions, will have increasing importance for mental health as the population ages.

The nature of the continuous immigration movements around the world seems to be a compelling issue on the consequences of health literacy and cultural competency in mental healthcare. In order to accommodate the underlying dilemma, more work and sacrifices would need to be initiated and implemented in terms of mental workplace diversity actions in political and health care organizations as much Bernie Sanders is trying to do in the presidential race of year 2016. The above analysis may be very brief, but the impacts indicated would be part of that process as may be presented and can be recognized in the Republican presidential debates heated by front –runner Donald Trump. If that is done, then a lot would begin to resurface in terms of mental health developments in universal healthcare administration and hence on inter-racial healing.

CHAPTER III

POWER OF A UNITED AMERICA WORLD ORDER

WHY IS AMERICA GETTING DISUNITED AND WEAK?

The biggest challenge in America today is to answer the question as to why it is vigorously being divided on racial lines between Africans and Whites in both education and employment opportunities. President Obama agreed with many scientists that racism is institutionalized and has been or is constituted in the DNA of the human species. He stressed that it cannot go away overnight because it has been instituted for 300 to 400 years in our nation after witnessing the racial slaughter of nine Africans in the church South Carolina in 2015. That is the same thing that is deeply instituted in education with some examples like Capella University online which asks African students to copy or simply propose dissertation research studies that are only suited to their interests in terms of culture and colonialism as well as many others without actually aimed at resolving any issues. While the current President Baraka Obama is getting deep into the roots of eliminating inequality, his opponents insist that then it means he does not love America. No single scientist has ever come up with a valid explanation as to why some or a lot of President Obama's opponents do believe that equality is wrong both home and abroad. However, it still proves that the greatest thing that has ever happened in America, the so called land of opportunities is the presidential election of somebody who can validate that description by streamlining the vestigial defects of colonialism and slavery in whatever forms it may be happening today behind some curtains. So what is the real problem and solution? Why do some people still think that Africans deserve to be poor even though they own piles of raw materials for every technological development while showing superiority in sports and other body power projects?

The following is an excerpt of receiving wrong education about identity and diversity in America as currently happening in the State of Missouri in the Ferguson city of Saint Louis as noted by doctor John Fitzegerald: In the photograph below, John who is a National Diversity Expert along with Principal and Chief Strategist of Criticality Management Consulting with experience in education serving as a former Associate Dean of Harvard College teamed up to talk about the lessons that were learned from the incident and how they should shape the future of racism in America.

In that excerpt, doctor Fitzegerald's analysis implied that the racial tensions in Ferguson, Missouri ignited by the shooting of unarmed black teenager Michael Brown had captured the nation's attention and the whole world to downgrade America as a weakling in terms of justice or equality for all races of people. It also opened conversations across homes, workplaces and boardrooms that are often difficult to introduce into any public or private lives in America. While a few have tried to initiate the defects of racism, many have brushed it off as non-existence ever since the 1960s even when racists have committed serious crimes that caused death. It wasn't by chance to note that since the race riots of the 1960s, tensions grew in Ferguson that finally exploded into mass demonstrations and civil unrest. Such a serious warning is real and that is why it brought to the fore the problems of systemic racial conflict in all sectors of American society that has forced a popular President like Obama to air serious comments on institutionalized racism that cause inequality in opportunities particularly in employment. Furthermore, in addition to the protests or even without the killing of Michael Brown, the American militarism that is supposed to protect its citizens displayed a different stance to the world arena in vision when the police headed for a show-down toward the victims who were unarmed or helpless in terms of defending themselves. Furthermore, the whole event in Missouri went so far and proved the existence of wide fissures of race relations in our country that many thought were disappearing in this generation or the immediate former one.

On the basis of the United States census performed in the year 2010 to update the status quo in justice, it was revealed that the Ferguson suburb of St. Louis is in the ninth position as the most segregated city in the United States. While the majority of the people in that city is African American in the population, the town itself as well as the whole state narrowly escaped both the civil rights era race riots of 1964, and such vestiges of racial tensions have continued to polarize the nation all through since because an institutionalized culture of civil unity and obedience. Such institutionalized structures of racism are still singing in many minds of the victimized African Americans even though they seem to have temporarily been silenced with negotiable peace and equal opportunity programs. Consequently, when the news spread and hit the right destination that Michael Brown had been killed by a white police officer, the Ferguson's African American community could not take it anymore. The final result was a call for major protests both locally and nationally while negative images could also be seen in countries as far as Africa, Russia and the world at large. The situation was a wake call that while progress had been achieved over the last few decades, a lot still remained to be desired and for which researches are not sure of what the real solution is to a problem ingrained in the genetic make-up of an organism as in these cases without appropriate therapy as in grass root education.

According to Doctor John Fitzegerald, I completely concur with him and president Obama on their analyses of the Ferguson incident in relationship to institutionalized racism in America which has continued to weaken America in conjunction with its worldwide affiliations. That will probably continue to be the case for years to come if a proper workable solution is not discovered and implemented. While the Fergusson case is not alone in our nation, it is true that racial issues are confined to all places in America. I do agree with doctor Fitzegerald that as much as I have experienced in the ten pharmaceutical companies some companies have adopted diversity strategies to offset issues like those of the Ferguson police department to calm down while keeping the real problem far from being solved. Like in my ten former employees and particularly the Pharmaceutical manufacturing corporations and other medicals, the strategy is to; keep minorities pacified but disengaged from the real process of meaning-making; hire one to cover-up the 200 non-African employees in racism, then promote just enough minorities not to be deemed racist; and that will silence any claim in discrimination suits in any courts where almost 90% of all judges are non-African, and dim the discord. The same in the Banking industry where as former United States Secretary of State, Hillary Clinton reiterated in 2016 town hall meeting that minorities are denied loans to start small business and instead directed to show how much money they have in account or the credit score bureaucracy. That is a must for any application to even begin or initial review as would avoid any serious conversations about race, prejudice, unconscious bias, and micro-aggressions that harm morale and productivity in trickle-down economics. Most truthfully all these are founded in racial bias resulting in a degradation already overtaken by China. As a consequence, these companies are more vulnerable than ever to the sort of race discrimination lawsuits that have tarnished institutions that include Universities and manufacturing companies like pharmaceuticals and including but not limited to a few like Quest Diagnostics, Bank of America, Johnson and Johnson, Nature's Bounty, Bayer, Merrill Lynch, Wal-Mart, Macy's, and Abercrombie and Fitch. However, all of these companies falsely deny any accusations, but have heavily been penalized, lost or settled race bias claims brought against them by their employees and customers around the world.

The above strategy is definitely not working and will never work to bring good or supposedly total peace that America seeks and for which it claims to be a leader in the world. In that respect, the "Corporate Diversity Report," that was recently released by the United States Senate, indicated that there is much room to improve in racial unification in representation at all levels of corporate America and possible only if we begin an initial thinking properly to avoid future similar incidents as those in Fergusson whose magnitude may not be figured by our simple imaginations. According to the report, when it comes to corporate boards, Hispanics, who make of seventeen percent of the United States population, have one if not the lowest of all American governmental representations at three percent of boards and three percent of executive teams. While African Americans, who are thirteen percent of the U.S. population, fare better in board representation, garnering eight percent of board seats, they are only four percent of executive teams. These dynamics are not significantly different from those of Ferguson, where African Americans have no representation in City Hall or on the school board, and are effectively shut out of public safety jobs. That is a clear indication that there is a lot to be desired in the future of America that claims to teach love and peace to the rest of the world.

Just like the independent movements in former colonial Africa that changed the operations of racial segregation, Companies and Institutions should learn four lessons from Ferguson's trigger on American and the third world war:

1. Racial tensions have to be resolved openly because they do not disappear by not addressing them. They simmer just beneath the surface until an event happens that disrupts conformity to corporate norms and then they erupt.
2. While evil people will always deny there is no racism, it does not mean they are the only rulers of this world. They can move to where they can apply the evil tactics and just as there is no "great white hope," there is no "great black hope". Consequently, it is quite reasonable to conclude that whether it's President Obama, Missouri State Highway Patrol Captain Ron Jackson, Richard Parsons who replaced Donald Sterling at the L.A. Clippers, or a company's "chief diversity officer." Racial tension abates when issues are addressed openly and self-reflectively.
3. Cover-ups are always the signs of a poor and evil leader. Poor performance from an evil on issues of race is harmful to their credibility and erodes the trust constituents have in the leader and that may lead to local or third world war.
4. History as well as the Fergusson incident confirms that the costs of suppressing racial tensions are far greater than the costs of addressing them because when wars happen everything is destroyed.

The question whether America can teach its Judges to be part of that solution by completely opposing racism and related hidden ugly tactics like saying that one is not a racist until he talks about it in words when they actually know that actions speak louder than words. That happens because in reality the companies want a shortcut to positive race relations without a clear concise analysis of a case or any situation. When it comes to issues of diversity, companies generally do not want to hear bad news or admit their complicity in adding to the climates of distrust and bias. Yet, the only way for companies to truly get beyond race is to weed out racial bias continuously until cleared genetically.

In view of the above, the question then is whether companies and institutions can over any long term resolutions on the issues of racism? While I will be offering my personal research-based resolution as a medical scientist in the future chapters, the following six strategies might be noted to be helpful:

1. Avoid the "Silence discord strategy" which a lot of judges use to dismiss racial discrimination lawsuits by reaffirming **commitment to diversity** through active engagement of minorities in the areas of corporate strategy, positioning, and revenue generation.

2. Welcome racial discussions in both private and public debates so as to implement internal, structured, diplomatically insured conversations led by senior executives about race and culture that permit employees to articulate and work through their concerns.

3. Introduce and implement company-wide training on "unconscious bias" and "micro-aggressions" to help employees be aware of the hidden prejudices they hold that could undermine them and their companies that are supported by institutionalized vestiges of racism.

4. Walk the talk by developing a broader understanding of diversity from both skin and cultural perspective that permits the company to move beyond the isolationism of race to a more inclusive paradigm of "excellence."

5. Upgrade education to recognize that diversity is not about superiority against inferiority," nor is it colors like black and white or others. Rather, diversity is actually about merit through excellence expressing itself as differences, similarities, complexities and tensions among all human beings. It is about uniting excellence across all business units and partners for the good of all people rather than sequestering it in human resources, and hold executives accountable for its continued development or get penalized.

6. Diversity is about peace as opposed to war and rather than thinking of diversity as "the elephant in the room," let America begin seeing diversity as the room. See success through true diversity because it is central to everything a company may

do from people management, to process design, to market segmentation all over the world.

In the past I have personally sued Universities and employers because of racism, but while we will not likely see racial protests in corporate C-Suites as we did on the streets of Ferguson, we shall most likely see more race-based lawsuits in the light of admissions by companies that "unconscious bias" has for years caused their hiring managers to discriminate against African American and Hispanic job candidates. In that respect, several institutions and corporate America need to recognize that there are a lot of Ferguson similarities in many of their management ranks, boardrooms, and stores that need to be eradicated for the well-being of their businesses and the people they serve.

Part of the solution to the above problem that would most likely bring down the world one day if a clear answer is not formulated is contained in my own experience through several institutions in America. Foremost, it was around 1989 to 1991 while working as a volunteer in the largest hospital in the State of New York by the name Kings County in Brooklyn that I realized the importance of identity in policy issues and development. As a full-time volunteer for one full year, the issue of improper identity was brought up by one Indian and two Jewish professional couple including a man and his wife in the same department and all of whom I trained with as a team in daily interactions. Then the man came up one morning and asked me, hey Henry I am just curious about something on identity. Go ahead with your question, I replied. Hello, Mangerere, why do you use an English first name and yet you are from Africa? Is Henry a really African name? No sir, I replied and said to him that it actually came from Britain. So you are using a slave name like most Africans do in the Americas and other countries, he added. Yes, I replied. He shook his head with disappointment saying that we Africans are missing something. I agreed, but to explore the subject a little further I asked him what his slave names were. However, he seemed insulted by that question and discontinued the conversation. However, I did confirm to him that we were brainwashed to believe that if we used English names then we could stand a better chance of getting employment than everybody else who didn't use especially the non-Africans in the European owned corporations. I then remembered an African American man by the name Cassius Clay who changed his identity name to his new religion while Louis Farakhan did not as was Baraka Obama, Kweisi Mfume, Jomo and Uhuru Kenyattas or Jaramogi Oginga Odinga. Twenty-five years later, I disapproved myself and all Africans that it is the complete opposite of what we were told as we grew up because the African Americans with full English names have always had the greatest percentage of unemployment according to the statistics on CNN and MSNBC news. At any capacity, that marked my turning point and became one of the most educative moments of my life that forms the basis of many working principles including the challenging public policy formulation projects in development.

For the past few years many movements and reclamations around the world have caused endless conflicts and wars including the current ones in Ukraine or Syria as well as the old types like the Israel and Palestine cases and the ones right here in the United States in the city of Ferguson in Missouri State. Such an ability to move is the cause and core basis of communication between all the tribes and races of the world. However, some communicators have claimed to be the better ones and to an extent that they should be the sole teachers of this world. Such an argument is being extended to the current educational operation systems of the online schooling curricula that are beginning to grow at an alarming rate. An example of that includes Capella University online which will be the topic of focus under the defects of its internet malpractice in educational research under the petals of knowledge, colonialism and slavery that some think should be punishable by discontinuation of postgraduate accreditation on a globalization basis in status. Thus, for globalization to work appropriately, it should be fair to everybody and acceptable by all people whether in healthcare policies or in any business transactions around the world. For that to happen, the roots of the current world crises must be explored and analyzed for proper solutions to be formulated and implemented appropriately. It is commonly noted that the essence of science is to discover identity in difference. Identity of race and tribe goes as far back as history can take us. However, history tells us that some tribes or races have moved faster than others so as to cause extinction of other tribal languages and the binding tribes themselves from this earth under the name of globalization. The current and probably the greatest scientist so far in the world, Doctor Chukwu Emeagwali who invented the Super Computer and became the father of internet, noted that it was totally wrong to be told by foreign teachers at his infant stages that his given African names were evil and worthless which needed to be replaced by European names. As he deserves to be as rich as Bill Gates or better than him for discovering or inventing internet, many people and especially Africans should look closely into what he has in mind for the Africans after promising to use his discovery to re-connect Africa. He is responsible for the development of all online schools and universities that are currently making billions of revenue in all countries all over the world except Africa. In those days, he states that he was told that to be a really human being he had to rename himself with an English name, Phillip blended with his last name. He strongly considers it a colonial sting and wished such a mistake could not have happened at all as he still holds the two identity names as Phillip Emeagwali.

As the author of this book, I strongly agree with Emeagwali that the destruction of the African identity as indicated as a mistake was the cruelest weapon of the African educational extinction ever planted in the continent that is still affecting many Africans into the current situation of darkness and poverty in all areas of life. It is generally agreed and whether in hypocrisy or truthfulness that when mistakes are committed and whether willingly or by error then corrections have to be made to re-invent the wheel on the underlying or challenging public policies or they keep on recycling and get worse in the name of globalization. If not, then globalization would simply translate into an advancement of colonialism other than enlightenment of the world masses living in poverty. This book is based on focusing on formulating and implementing resolutions that could correct the above mistake because Africa is the only continent that according to Emeagwali, has more people speaking English than the whole of the United Kingdom, more people speaking French than the whole of France, and the same with many other European nations. It was inspiring that Emeagwali invented internet and promised to use to interconnect Africa. Such a promise could remain a dream unless a workable public policy formula is designed and implemented and serve as of one the fruits of his invention. That is the purpose of this book and starting with this chapter which emphasizes the defects in education dating back to slavery and colonialism as quoted by doctor Emeagwali.

For the past several centuries, globalization has been translated from its cultural past to implant the belief that education as a whole is the basis of industrial development. Among all the world's continents, only Africa falls short of defining the official meaning of education. Such confusion has continued to dwell among the so called African professionals because most of them have been trained either through the Eastern or Western education systems. While my sister received her medical education from the eastern block of Russia, I received most of my modern pharmaceutical education from the Western world of the Americas. The same case applies to most Africans whose most first names align with the region that served as the colonial master a few centuries back. For many people especially those from the developing world, education which used to be a guarantee to job placement and security is no longer the case. It only comes as a big surprise and tragedy to discover that after spending so much time and life energy reading and researching to earn degrees and certifications, it is often found that one either knows very little or can never find any related employment or it is an apparent mental health repercussion. That finding is commensurate and with particular reference to Africans wherever they may happen to be other than home. As a young boy in Africa, my grandmother always stressed and told me of the importance of working extremely hard to gain entrance and immigrate to America for better education and guaranteed employment in my future. While my attitude did not fully change about my African nature, I still ended up developing some little attitude positivity towards light-skinned people until I read about Jewish and African holocausts of slavery in the past centuries. Consequently, when my Germany-born priest told me that he was taking me to study medicine in Germany, it became a heartfelt celebration with my father especially excited while working as a chief accountant for a British company in Kenya. However, that never happened because my priest was transferred back to Germany before I completed high school. The significance of this information is that globalization had been so deep-rooted that nobody existed that could educate me and others that the African people were not recognized to be equal to other human beings on the planet earth. Equality is still the hardest thing to achieve for any African outside Africa as the United States President Baraka Obama emphasized on that particular development in 2014 or during his second term in office. Thus, if the internet discovery by an African scientist, Emeagwali is the basis of modern globalization then it can serve as the root base and right tool for educational equality that will open doors for global equal opportunity employment.

While voyages of education are the main bases of globalization in many parts of the world, Africa remains the major pinnacle playground on such an exploration in development. In terms of educational definition, we had always been told that education was never an original African affair as it was made known to us that an African had no education to offer on anything in the world. We are made to belief that it had actually come from the light-skinned people wherever you find them other than dark-skinned people from the Dark Continent. That information came from my own mother and many other senior people in the community, but I found it extremely hard to belief because I had been told of people like Jomo Kenyatta, Kwame Nkrumah, Nyerere, Mandela, Lumumba and many others' legacies in independent Africa. My mother was particularly useful in defining the initial life stages in both the colonial education of civilization as well as my own cultural values. Unlike my father who was an accountant, my mother did not even go through or beyond grade three of the western classroom education. My first and main question to my father who worked for a British Company was why he used a British name as his first name and yet the British are the same people who were fought by Jomo Kenyatta and others for almost a century in order to gain the Kenyan or African freedom. My father's answer to that question was two-fold. The answer was that the world was operating under the dictatorship of colonialism for which many Africans had to give up their first given names for a British or Christian name. He couldn't attach any particular reason of substance that could give a plausible or concrete explanation because I asked him why Jomo Kenyatta deleted his English name as the Kenyan President including his son Uhuru Kenyatta who later became Kenya's president too in the new century. However, he reiterated that Kenyatta was a hero who fought for our independence from Britain for almost 40 years including 7 years in prison for that same cause as a freedom fighter. He had all the guts to drop his colonial name to certify his anti-colonial sentiments that are often referred to as slave mentalities. So are you still living under such a mentality, I asked my father? To some extent yes, he answered. And so can we conclude that all those Africans who replaced their African names for foreign names are still living under the same mentalities of self-denials on their cultural roots as to cause extinction? That is partially yes even though we have to continue regretting it and seek solutions of repair, he replied. Dad, tell me what you mean exactly by partial, I asked! Well, by looking as the former real slaves and the current descendants of slavery, you can see that they completely lost their African names into English names during and after the transatlantic slavery and slave trade. Those are the identities that are completely colonized that need a major repair or so called an overhaul in that perspective from total English identity to full African identities.

The words slavery and colonialism are quite uncomfortable to those who feel guilty on behalf of their ancestral parents who actually committed the victimization of Africans and other people in the name of education. It is actually uncomfortable for both the children of the former slave masters and the children of the former slave workers even though it is more severe in guilty for the wrong doers. The main reason for that is that for one, the victims suspect that they might actually be touching the old healing wounds which might cause pain to both parties. The victimizers simply try to avoid it because they suffer from extreme guilty which pinpoints to the attachment winds of an evil commitment. They are the children of the former slave owners who could feel terrible as to how their ancestors depict an unpleasant nature in the African arena. The children of the former slaves could develop that feeling that after having been owned for so long as free laborers, their contributions are the main basis for greatness of America in terms of accumulated wealth as displayed by the World Bank or the International Monetary Fund. Consequently, there are two types of children in America today including those that are native born and the descendants of the new and old immigrants from almost all over the world. Those children were recently referred to as "We are the world" on a musical title by the greatest musician that ever lived known as Michael Jackson. The title of the musical production originated from an invitation of most musicians from all over the world to compose and produce the song. It was a clear indication that America was and still remains a structural feature made of immigrants according to most believers.

As much as Michael Jackson phrased the song, America is the real global icon representing almost all the tribes of the whole world. Thus, for real change that can be trusted, the best point of starting such a development is America and for a long lasting unity and trustworthiness. During the peak of the Civil Rights Movements of the 1960s, Doctor Martin L. King Jr., delivered the famous speech popularly known as "I have a dream" Doctor King foresaw the future as that one day that the white brothers and sisters would join hands with the black brothers and sisters and match together as one nation. Fifty years later, that perception has been translated tremendously from being an African American vision into a worldwide global development. That has been extracted from two major events including the invention of the internet through the supercomputer discovery by the Nigerian African, Chukwu Emeagwali and the Western World American election of the first African American president Baraka Obama. On these particular individuals two major accomplishments are extremely considerable on the question of education, colonialism and slavery. First, on his article on globalization, Emeagwali talks about the childhood re-identification of his own names which he was forced to adapt to English names. Secondly, the first elected African American president explained how he acquired his two African names while touring the Middle East Jewish nation of Israel and one African country of Egypt. It was shocking to the world for president Obama to elaborate to the press in both countries that his name Baraka was a given name from his Kenya father directly translated from the Lugha Ya Kiwashili language that means blessing or lucky. While in Israel, he also confirmed to the Jewish people that it meant the same thing in their language as much as it meant the translation in Arabic Egypt. That was amazing as to how one of the two African names could stand for the same meaning in three completely different countries in terms of belief and culture. On personal note, it created a different notion in terms of global Literacy and cultural competence. The information spread throughout the world like fire and it seemed that the usefulness of the Emeagwali internet invention through the super-computer and the emerging online educational institutions could not be over-emphasized. However, Capella University do not accept many research dissertation studies for post degrees that are likely to discuss racism and geared to solve the problem of inter-racial conflicts in the world as it is. Some of the examples include the selection of research plans to explore dissertations on Health Literacy and cultural competence among the chronically sick elderly African Americans that they felt could be against the core principles of colonialism and slavery. It is true that Capella University has never allowed that to happen and for which reason all Africans should be well made aware before they waste their time and money on tuition on incompetent and unfruitful education. Their intention seems to most likely block any development that could justify a fair and proper globalization of educational research for the implementation of equal opportunity systems for all humans. In such institutions, many programs are usually more than a 4-year paid education program worth more than $200,000 in costs, tuition and other expenses that may be described as a complete daylight theft without violence from poor Africans denoting events dating back to the past centuries of colonialism and slavery. The question that remains is whether Africans should keep on buying wrong education with this kind of theft that usually doesn't earn them anything worth when we remember about institutionalized racism as indicated above in the previous chapter. The failure of most Africans to utilize internet to reconnect Africa by their own online schools grounded with beneficial interests and Universities in all areas of education is a call that Emeagwali continues to preach to the racial victims around the world. Africa will continue to extend the past serious mistakes of colonialism and slavery in the name of online education as in the above case of Capella University and others in order to maintain the status quo where an African can invent something like the internet on the basis of Emeagwali example in the above case and only end up being used as a weapon of destruction against themselves. The question as to how that problem can be resolved through a public policy formulation in development should be a constructive priority and the actual purpose of this book on educational proliferation. Can we keep buying the strategy of silencing the discord as indicated above whereby any approach towards the eradication of the 300-400 hundred years of institutionalized racial biases is still being silenced by the bogus strategy?

The answer to the above question can become more appropriate if the specifically obvious determining factors can be closely examined to account for the past errors committed by the respective groups of people in human history. If global education is expected to be fairly utilized by the internet skills, then the most recent American election is the most profound analytical tool. It could have been so difficult if not impossible for America to elect a minority African or Kenyan American if it weren't the skills of the internet communication around the planet. That is a clear prove that the fruits of the African Nigerian, Emeagwali who discovered the internet are beginning to be sowed. It served part of the realization of the dream made by Doctor Martin Luther King junior in the last century. One of the major leaders who recognized Emeagwali was former United States president, William Bill Clinton. President Clinton was one of the most popular presidents then and even now because of his successful transformation of the United States economy from a terrible recession under his predecessor George Bush senior before 1992. As far as this chapter is concerned president Clinton's popularity translated into something even bigger on the issue of globalization under the terms education, colonialism and slavery by apologizing on behalf of his ancestors' mistakes. President Clinton apologized for the slavery of the Africans and instead of being embraced; he received a lot of negative attacks from his fellow republican opponents. It was one of the greatest moments of the American presidency which started the healing of many old wounds often expressed by discrimination and inequality in economic opportunities, health care and employment for the African Americans. As mentioned earlier, Clinton was the only president to embrace Doctor Emeagwali after inventing internet through the construction of the super-computer. The challenge is about where and how the repair of the overhaul mentioned in the above question is going to start? While it may start from such points as the destruction of healthcare disparities as tackled by the development of the Obamacare under the description of Affordable Care Act, many do think that it will start from the early stages of development as in the children and grow gradually.

As much as we continue and strife to live with our natural moral values and activities, many of us believe that children deserve to take the challenge under the guidance of the systemic correction of the above mentioned identities. Globalization will come to a collapse if people especially Africans continue to send their children to schools and expect the formal education to translate their copied identities to be corrected under the teachers' instructions of the same education. It would definitely take more than a formal education to renegade the desired development in the reclamation of the lost identities that are heading for extinction unless checked and corrected on time. It takes more than just a formal education to devise and implement a generic formulation of a long lasting imprint of solutions on the disordered elements. Consequently, it would take more than a simple follow-up of a given syllabus in an African institution to produce a long lasting remedy for the infiltrated identity as the case of the given slave names that are still expanding in the name of education. One of the challenges that were encountered during the time of Clinton's apology for slavery is that the Ugandan president Yoweri Museveni went on to collide with a rejection of the proposition. President Museveni publically exclaimed that it was incorrect for an American president to offer such an apology on behalf of his ancestors because it was actually the Africans themselves who were at fault and responsible for such evil acts on the humanity of their brothers. He stressed that the whole blame should be directed to the former grandparents or ancestors to the current African children all over the world. However, contrary to the goal of this book president Museveni did not offer a viable solution to the current globalization crises based on the colonialism, education, and disparities based on the vestiges of slavery and trans-Atlantic slave trade of the 14th century.

Many world leaders often find it easy to criticize without offering tangible solutions. In the above narrative, it was obvious that President Museveni who has been in power for more than 34 years was simply basing his argument on the syllabi on which he was educated. Unlike the great African Scientist mentioned earlier as Emeagwali, it was amazing to note that it is the same syllabi that educated Museveni that is still being used to educate our current leaders and most of whom think alike. It is even more amazing to encounter some African Americans who closely think like president Museveni and strongly criticize President Baraka Obama for expressing a non-slave mentality by using an original cultural identity bearing two African names. Reverend Jesse Jackson has previously taken a keen note on that and said that regardless of whether Africans are bearing the American status or the indigenous type there is still a colonial mentality troubling a large percentage of them. That is why one African American article recently quoted that based on what was happening in America today, we as Africans are still slaves under the consumer theory.

The quoted article mentioned above developed into a new emotional debate on many African forums online where a lot of intellectuals were either sympathetic or blameful to one another for doing nothing or less than expected to affect true change. Of course it is always an African to become free or gain independence on ridding any vestiges of slavery, but it is made to remain a distant dream when Africans themselves cannot stop thinking like slaves. The article clearly states and calls it the theory of containment whereby everything is placed in a book in a syllabus by the slave master and thereby to be consumed by the children of the slaves. The consumer has to be conditioned classically to a big scale of an extent looking similar to Pavlov's theory and so much regulated to remain deeply rooted like a stamp of the fig tree. Even when president Museveni clearly understood the theory of theology where people have to learn how to fish and keep it on their own, he still advocated for the opposing side of the isle mimicking the exact likewise supporters of the consumer theory. The problem in such advocacy is based on deep-rooted nature of education over the centuries that is about to be resolved by the discovery of the super computer and internet reach out with online business practices. It may be the turning point for the exposure of all the fallacies of education over the centuries since the industrial revolution.

One of the most fascinating issues in formal education is whether it is fitting globalization and everybody for equal opportunity or it is there to be used as a weapon of containment in whole or parts of the system. Can it teach people to be fishers of their own tribes and races to avoid the defects of the consumer theory? Many don't believe the existence of any major controversy, but if one individual teaches his neighbor how to fish in the river with full honesty then the learner should be able to perform the job and feed himself to full-time independence. That is why the world has been watching China and India develop and grow at alarming rates in the past few years to become major economic world powers to the extent of even lending money to America. That is true even when the two nations happen to be the world's most populous countries and actually holding more than a half of the whole global population. While the statistical census confirms the population similarity, China is actually a little different because it never fought for independence as India, America or many African countries. In fact, it was never colonized by anybody from anywhere in the world. Thus, China like many developed nations has never been subjected or suffered from the plagues of the consumer theory. China just attained its independence from Britain in 1947 or a few years after the Second World War. The big lesson for Africans to learn is to ask for answers as to how China under the communist system could transcend to the top within very few years while Tanzania with a partially similar lifestyle is still slow to pick up. The question as to how China has achieved that should not be as amazing as it may sound, but it offers many developing nations an inspirational instrument of future self-analysis.

It should be in clear vision that if India could gain full racial respect from former colonizers and around the world after gaining independence from Britain then anybody can actually perform the same task without being stuck at the bottom on the basis of the consumer theory. Thus, it is quite conceivable that it does not matter so much as to whether one has been or stands as a descendant of slaves as in the case in America or if there is any heritage from a colonized past. That statement concurs with the contents from the 1984 Jesse Jackson Speech at the Democratic National Convention in Los Angeles, where he was quoted as saying that "by the fact that one is born in a slum, it does not mean that the slum is born in that person" The person can actually rise above the slum and see the sunny side with brilliance in a high standard of living in shining conditions. That was a direct translation that by the fact that some people were born as slaves or descendants of slavery, it does not mean that they are stuck as to be identified by slave names, think like slaves and live in slavery conditions of the poverty in consecutive depressions and recessional economic systems. That is the greatest factor in the much needed educational overhaul as proposed in the turning point through the online systems of awareness. However, without a proper interpretation and understanding with respective implementation of the parabolic expression, the dream will still hang in a pipeline in a bridge to nowhere. The beginning of it all is to re-examine the whole system of education and the related syllabi to screen all the deterring elements that continue to plague other people into the same disparities from generation to generation.

In the past few years and particularly during the past decade, many of the affected professionals have tried to search and research on many of the related above issues in the most of the world in which we live with many hypotheses. The hypothetical remedy to identity destruction seems to depend on two or three differential factors. Those are based on either a colonial descendant or a slave descendant who can be implicated on the turning points of globalization. Like any dreamer, I dream of remaining a peacemaker other than a warmonger. Consequently, I dreamed and presented my hypothesis in the year 2000 to many modern and traditional African professionals in various fields because of my belief that charity begins at home. While I did expect some critique on that presentation, it was surprising that I received a red carpet on that particular content. That was why I later on volunteered to perform some theological work as a preacher in a small church in my community. The proposal gained a lot of momentum and convinced me that it could be applied to several areas of research if not universally so in all of them.

Just like the days of Albert Einstein and Chukwu Emeagwali, it is not easy to conceive and implement a workable formula that can create really freedom to those who are desperate and need it most. There are always roadblocks around the globe in the name of globalization. Thus, it has to take root in different horizons to produce a reasonable and tremendous result in the long run and out of simple substances using a workable formula. It could be a simple mathematical or physical formula which if well designed and constructed it could require a small force in application, but the end result is a big impact in resolutions that can be continuous for many generations. Consequently, the main idea behind the current bureaucracies of scrambling systems for developing nation traces back to the delivery of controlled social behaviors. In the controlled social systems of slavery, the long term results come out of a small force in initial applications as exemplified by the divide and rule ideology in technology that eventually expand exponentially to reach out to highly intensified proportions of human populations.

On the basis of the above information it is important to note that the first hypothetical formula was closely under the guidance integrated in the formal understanding that slavery in developmental education is made out of simple substances. The substances are formulated into groups which we see as human beings of two major types in white and black. In that respect and whether one is a theologist or scientist, there is actually one firm scientific and scriptural belief that all human beings are made out of the same flesh chemical ingredients or dust. That agreement tends to confirm the authenticity of the above hypothesis because many worldwide operations have criminalized racism based on skin color, tribe or national origin. It is based on the scientific principal that chemical substances contained in that dust are what make a human being and other animals according to species and specialized manipulation at the developmental stages of life. Consequently, the number one characteristic whose manipulation at an early age can result is tremendous changes as desired at a late age are that of identity. Without such an initiative, true change could remain a pipe dream in the waiting. Accordingly, such a developmental impact can be initiated and even implemented in the form of a theoretical classical conditioning where a new language is created as in the case of computers or in the processes of rewards based on learning merit. On such a criterion, it does not matter whether an individual is Black or light skinned and from any particular tribe or ethnic group. It is simply to identify an Indian by an Indian identity and Chinese or African by their proper identity at an early developmental age. Thus, it is solely dependent on the parents understanding as to what it really means to have a slave name as previously mentioned and to implant the same on those receiving new identity. The understanding would be passed on to the next generation and the ones to follow and thereafter from generation to generation. It is as scaring as anything in the lives of those who would like to keep others under the umbrella of slaves because it retains superiority within the baseless foundations. While they could shy away, it is proven to be the only solution to a long lasting eradication of several disparities in education and development under the auspices of globalization, colonialism and slavery. However, it is worth the exercise because even former South African president Nelson Mandela said in other terms as "there is no easy walk to Freedom"

Along the above initiative and understanding it is a common knowledge to experience different reactions to the given developing theory. As far as the Africans are concerned, there are two types of stories commonly presented. For one, those Africans from colonial Africa do strongly believe that there is great economic success under their own definitions if a child is born and given a European name as in Germany or English. However, if one chooses a simple African name like Kweisi Mfume or Baraka Obama then that choice limits a lot of sweet pies ahead of their lives. At the current time in world history, we had Kweisi Mfume and Baraka Obama as president of NAACP and the United States Government respectively. Those are some of the greatest names in the history of globalization based on proper identity.

The issue of identity whether in self destruction or reconstruction along the given guidelines has only been slightly tackled even though research has been conducted in various diverse conditions. A particular personal incident to prove that slave names are actually non-profitable occurred to me while performing my job in a company by the name Quest Diagnostics as a regular employee. Before I started working there the company had just been sued and forced to pay about one million dollars to an African American victim of racial discrimination in their employment. According to my case of the story, I happened to have been the most qualified academically in that department as the only one with a Master's degree among my co-workers. It also happened that I and another Arabic individual were the only ones with expired work-permits or actually without working permits ever as in the case of the Arabic worker. To prove the point on a personal perspective, the Arabic employee had both his first and last names in Arabic while my first name was English and second one in African. At the time of full-company sponsorship it was only the Arabic nationality that was selected with full benefits as I was shown through the door claiming the company was not doing well businesswise with a few misunderstandings. That proved that the company had learned nothing from the previous suit against them on which they were forced to million dollars. That was contrary to what the famous world class athlete, Carl Lewis said that "the best weapon against racism is best" While filled and suffering with trauma I did not sue the company because of my belief that one sows what he reaps which they sowed later on in the famous 2014 class action lawsuit by a group of women. My belief is as good as a curse because for the last ten companies that I worked for who displayed the same kind of concept ended up reaping the plagues that I prophesied because they sowed based on my treatment with racial biases displayed on unequal opportunity while being the only African in that department. The question is whether any given law that is passed can ever be implemented and enforced without the old forms of bias on education, colonialism and slave mentalities. The Supreme Court is probably the only one that I can consider to be fair in that perspective. A recent notation was witnessed in the year 2008 during the Presidential election campaigns in the United States of America. During that electioneering period and similar to other previous ones, rules had been set before the campaign launches for which all the candidates had agreed to abide by them and closely follow during as well thorough the end of the game. However, towards the end of those stiff contests so far described as the most historical bitter disagreements cropped up.

In the given circumstances on identity and while watching news on the popular CNN live channel, it was broadcasted that law makers were facing big challenges on the already setup rules for the election game. In one instant the game that was sounding interesting and overwhelming was being presided and analyzed by Donna Brazil often described as an independent in the American politics. While in Michigan, Donna Brazil had watched witness or speaker after speaker present their personal testimonies until she said that she had learned the good manners of games contests from her mother. Michigan had been disqualified as a primary contesting state in the ongoing election primaries on the Democratic Party. Being one of the referees, Donna Brazil was unanimously quoted as I watched her on television that there were one criteria that her mother taught her about the rules of any game when she grew up as a girl. She said her mother stressed by telling that the most important part of any rules that are set for any game is their validation and abiding by those rules until the end conclusion of that game. That her mother told that whenever she had to go out for any contest game she had to make sure she completely understood the rules set up for that particular game and to follow them accordingly to the dim end. Once the rules have set up and the game has started, you cannot change or amend them until the game is concluded no matter whether you are favored to win or lose. Amendments are only possible and allowed after the game is over. On a personal perspective, I strongly thought that Donna Brazil was responsible for delivering the most powerful statement to the best competitive game ever contested in a democratic primary that was heading for the general election. Consequently, the favored candidate Hillary Rodham Clinton ended up losing to her long distant underdog, Baraka Obama that shocked America and the whole world. It was the greatest moment of democracy because merit was allowed to prevail after extended dialogue that tried and almost succeeded to deny a minority African American candidate from becoming the first in the American presidency. While many Americans and people around the world may not realize the importance of that and its connection to globalization and identity, the two African names of Baraka and Obama actually became the greatest revolution in the democratic world that initiated the beginning of the end of slave mentality constituted in education, colonialism, and slavery. It actually attacked greed, selfishness and ignorance all over the world.

Education is and cannot buy wisdom, but it is all about both enlightenments for personal advancement and competition for survival of the fittest. However, for the last few centuries the conspiracy of ignorance has become so rampant that it has led to many contradictions so as to question the advocacy of educational justice and liberties which make them look like a pipe dream. A few decades back the educational expressions under the civil rights movements such as the famous quote as "all men are created equal" had spread throughout the world. One of such ignorance factors resides in the education on energy resources. One of the most intelligent presidents in the history of America, President Baraka Obama has always stressed on the importance of becoming oil independent and efficient to avoid unnecessary wars with people whose countries own most of the world oil, but we have never developed good relations with them. It is very ignorant to continue describing one as an enemy from generation to generation because of their faith and other things and yet remain full dependent on their minerals and oil-rich deposits under their territories. That is simply short-sightedness with limited time offer for generations to come. It is internationally agreed that short-sightedness or short-term goals are a destructive priority given the circumstances encountered with the past conflicts of territorial wars when the validity of ignorance-based enmity on the way to development is not realized.

One of the great American stories resides along the lines and sacrifices of President Abraham Lincoln which made him the best among them all. His main history lies on his hard work to save the union now called the United States of America. As great as it was he passed the great parable test of "a divided house does not stand" America has recently hinted on some States receding, but Abraham Lincoln noted that all men were created equal and actually freed all African slaves on his term by taking his own life in assassination. He closely wanted to abide by the United States constitution which stated that everybody in this world deserved a decent life where he could realize peace, liberty and pursuit of happiness as he reminded the Americans that they had forgotten about God. The current world wars and the potential to the third major war in that series is based on that misunderstanding.

The education under the influence of the consumer theory mentioned above does not look at the world as a house that deserves to focus on freedom, liberty and pursuit of happiness by all its residents. That is why many of us talk about pursuing personal interests other than public ones to initiate self-dependence national and international strategies. It was amazing to witness former Republican Party Secretary of State Collin Powell extend his whole support to the opponent party to elect Baraka Obama as president in the historic 2008 general election. Among the most intriguing encounters was that Collin Powell reminded the world that as African Americans we have been tuned to an education that drives us to continue believing that we are able to produce to a limited level. Collin Powell who was a former General and head of the United States Army became one of the fewest cases to make a turning point in the Republic Party when declared to be well uncomfortable when he sees a lot of African homelessness in Washington DC streets and others while he and few others were living in luxury conditions. He went ahead to advice against the Iraq war as the secretary of state for which he was later expected to resign as he did because it was an idea based on no specifics or valid causes other than mere suspicions. The difference between Collin Powell and his party or Vice-President Dick Cheney that forced him to resign later led him to quote these words "the bastards can't drive me out" I will leave when it is appropriate, declared Collin Powell. While the language may have been bombastic for a professional like Powell, it marked a major turning point or part of the beginning of world hope on inter-racial healing. That is why he ended up endorsing a democrat instead of a Republican in the 2008 United States presidential race between John McCain and Baraka Obama.

Around that same time during the Bush administration, Fidel Castro, the leader of the communist country of Cuba threw another bombshell on poverty among Africans all over the world while attending the United Nations conference in New York. He reiterated with anger that the main reason as to why poverty was still rampant among Africans was because it is deep-rooted on slavery, colonialism and education. While watching him speak on television, his facial expression could explain how angry he was on behalf of African on talking about slavery. While I did not watch the whole excerpt of the speech, I could expect somebody somewhere in the world to begin searching for a specific or general solution to such an underlying problem. A sympathetic view to such a speech could and must be the starting point and much the same way as we did with the Jewish holocaust in the Second World War where former United States Secretary Doctor Henry Kissinger was one of the escapees from Germany tragedy. Such sympathy seems to be held hostage because of the issues of ignorance, greed, selfishness and identity all of which are based on education, colonialism and slavery.

The above issues are based on the type of education people receive during their lifetimes as opposed to the firm or controversial beliefs that correct education is the foundation of any good human development. It is still a big question as to whether Africans are paying for the correct identity and the education that can actually get them out of poverty and compete with the developed world in the coming generations or just a design for a continuous mimic of the same old trends of curricula that doesn't produce, but stay dependent and partially pending towards evil. The word evil in this context is referred to a phrase that was one time used by former president George W. Bush before his re-election. He said that he did not belief that there will ever be a single time in the future history of the world that people will be free of evil. You are either with us or with the enemy, he quoted and a direct reference that one can't serve two masters according to the scriptures. France declined to support the war and was quoted as being supportive of one master in Iraq as well as then Senator Baraka Obama who voted against it. Thus, the only catch is when the same expression is utilized to identify a whole tribe or religion as one master at the expense of one individual like Vladimir Putin, Fidel Castro, Muamar Gadaffi, Sadam Hussein or Louis Farakhan. Former South African President the late Nelson Mandela posed the strongest language on opposing that war. All this could remain a misunderstanding as it sounds unless the turning points are taken serious by both the victims and the non-victims as to influence the systems of education, colonialism and slavery mentalities.

On the same issue of education, former New York Governor Mario Cuomo appeared before a television interview and rephrased some reactions to the bombing of the world Trade Center in 2001 on behalf of terrorism. The interview was as follows:

Hello former governor Cuomo and how are you doing today, asked the journalist as he greeted him? Quite well and thank you, he replied to the journalist. Now, as far as the issue of terrorism is concerned, do you think President George W. Bush is doing a good job and he is well educated on that issue? The journalist asked the governor. Governor Cuomo replied to the journalist that President Bush did have the slightest idea on how to deal with terrorism.

Caught in laughter, it was quite amusing and yet provoking for me and many on the watch to hear such a comment about the former president's performance in foreign policy affairs. Terrorism is an evil business and belief wherever it may occur, but does the current public policy on education, colonialism and slavery contain the substances needed to deal with it towards a brighter future in the generations to come? Is the use of force as in slavery going to advance education to a fair playground by all human beings in the world with negligible poverty in that operation? Is forced education not part of the causes of the large majority of homelessness based on idleness and caused by unemployment on many Africans?

Part of the answer to the above questions resides on the methods of education based on colonialism and slavery that end up affecting the lawmakers as well as the implementers or the law enforcement itself. It is true that if a violation of the law is committed by a lawmaker then the majority of the followers tend to explore the matter as an opportunity to commit crime of any type at any cost and capacity. That is particularly true when an educational lawmaker commits a crime and for some reason tends to get away with it by biased judgment through the prevailing court systems under the procedures of criminal justice. The same applies to university educational suppression tactics as mentioned earlier on Capella University online where an African talent is considered inferior and worthless and hence agrees with Emeagwali's article on identity issues in globalization. The introduction of videotaping by then Senator Baraka Obama into the law enforcement operations of police departments whenever they make arrests or initial interrogations was a great development and achievements continue to surface. While total achievement is far from being realized because of the identity issues, it serves part of the answer to the above question or the issue at hand without looking back to the old wounds as with the Rodney King of Los Angeles or the Louima Sodomization in New York a few years ago.

As progress continues based on the past few years on the issues of identity, a major breakthrough came into being that can prove the worthiness of this book and its recommendations. That happened about thirty years ago or around 1985-6 with assistance of the Reverend Jesse Jackson when a campaign was ignited to change the identity of Black Americans to African Americans. That was the first and the foundations of several turning points that was a real new turning point that is yet to be realized in terms of its significance by the children of the former slaves. Reverend Jesse Jackson agreed that it was no longer making sense for black-skinned people to be identified by the color of their skin other than by the content of their character as originally quoted by Doctor Martin Luther King junior during the civil Rights Movements of the 1960s. The usage of the word Negro that stands for offensive or Black people in identity began to disappear during that struggle, but the slave names remained. The purpose of this book is to continue to correct the identities in the same respect until the mission is accomplished for the pursuit of happiness for all under the World Constitution as could probably be led by America without any bias or favoritism. It was as challenging for the victims then as it still is to some extent for black Americans to accept identity change because of the past presentations about Africa as a dark continent full of diseases and poverty. However, it opened up some avenue from which further corrections could be initiated as in this publication.

As much as it is well known is that for America to succeed as a union it has to solve its own problems of disunity before it solves other nation's challenges. That is because of the fact that a divided house does not stand as much as the union representatives are very much aware. The issue of division has been hinted mostly by Republicans including the recent proposal by some to the State of Texas to secede from the United States of America union and particularly when the minority first African American President took power in 2008. In many perspectives, the election of Baraka Obama was very instrumental in keeping the Union intact and binding as well as serving as a lesson to the whole world in the same awareness. President stressed that things don't change from the top heading down, but the other way round. When he stopped in Israel to address the Jewish nation the foremost priority was to identify himself in detail because that is what matters most and especially so in such countries. Consequently, he explained the meaning of his first name Barack in Hebrew which is spelled differently in different countries. He confirmed to the Jewish people that Barack means a blessing or lucky. At the same time, however, he also took the initiative to explain the origin of Barack in terms of the Kenya African American ancestry. It was quite overwhelming and so interesting to hear him say that Barack actually comes from Baraka in the language of Kiswahili. Just like in the Jewish Hebrew language mentioned above, Baraka in Kiswahili means blessing or lucky. That presented a powerful image or symbol of world unity at least to some extent than never before. The same was true in the American political and cultural history and integration towards a new healing or turning point in education and healthcare economics as opposed to the subjection of the vestiges of colonialism and slavery in consequence. To complete the project on identity, the future to be of an American President in translation, Barack Obama proceeded to Egypt to address the Arabs on the basic issue of identity in terms of meaning and the origin of his names. As before, he confirmed to the Arab nation that Barack in Arabic stood for blessing or lucky. I thought he had done an amazing job to deserve winning the highest office in the United States of America and as a symbol of future unified world order in justice that represented the whites, Jews, Arabs and rest of the world as gentiles in the usual description.

Just like myself and many people who try to bring new ideas and talents for positive changes, the then Senator Obama had opponents while delivering such an important educational material and actually some from his very backyard in Chicago in the State of Illinois. In that backyard he had some of the most educated African Americans by the name Doctor Jim Keyes who presented himself as a political opponent and a member of the Republican Party. One of the worst confrontations to Barack Obama included his open utterances of distraction or wrong education about his really identity as explained above in several occasions and that of people like him. Doctor Jim Keyes claimed that Barack Obama was not a really African American because he is not one of the descendants of slavery as his father was a Kenyan who had repatriated and died in Kenya in a road accident. While that was being debated, it was also disclosed that Barack Obama's mother had blood relations to former Vice-President Dick Cheney and his grandfather was actually a former American veteran of World War II. Doctor Keyes, who was a professor and a graduate of Harvard University also attended by Dick Cheney had actually managed to convince a few people that on that basis, Barack Obama was not a descendant of slaves and therefore not qualified to be a senator even though he was born in the United States of America. The wrong or rather mis-education actually started spreading fast and deep that it even caught with prominent people like the Reverend Jesse Jackson to be so convinced and trapped on video quoting that Obama looked down on Blacks who later apologized. He had a similar issue the second time, but later apologized and forgiven accordingly because it all depended on the complexity of education, colonialism, and slave mentality issues based on the roots of identity. Even a co-worker African American lady at Bayer Pharmaceuticals where I experienced some racism on employment like many other companies in various instances disclosed to me that Barack Obama was not a Jesus after all and she wanted McCain to actually win the presidency. The only radio station she listened to and almost all research laboratory co-workers was the one handled by Rush Limbaugh often referred as the leader of the Republic party and descent by the Reverend Al Sharpton on MSNBC show. That was an educated African American lady holding a master's degree in Chemistry, but with a similar trend of thinking like Doctor Jim Keyes as mentioned earlier.

When examining the above examples that specifically target the issues of education, colonialism, and slavery, one is able to analyze the defects of the William Lynch theory proposed in 1742 that he promised could last about 1000 years or longer in validation. The retrospective theory is the one that talks about the creation of the slave at the Riverside Bank and is the basis of the current consumer theories mentioned above affecting many Africans and African Americans that is beginning to be repaired accordingly and with respect to this writing information. The theory actually agrees with the above mentioned rhetoric of former Cuban President Fidel Castro's speech as indicated earlier. It confirms that if one plants a genetically engineered seed in a given environment and it is well guided with adequate growth requirements, it could actually develop accordingly to bear fruits as originally planted. Such a seed will then keep producing more of the same seedlings from generation to generation and in this case referring to the slave seed and colonialism. However, after only one hundred years President Abraham Lincoln detected something wrong with that theory and belief by foreseeing such a program as a threat to the future survival of human existence. President Lincoln noted the underlying program was one whose foundation was hypocritical lies. However, the legend still lives while the whole world agrees that no lie lasts forever. For many of the times when a lie is discovered it causes serious fears and turmoil just as with the case of any thief who may be caught stealing. Just like the father of all lies as mentioned in scripture, some like Cliven Bundy in the picture below in this year of 2014 are still opponents of President Abraham Lincoln and conservatively supportive and confident about William Lynch theory on slave creation and development that was designed to last may be up to one thousand years.

Cliven Bundy Defends his speech Saying Blacks Were Better Off as Slaves

Cliven Bundy, the Nevada rancher claimed in his speech that he did not recognize the governing land laws by blasting a conservative folk hero for doing the opposite of that on supporting the government. The issue was encountered when the folk from the federal government's tried to stop his cattle from grazing on what is designated as public land. That is the time he reiterated that he stood by his comments and he couldn't see source of the uproar that he watched on several headline news. His main point was that he definitely thought that and suggested that African Americans might have been better off under slavery laws of the past generations. He sees blacks as slaves no matter what they may be capable of doing as in sports or more precisely in both education and physical wellbeing under sheltered places or in homelessness. He went to certify his claims because, in his view, he claimed that there is nowhere in the Constitution that it is spelled that Americans should and cannot use land owned by the local or the federal government.

Respectively and as recently as in the current year of 2015 or about three months ago at the writing of this book, America and the rest of the world were shocked to read the article related to the above story by Cliven Bundy as seen on television broadcasts all across the planet earth:

While Donald Sterling was recently fired from National Basketball Association (NBA), he added more impact to the above excerpt in issue by stating that he was the responsible feeder of the African professionals of the NBA teams in every aspect of their lives. However, the above article confirms the current case on education, colonialism, and slavery as it affects not only the children of the former slaves, but also the children of the former slave masters. This is the kind of belief that is based on lies that almost dismantled the United States of America if it weren't because of the brevity of such people as President Abraham Lincoln who gave up his life for that cause. The greatest lie that ever lived at that time and now was that in the world that we live one racial identity must be made to feel inferior by the one which thinks it should be superior and for thousands of years if not indefinitely. This lie is the basic cause of world conflicts and wars that never seem to end unless the information in this book is well documented and the contents implemented accordingly. That is why some recent article news commended more or stronger independent strategies by Africans in quote "Jason Riley: 'Africans or Blacks Ultimately Must Help Themselves" I interpreted that to mean everything that Africans need to do to compete with the rest of the world without the slightest reliance on foreigners.

After reviewing a few historical events as in the current Capella University case as well as in the past generations on the issues of identity and going back to the twentieth century, a development of a gradual level of a theory of developmental stages came into mind. I named the prospective project as the theory of permittivity development. I had come across the popularly known as the greatest Boxing heavyweight in history changing his slave names from Cassius Clay to Muhammad Ali. It is with most honest truth that he did not carry anything related to Muslim blood that anybody could associate the boxing champion then. I met Muhammad Ali first time around 1979-80 when he visited Kenya at which time he had received a heroes' welcome as one of the most influential men of the 20th century. I asked the boxing champion why he had changed his name from an English name to a religious name rooted in the nation of Islam and yet his ancestral origins were traced back to Africa with names he could choose from. He said he had been converted to a Muslim faith and thought by so doing he could rid himself of the slave names as quoted earlier by my friendly Indian and Jewish co-workers at Kings County Hospital in New York. However, it was a learning opportunity for the former champion because I made him to discover the answers as to why some people like him and the first president, Jomo Kenyatta reclaimed his African identity after having used only English names. Probably he could have changed to the right names, but conversion time was out of his way with age to display the much needed sense because he had already achieved his place I history. Despite the politics that surrounded him, Muhammad Ali was voted as the sportsman of the century.

The proposed theory of permittivity mentioned above tends to align with many daily life examples like the one describing Muhammad Ali. It tries to view every process behavior in life as a result of the behavioral patterns of the dust particles or chemicals in the underlying content which can be well programmed to resolve the current conflicts rooted deeply in tribal or racial identity. It does not discriminate between psychological or physiological principles even when the dust may be as invisible as the oxygen that every living cell breathes or lives on. Thus, identity on the basis of education, colonialism and slavery should be viewed as having been impacted by some repairable changes within the scale of dust particles in that perspective.

The issue of complexity on identity has been so significant that it needs to be communicated appropriately for treatment and educational recovery on the basis of the current syllabi and curricula. From a personal perspective, the renaming of former heavy weight champion Muhammad Ali and Kweisi Mfume formed part of the beginnings of the root cause solution to that issue. Those identities should have come the same way they did for President Baraka Obama at the time of birth or what I describe as the root levels. That is the time a newborn discovers the new world and the best time to initiate change to grow with it both chemically and physiologically.

Some of the unfounded conspiracies against the above theory of permittivity reside on the primitive beliefs that equality is a crime because skin complexity is different. It is such a primitive thought in belief that made it a good reason to classify President Yoweri Museveni of Uganda and Mobutu Sesseseko of Zaire as products of the consumer theory.

On another perspective, there was an encounter mission when former president Bill Clinton made a trip to Africa and visited Uganda. At that time, I had actually expected Clinton on such a mission to deliver world class political democratic education on globalization to his friend President Yoweri Museveni. That was extremely important because he created a legacy on apologizing for slavery on behalf of his ancestors, but was opposed by President Museveni who blamed the Africans themselves. Many if not all Africans went ahead to condemn President Museveni and particularly the African Americans that are still most affected by the triangular relatives of education, colonialism and slavery. President Museveni was completely ignorant of what Clinton was up to and particularly contrary to Doctor Emeagwali's message mentioned above on identity that is strongly in need of the knowledge on the applications of the proposed theory of permittivity.

On the basis of both the scientific and historical theories on globalization including the proposed one on permittivity, the belief that still stands is that dust cannot be created nor destroyed and regardless of the various formulations or renovations along with evolution. Consequently, the beginning of such a theory as expected can be exemplified by the mention of the virus that causes AIDS that emerged into the world less than forty years ago. According to science, the virus had evolved from other known viruses through small chemical or dust manipulation that made it to become resistant to the available treatments in the world. The treatments currently available have resulted from the scientific manipulations to counteract with viral behavior. According to the proposed theory of permittivity, it is through the same original process of creating the slavery by the slave names that the final treatment would be achieved. A simple apology for slavery as done by President Bill Clinton was good, but not strong enough to treat the underlying slave mentality in education, colonialism and globalization. Since current and future worldwide globalization is bound to affect all human beings, the treatment is urgently needed to avoid a repeat of history that is seen all over the world as conflicts of crime and political civil wars based on identity. The big question is to find the best method of communication that could compel most of the victims of slavery so as to have the treatment on call initiated as proposed.

Part of the answer to the question above resides on the identification of a unifying tool of communication and starting from Africa that is still in great suffering on the basis of the vestiges of education, colonialism and slavery. On trying to do that, an initial strategy had to be a structural implementation based on the above proposed theory. Such a tool had to be one identified to communicate a common theme and a continental approach for the roots of the affected identities and victims. On something to do with Africa, I foresaw a unifying documentation system for the newly formed Africa Union that was taking place. After studying and observing the major dialects of the continent, I thought that most of the fifty African countries could chip in and devise an easy workable tool of communication based on their culturally united roots. Upon several chats on various forums, the African Union leaders ended up gathering at their continental headquarters in the African township of Addis Ababa which is the capital city of Ethiopia. It was such an inspiring meeting whose results led to a united vote on continental documentary communication in administrative systems. Out of that conference they had voted that the language of Kiswahili had to become the official African language without any assistance of foreign intervention languages or rocket sciences. Consequently, the meeting led to a new kind of focus with a new kind of inheritance as witnessed by the whole world in 2010 within the abiding countries.

If it is to be accepted that problems don't just happen without being caused or committed by people, then it should also be true that solutions can't simply occur without someone figuring out a way to tackle them. In actuality, it is very true that not even the simplest solution can ever happen without an initial approach taken by someone out there spending time and energy. About two to three years before the assembly of the African union leaders and the historical voting of the Kiswahili as the official African language it had become clear that the problem of identity was beginning to be resolved under the permittivity theory as proposed. The same principle should follow for the correction of the personal African identities as exemplified by the former boxing champion Muhammad Ali in the last century and followed by others like Doctor Matunda Nyanchama and Professor Kivutha Kibwana. On behalf of great organizations like NAACP (National Association for Advancement of Colored People), it was a serious notation to research the backgrounds and origins of the former president by the name Kweisi Mfume. In particular, it was Doctor Matunda Nyanchama who reminded many professionals on an African forum that we Africans must insist to discover the point in time when the rain started beating us. That implied that if we determine that significant time in history, then we shall be able to formulate a repair mechanism accordingly in the same respect. However, it was encouraging to have professor Kibwana in complete agreement with my proposal on the proposed theory of Permittivity because it strictly addresses the answer to the question of root causes.

The saying that tells human beings about sowing and later reaping the same thing from whatever was sowed actually confirms that our future expectations are based on what we have performed in the past and ranging from as early as yesterday to many generations back and even centuries. Consequently, there is no way anybody anywhere can actually reap what he did not plant. If one sows love and respect, that is exactly what he or she should expect to see in their future or their generations to come based on history. Thus, it then translates into a clear analogy that if a person or group of people prefer to sow hatred in themselves or their siblings, they should expect the same payback in return at some point in their lives or in the future generations of their children and grandchildren. Intelligent people would more preferably sow love and respect as much as they would like to be respected and loved. That is why Civil Rights leader, Doctor Martin L. King said that we must learn to live together like brothers and sisters or perish like fools. As far as the identity correction is concerned, sowing was based on planting ignorance, greed and selfishness that continues to operate in education, colonialism and slavery under the theories of consumerism and permittivity. Ignorance was planted when the African identity was thrashed by the British according to the Emeagwali story given earlier when he called for a repair mechanism to that seed after discovering the super computer that later translated into internet.

The challenge of identity in the given perspective has been one of the most controversial issues in several African institutions and University campuses, but the number one priority in the highly required resolution on the expected formulations. While the alienation of the African from his cultural past continues to drill into the outskirts of their educational development, it is still an estrangement caused by the explosive political atmospheres along the partner states within the continent as well as in the diaspora. That happens while all other nationalities try their best to retain most if not all their cultural names. That is true with the Chinese, Indians and so forth who have always asked me why Africans like using other nationalities names other than the original African cultural names. I said to them that it is not everybody who does that with the best example being President Baraka Obama himself whose names originate from Kiwashili language meaning blessing. Even when he got baptized by the reverend Jeremiah Wright his names still remained the way they were as an African American. There is no way anybody can accuse him of not being a Christian because his content in character confirm the same to be highly true. Thus, in that respect, it shows that identity correction is needed now more than ever in order to treat the current defects that lead to great unemployment numbers for Africans. That is the genius of this proposal and similar others to follow.

On further analysis of the above examples there have been occasions when the choice and use of foreign names makes some people to feel great and comfortable in various conditions where the depth of the cancerous infection is very difficult to remove as the underlying ignorance. In some examples or cases like that of the former King of Rock music, Michael Jackson, he could try to transform his identity both in description and in skin color. He kept on being criticized, but stood resistant to such an allegation by denying any trials to actually change his skin color from black to light brown or yellow. One of the main reasons as to why Michael Jackson denied such an allegation was because of the fact that a serious embarrassment could hit him hard to make him look like a self-hater. That could translate to the view that he felt God did not know what he was doing by making him African and dark-skinned. In one way or another, Michael Jackson rolled up to become the greatest rock music star entertainer of the century. His fame continued to spread like fire and particularly when he composed the popular song that was entitled "We are the World" after successfully managing to bring almost all his fellow musicians together. However, his root-cause that drove him to skin color inferiority and led him to believe that by changing it to light brown could make him superior was based on the type of education, colonialism and slavery on behalf of the consumer theory on slave mentalities. At the same time that theory could be seen fading away when Michael Jackson immigrated to South Africa to become a citizen and something that was contrary to the consumer theory, but a representative of the turning point on the inter-racial healing hope. While many could not explain why Michael Jackson decided to denounce his United States citizenship in the country so called the land of opportunities, it was intellectually visible that the healing process was taking place against the consumer theory. Somewhere along the line he could and was actually going to denounce his European names to acquire the original African names within that new home country in South Africa. The big question is to find out why Africans could dislike their skin color even when they have learned the bitter side and background of history and scientific merit of the contents of every human being in the world under globalization developments. That question still stands even when the Reverend Doctor Martin Luther King stressed the point that black is beauty when whitening creams were becoming a big commodity in the African markets benefiting pharmaceutical companies while unhealthy and unsafe on side effects. One New York Lawyer who was extremely angry and without a joke or smile on his face, said during a television interview that for Africans to receive the same justice as the white people do they have to turn white. I was left in a big dilemma and a big question to seek the right answers after watching that interview throughout my life. That made me to seek the development of the theory that could try to answer many related questions through a unified principle.

The issue of identity justice is a crisis both racially and ethnically and for the world to come together and get out of crises as the current ones between Russia, Ukraine and United States or Israel-Palestine, the root cause has to be resolved or they perish like fools. The seed that was planted that gave rise to these crises and referred to as the time the rain started beating us has to be well illustrated and resolved. All these crises are due to specific causes deep rooted in identity differences across the human species on the basis of egocentrism and self-preferences over other peoples' existence. As former South African president Nelson Mandela once said, there is no particular force that can stop a determined group of human beings from achieving their rights and freedom. The truth is that not even a country that may claim super-power aspect of superiority can influence the suppression of such a determination with a special reference to America and Russia.

As the common knowledge reminds many of us is that America is basically made out of immigrants who moved in from almost all countries of the world. Thus, it should formulate policies that emulate that descriptive representation without the slightest of any prejudice. However, contrary to that dream, America is still struggling and short of the best formula on how to deal with racism in its own land before even trying to stop it elsewhere. It must lead by example or discontinue the walk while the talk sinks. The growth and development of the new and old American culture would depend more on the exploration of the American dream that calls for freedom and equality for the pursuit of happiness for all its citizens. The ideology of suppression of one or more identities by another as prescribed in the consumer theory on the basis of education, colonialism and slavery has continued to dilute the prosperity of the American capitalism and corporate investments because it is based on greed, ignorance and selfishness. Thus, the greatest remedy to the current world crises is the recognition that every identity is valuable and is the focus of the great suppressions of the world as displayed in constant conflicts. The most important development and achievement is to walk the talk without double standards on the issues of identity conflicts by utilizing the root causes which are determinable by going down and right back to the year 1492 during as well as after the discovery of America. As much as many people pose the question as to what is really missing in education that makes the various occurrences of identity crises to happen, it is agreed that the root cause of problems are the central turning points in proper public policy development formulations to alleviate and even eliminate most of those misunderstandings. The same principle should apply in most if not all other areas of research and development.

As the world gets more and more populated, there is significant time being spent by most leaders and their people as to how the world can get properly led and re-united on a long lasting mission to avoid the current wars and irrational conflicts. Since the cold wars are beginning to re-ignite cultural significance would definitely become a priority for those who played the major role in the past as it boils down to clear nonsense for anyone to initiate unnecessary wars and conflicts in the modern era. Consequently, as much as the world leaders struggle to come together with a United Nations inspiration, many different world faiths and beliefs have to find a common play ground as opposed to a mere call to wars or hateful conflicts of mass destructions. The methods as to how such a mission can become an accomplishment are a subject that has attracted a lot of attention to many scientists. The way the world has been shaped to current changes through globalization, religion, colonialism, and slavery is not only amazing and challenging to many scientists, but to a lot of world leaders and upright human beings.

Part of the answer to the above question resides on the change of global policies by the major world governments particularly the superpower nations and assisted by the United Nations encompassing the small countries. In that respect, the United States president, Mr Baraka Obama, won the presidential elections of the year 2008 on the grounds of hope for change. President Obama frequently talked about a world that was so thirsty for change and with a hope that if America changed, the whole world could follow within the next few years or generations. The expression that he frequently used in his speeches as "Fired up, Ready to go" took a lot of my attention and commensurately accelerated the finishing of this book that I had been focusing on for the last few years. That was an idea of which invention has to start from one person and spreads evenly to initiate change in the whole world regardless of how long it may take so long as it is the human right towards freedom, justice, liberty, and pursuit of happiness for all people.

It is an indisputable fact that true change is deep rooted in attitudinal overhauls which are sometimes initiated and caused by generational revolutions on different scales of life as the 2016 United States of American presidential candidate Bernie Sanders presents his case on universal healthcare and education in political revolution. In that respect, a lot of world leaders would initiate change through a total overhaul of attitude. Many examples can be cited and Obama still serves as the best example as to how the world can initiate that change of attitude. When Obama talks about change we can believe in, he actually means a change of identity attitude for the current and the future generations. Globalization towards acceptable world public equality policies seems to be the only criteria for justice and peaceful solutions. Such a fact is revealed in a transcript from a speech delivered by Philip Emeagwali at the Pan-African Conference on Globalization in 1989, Washington, DC USA. Philip Emeagwali helped give birth to the supercomputer - the technology that spawned the Internet. He won the 1989 Gordon Bell Prize, which has been dubbed the "Nobel Prize of Supercomputing.

According to Emeagwali, identity is crucially important that for a proper and fair formulation of a super public health policy and other similar structures to be implemented the following information has to be well taken. The message quoted that "I speak of the price Africans have paid for their education and "enlightenment" from personal experience. That, I was born "Chukwurah," but my missionary schoolteachers insisted I drop my "heathen" name. The prefix "Chukwu" in my name is the Igbo word for "God." Yet, somehow, the missionaries insisted that "Chukwurah" was a name befitting a godless pagan. The Catholic Church renamed me "Philip," and Saint Philip became my patron and protector, replacing God, after whom I was named, he said.

The author insists that, he had to argue that something more than a name had been lost. Something central to his heritage had been stripped away. This denial of our past is the very antithesis of a good education. Our names represent not only our heritage, but connect us to our parents and past. As parents, the names we choose for our children reflect our dreams for their future and our perceptions of the treasures they represent to us.

His indoctrination went far deeper than just a name. The missionary school tried to teach me that saints make better role models than scientists. I was taught to write in a new language. As a result, I became literate in English but remain illiterate in Igbo - my native tongue. I learned the Latin language which I considered as good as dead because I would never use in the modern world while it was the official language of the Catholic Church, which owned the schools I attended.

Today, there are more French speakers in Africa than there are in France. There are more English speakers in Nigeria than there are in the United Kingdom. There are more Portuguese speakers in Mozambique than there are in Portugal. The Organization of African Unity never approved an African language as one of its official languages. We won the battle of decolonizing our continent, but we lost the war on decolonizing our minds". Quoted Emeagwali!

There are two major alienations that the world has recorded in its history. The American alienation through the discovery of America as well as the greater part of Africa in terms of transfer from its cultural past to the present time. The alienation of the African from its cultural past is still one of the most controversial ideologies in several learning institutions around Africa, America, and the world at large. Time after another, it keeps exploding in several African University campuses and most of which are accelerated by various estrangements from within the continent that are fueled by the explosive political atmospheres. Consequently, the American and African lines of identity contain the strongest roots of attitude change that would be attributed to a long lasting change that the world urgently desires in order to achieve a lot of missions.

One of the greatest achievements that a change of attitude would inspire is the development of a root based self-appreciation. Such an appreciation would strengthen the belief that a human right is a human right, and that all human beings are created equal in all the rights that exist under God. The endless wars based on race and ethnic backgrounds, would be healed by deep-rooted attitude change including the most victimized under that basis.

The issue of attitude change is just an example of a case in which a small change in attitude can lead to tremendously big resolutions affecting the world. That is true for the fact that many people around the world have been trained and brainwashed to the attitude of judging by either appearance or simple identity other than the individual character quality. It is not quite easy to concede that the above statements are quite true, but the big question is yet to come. It is the question targeting the large scale method of determining the identity effect in terms of penetrating through the human hearts to effect real changes that the world urgently desires and longed for many years from the core principles of happiness.

Part of the answer to the above question resides on the human politics of religion and trading policies. This may only serve as the partial answer, but in actuality, it grows to become the greatest one and as much as the major description goes in terms of trading patterns on main street in modern lives of mankind in the developed countries. Consequently, it makes some sense to start the analysis with a reference to trading and globalization by close examination in accordance with the likely forces or factors that might affect the definition in relation to the various religious terms in the world. It is quite imperative to realize and recognize the true facts of trading as much and as far back as it can go into the ancient civilization. By going back into the dim past into the ancient civilization, many people plainly accept that there are as many opportunities and talents as there are people in terms of numbers. Consequently, there are five major opportunities and talents applicable with respect to the five world continents. In that regard, there develops a new ideology of translating and defining opportunity with respect to location and talent. Thus, by subscribing to such a definition, a person can determine which trading skill suits his or her talent for further developments. However, modern civilization can weaken that definition when a whole continent such as America, Africa, or Asia, decides to merge or split with others to rebuild one special unit under the influence of politics and power. Many people around the world would keep wondering what the real cause is that still stands problematic in trading and religion as to pose a lot of threat to world unity of an originally united mankind. A specific identity of a problem with a respective resolution would sound more appealing than any other option.

As far as the term trading is concerned, there is always a question of power murmuring in relationship to money as utilized in the commercialization activities, and which has consistently been mentioned in many historical books and principle records. History has quite revealed that trading has occurred in many different types of formats around the world for many generations, but the prime objective has been wealth accumulation and power enrichment. Mankind has been inspired through many races around the world, but no race has ever been more intense than the one related to money and power. Consequently, there is a huge requirement of especially enormous commitments and energy before such an accumulation of money and power can be achieved. The basic law of human needs clearly states that food or energy is the most important requirement, but energy extends beyond all aspects of that language with a phenomenal structure of identity in world politics. In that respect, many scientists throughout human civilization have invented various devices and particularly those that are electrically driven such as batteries which are capable of storing energy and serve as alternative sources of power supply which can even aid some special patient needs. However, energy remains the major basis of industrial development and as a source of power and money that still stands between worldwide controversies threatening to split mankind into poor products or simple dusts of extinction. The issue of posing a big threat to mankind inspired all the collections that led into the authorship of this important writing. Once the issue of energy as a world crisis and a main trading problem is resolved, many other related issues in that political arena would fall prey under the same resolution. It would stand as a senseless priority to plainly attempt to resolve a worldwide financial crisis if in fact same old traditions of operation are kept intact as far as energy trading is concerned.

On humanitarian requirements, energy remains the most important basic need. In that regard, it becomes quite imperative to conclude that only a long-term energy crisis resolution would serve as a sensible ideology. There is a clear indication from historical and religious books that to eat we must want to work. That is an intuition that comes as an equal opportunity employer for all humans and right from early childhood developments. Consequently, many crises tend to crop up in several environments at any time the equal opportunity is violated. Such a violation has served as the root cause of all conflicts around the world and particularly in trading activities. In that respect, it becomes a worthwhile idea to engage in the discussion of the five continents as previously mentioned with respect to their opportunities and talents.

Since the world has ever been going through financial crises in its history at one time or another, it is a universal duty to keep searching for respective and fair resolutions with a long-term investment objectives. The special reference of such resolutions would strictly follow through the origins and often described as root causes of events. That is a particular avenue that once opened, would in fact access more pathways through which other developments would most likely follow pattern. Interestingly, however, it may become quite necessary to devise a prediction that can be used to formulate a working system utilizing the five opportunities and talents as stated.

To elaborate the methods as to how the above mentioned opportunities and talents can be well utilized, it would be necessary to realize that they are as many as the number of people under normal conditions. In that context, an exemplary oil producing country like Russia or Nigeria, would be holders of large deposits of energy in crude oil, but lack a trading consumer partner that would buy the product. In that respect, the relative talents and opportunities might be well underutilized or actually never be used at all. While that may be happening, the likely consumers or potential buyers for that matter, could be desperately in need, but then suffer the inflation for lack of accessibility and finally death. Dying of cold and hunger is one of the most embarrassing tragedies witnessed in many parts of the world in all the five continents, but easily preventable. The whole world made by several governing bodies keeps watching crises and one after another on which most of them claim many lives, but very few realize what the root cause happens to be as well as the respective resolution. Crises would always be a dwelling catastrophe among human beings so long as the sources of energy and it uses have not been well understood and relativity rationing implemented. Energy as the sole element of all growths and developments would keep holding life in a complex situation because lack of proper rationing, actually causes hunger and weakness both of which lead to death through famine, crime and insecurity. A lot of debates have been presented to argue that crime and insecurity are caused by the nature of evil desires and traits. While that may be valid, it is also true that most of it is related to famine and poverty as witnessed all around the world.

While many energy crises are still being evidently witnessed around the world, the truth of the matter is that modern economic scientists have invented various machines that can produce enough energy for almost all the necessary operations for daily activities. Even at that, the world is still subjected to energy related wars and conflicting crises. Consequently, it has become an apparent necessity for the world to see through such crises and advocate on cooperation other than mere competition as we know it. A mere competition without cooperation is the most destructive priority the world can ever opt to see now or in the future generations. The world has witnessed as to how many modern leaders stand up to advocate for competition and most of which boil up to short term investments. It has been quite conceivable that almost every short term investment usually ends up in the recycling of the same egocentric crises of traditions as witnessed in the past generations with a trivial repeat of history. One of the most complex challenges that can ever be imposed on humans is one that is deep rooted in the change of attitude and still stands as mankind's greatest investment in long term investments. Failure to achieve deep rooted changes in attitude has resulted in a shallow smear of the real crises as the issues keep repeating themselves from generation to generation. It is thus, generally agreed that in order to learn, we must grow from past mistakes and develop a special desire to be taught. Only then can the small world we live in can work together to avoid unnecessary conflicts which keep on recurring and where anybody can be a launcher, but everybody remains a target.

A deep rooted investment on attitude change is nothing, but a new and renewable different type of education and inheritance which has to give great consideration into the importance of co-existence. such a consideration would be possible when an old parable or saying is well utilized for that purpose. The saying clearly states that education is the foundation of all developments. However, with both the current and the previous crises lessons that the world has witnessed, it is quite imperative to rephrase it by saying that proper education is the foundation for proper developments. Some politicians would of course make it look like a political game on launching interrogations to question what myself or someone else may mean by proper education. In so doing, they might be subjected to some criticism and turn the proponents of such materials into useful features for the majority. Most of the educational materials come by the theoretical process of hearing and through a subscribed instructor who is usually described as a certified or qualified teacher. Thus, the question becomes difficult when we try to enquire more about the basis of the qualification or certification at hand and as to whether it is a mere status quo or a different type of inheritance. For the most part, the current and old world crises and conflicts have been settled under the old textbook educational tactics. However, when cross analysis of the results and fruits reaped through various settlements is performed, it is concluded that proper education has the highest obligation to re-invent itself with a new type of inheritance on its systems of which the best option is total overhaul or high level innovation on the current educational roots.

A few people, who closely examine the current educational system as a whole, do actually experience one controversy which a lot of professionals tend to overlook. The overlook happens to be the real number one priority that needs serious revision in order to nurture a new type of inheritance. The overlook is overwhelmingly based on the failure to examine the roots of our current identity and differences ranging from religion, culture, as well as the racial similarities through the generations of our universe. As much as we would like to make ourselves faithful and compliant with the past educational inventions and achievements, it is similarly important to expose all facts whether they happen to be in favor of one group or not. Consequently, if an educational advancement is explored to prove evolution in one aspect in order to satisfy a certain desire, then it shouldn't be a problem when a new chain in the same advancement dissatisfies the respective interest. For the past few years, religious education has been considered the best razor blade that can be used to shape political exploration as much as attitude through inspiration in justice is so much accomplished. Most religious institutions and groups around the world tend to share very basic values and common practices even when their prophets may be seem to be totally different. In that regard, most of them would share the same thoughts about justice, respect and unity while others would fall short of trusting one another in terms of the rules on freedom, theft, murder, immorality and lying in general. These are among those factors that a wide survey throughout the world would serve as the basis of the underlying argument.

The United States of America is one of the largest examples of outstanding freedoms in terms of religious practices despite the. On the basis of the above argument in proposal, it is hypothetically true that religion is the number one and the foremost element in education that has to be dealt with and appropriately if there is to be a hope of recent incidents in South Carolina that resulted in nine Africans being killed in the church including their pastor. It seemed to have started rising to a new level with a new type of inheritance. A few religions believe in spiritual life and without respect, some political scientists have taken room to misinterpret the faith in order to counter attack with terroristic methods on a race to superiority. While some are fighting for spiritual superiority, some are deadly racing for material superiority. However, the common result is premature physical death with many casualties through various preaching conflicts. Material superiority has been the most controversial issues affecting all people in the whole world whether Christian, Muslim, Jewish or gentile, Juda or Hindu, etc. Many Christians and Muslims share the belief of having second life after death, but it would transcend to serious mis-education for a system to teach to the faith that unleashing anger through a suicidal bomb would be as good as appropriate. Whether it is Muslim or Christian, it would display a mis-education of the worst quality and not from the real Christians hierarchy.

On another aspect of philosophy, the major world religions share a common belief on the existence of the evil powers originating from the evil spirituality. The commonality of that sharing kindly tends to create a negotiating ground towards a workable playground. The playground converges to a point where a clear understanding is uplifted to a level of singing one hymn that if evil exists, then it has to be dealt with accordingly and using one yardstick. Consequently, if murder and stealing are wrong and painful to all human lives, it should become a universal presentation in every educational curriculum of the new type of inheritance as mentioned above. In that regard, any mis-education should be rooted out collectively with respect to that inheritance. The translation then boils out to the common understanding that if the Jewish holocaust was wrong for one group, it should be wrong for everybody else without the exclusion of the 1994 Rwandan genocide or the 16th century African slavery and slave trading across the Atlantic Ocean. That should become an enforced principle in all religions with different faiths because pain is equally felt among all people. It should be the same principle applicable to democratic systems for if they are to work and by so doing, they better be rooted in clarity, honest, and transparency or never work without pretense. However, the existence of the evil nature in certain human beings as believed by many religions still leaves a lot to be desired and solved.

Former United States president George W. Bush once said that he did not believe that the world will really ever be free of evil. While watching that speech, many would translate it for the benefit of the circumstances at that time after the bombing of the various American cities including Nairobi and Dar Es Salaam and the qualification of the continuity of such counter-terrorism as witnessed in Iraq. Others would still certify on the basis of biological weapons investigation reports announced by the intelligence agency through former secretary, Collin Powell that eventually turned out to be false. It became one of the greatest challenges of the Christian faithful because most have never reached to a point where they can support war on the basis of their faith. Well, some could describe it as ignorance which is forgivable because even his own father at some point during the funeral of Rev. Dr. Martin L. King Jr. his wife, Coretta, said that he lamented some of the things he supported or found himself part of at the climax of the civil Rights movements. The former president revealed publicly during the funeral that it was all out of ignorance. From a personal perspective, that sounded to be the greatest statement from the former president from which many would develop a new type of inheritance as they seriously suffer from the same ailment without their wishes. A lot of leaders would shy away from such a remark because of stomach politics, but I said to myself that if he had presented closely related statements, he could have raised his popularity to a probable tie with president Bill Clinton for the importance of any good leadership is based on the strong ideals of justice for all other than the privileged few as repeated many times by former senator, Ted Kennedy. However, former president Bill Clinton did even better when he threw a bombshell on America by apologizing for the evil acts of slavery on behalf of his ancestors. While he wasn't the strongest Christian or religious faithful, he still surpassed many who seem to be more faithful Christians that might most likely shy away from such a pronouncement that the whole world would admire as a new type of educational inheritance. It is the kind of religious education that the world really desires to formulate in its overhaul hypothetical proposal and particularly in the justice or righteous institutions. However, world religious freedom allows all religions to co-exist.

It is not clear whether a righteous institution is necessarily a religious institution, but the most probably greatest element that inspired the above idea was based on the faithful philosophical knowledge and belief as well as a professional on development in healthcare working as a researcher and pharmaceutical development scientist. That was the time I came up with the proposed theory of developmental permittivity (Root based scientific and cultural correctional theory) (RBSCCT), after having been inspired by a unifying characteristic between religion and science. Both religion and science agree on one interesting phenomenal feature that would be expanded appropriately in many explanations. It is the belief that regardless of whether one is creationist or a scientist, life is based on the processional development from simple particles which may themselves be non-living at the particulate level. Consequently, the particulate level that is often referred to as dust reformulates to become living according to religious beliefs which goes back to dust once the oxygen and hydrogen are removed. The dust content may be encountered in many materials used by scientists to develop parts and machines like robots and rockets, but all out of the same simple substances. Thus, the proposed theory of permittivity unifies the two beliefs to prove that everything that is desired to be developed is based on the same simple substances and only processing changes would revolutionize the products. That would supposedly be true for tooling and machines and probably so for human attitude in development whether it is race or simple ethnic conflicts. There is still that strong belief that the essence of science and religion is to discover identity in difference and in so doing to try to bring the world together out of numerous conflicts. After launching the above proposed theory of revolutionary development as it was later named, it received unanimous support from professors and other politicians in the year 2001 on American internets on the chatting forums and became instrumental on further authorship.

Despite the continuous conflicts, the above proposed theory suggests that a proposition to unification must be defined at the early stages of childhood development. Scientifically, it may not sound like the particulate level for which the basis of the theory was formulated. However, unanimous support on various forums leaves a minute room for any viable criticism on the proposed theory. It is quite conceivable that some scientists would seek more on the subject to a certain relative peer review acknowledgement. Within many limits and prime substantiated proves, there is a lot of hope that the world can still be brought to a common understanding under the general agreement that "the essence of science is to discover identity in difference". Many compromises are quite inevitable for the several world conflicts to be brought to reconciliation for which the above proposed theory projects to. The hypothetical proposal received total support without any objections at the time of its launch in the year 2001 and ranging from regular members to politicians and university professors.

As far as the religious conflicts are concerned, the above theory in proposition suggests that a proper and concrete unification process must be clearly defined at the early stages of childhood development. From both general and scientific principles, it closely sounds like the particulate grass root level at which the proposed theory was formulated. The only challenge then becomes the process and success of the likely implementation of the proposition. According to the theory, the implementation with respect to the projected goals would depend on the ideology that the early stages of childhood development during learning, many new and specific lines of transformation sites can be detected and marked or cited. That would closely simulate the methods similar to those used by biological or medical doctors in the clinical practices in prenatal care, but on a larger particulate scale. If such an experiment is well structured and carefully conducted, it is likely to follow the same principle for the respective change desired and from generation to generation. That is because of the famous theory which clearly states that matter neither be created nor destroyed. It can only be shaped and reshaped in several assemblies to produce different goods, but content would always remain dust as we see or know it and as we come and go out of this world. World innovation is all based on reshaping or more precisely described as formulation or reformulation which is usually determined by environmental conditional changes particularly temperature and light variations among others.

As mentioned above, the foremost priority is the revolutionary desire to impact on the set-up systems change that would inspire the world community into becoming a unified organization. Such an organization would closely enforce a unified agreeable regulation that respects one another no matter what religion and so long as it preaches truth and reconciliation while supporting all mankind survival with appropriate punishment. Severe punishment should be strongly imposed on any religion or organization that believes in killing others as in mass destructions for material gain and survival. Humanity in history has of course recorded extreme cases of greedy conflicts that led to painful genocides such as the most recent Rwandan tragedy of 1994. That tragedy alone witnessed the slaughter of one million people all on the basis of ethnic and cultural or religious differences. Mankind has also witnessed the holocaust during the second world war as well as the famous transatlantic slavery and slave trade in the 16th century and as much as we recognize it in Darfur in Africa's largest country of Sudan. While many people would dismiss any connection or relationship between such crimes and religion, it is sometimes quite suspiciously true that there are devil followers in existence that are responsible. However, in several politicized environments including world leaders do agree with or without reality that most of such acts are simply committed out of ignorance as well as the misinterpretation of the civil and human legal rights of living. After former United States president Bill Clinton apologized for slavery on behalf of his ancestors and all who committed the evil trading of African human beings, a few digested the matter positively as exemplified by his predecessor George Bush. Actually, George Bush summed it up very well and described it as an evil act committed out of ignorance. I do find both apologies very acceptable and useful teaching instruments for the above mentioned religious factor. Consequently, I find it quite convincing and reasonable to conclude that most if not all religious conflicts including the so called holy wars are usually acts committed out of ignorance. That is the kind of ignorance that still stands as the greatest threat to the survival or future existence of human species. Consequently, it is only through proper education as an overhaul as mentioned earlier, that can eradicate such ignorance that have cost the world a lot of millions of lives and possibly all if not checked in the future. On that making, we are bound to agree that ignorance is the greatest weapon of mass destruction. Every time I address the issue, I actually do it philosophically by rephrasing it as "ignorance is a weapon for which anyone can be a launcher, but everybody remains a target". To expand on the same point, it becomes interesting to quote the Iraq war ignorance as one of the most controversial until the truth was conspicuously exposed in the middle of the first decade of the new millennium of the year 2000. For the former United States president to have been re-elected, it was clear that a lot of people had found it easy to believe by simple verbal hearing under suspicion without physical evidence. The few, who were opposed to the war including President Obama, were proven to be correct later on after the world tragedy in experience that served as part of the causes of the global financial crises and depressions. However, the lessons learned are still fresh and would be unforgettable on a long lasting fashion while leaving a lot to be desired. Whichever way it was formulated and presented as a case for consideration among allies and other worldwide leaders, it is a teaching instrument that denotes how wisdom should be viewed as the only way out for a long lasting world union. Many have come to realize how such an event in shape actually ended up changing the world politics in various hemispheres because the power to make the right judgment is the best weapon of peaceful living and more so in avoiding world crises as those encountered. Misuse of power has led to the current global financial depressions and is one of the most delicate emotional factors that is driven out of ignorance. Under the same criteria, terrorism is likewise driven with origins deep rooted in ignorance and only treatable an evolutionary educational overhaul of the same scale from the roots, but opposite in direction.

Nevertheless, in this chapter, I have tried to dwell on the most important factor that the world needs to urgently address and resolve in order to begin investing in a future world order based on long lasting freedom and peace. That is the world dream that everyone longs for, but often derailed by a few elements out of ignorance, greed and selfishness. The significance of religious identity and understanding to underscore respect can be debated in many terms, but it is time the world had better taken the initiative to make it workable for all under the same scale of measurements. In the subsequent chapters in continuous publication, more discussion would be closely injected under the same principle so as to encourage the world union in a long lasting foundation. However, to do that it is important for the world to realize that if all people are created equal under God, then equality is universal among human species. In that respect, whatever the factor that one encounters with pain, it has to be a human pain for all without the slightest exemption or nothing prospers on the objective of achieving a long lasting and fairly justified world order based on the principles of the inter-racial healing of hope.

CHAPTER IV

WORLD ORDER BY FINANCIAL FREEDOM

Healthcare Financial mergers – Public Policy Base for the new world order.

The word finance actually refers to monetary related factors and sometimes it is even stated that too much greed for money is the root cause of all evil. That is especially true when only one class or group of people or race aims at having or owning it all and obstructing many or everybody else in other groups from having similar or equal rights on such related matters. One of the greatest political fights in American history is that based on the development of a financial health insurance healthcare system policy that can unanimously be accepted by most citizens and extend some benefits to the disadvantaged groups of mostly African Americans over the centuries. That civil war starts from the fight between democrats and Republicans on the basis of validating or repealing of Obamacare that is often called the Affordable Care Act of 2010. The fight is seemingly endless and to some it looks like a civil war that is beneficial to the rest of the developed world like Canada, Germany, China and Russia because they view it as the most serious weakness of the United States of America and truly looks correct as it translates the weakness to a roaring cold or hot Third World War. However, for that to happen, America has to walk the talk of diversity in all its operations in this place they call the land of immigrants and digest the Bernie Sanders' inspiration of financial debt-free education for the young and the future generations through a democratic revolution.

After almost one hundred years without a workable health insurance system, the election of the first African minority president marked the initiation of such an institution that has caused a lot of heat in the American political nature. The introduction of the Obamacare so called the Affordable Care Act of 2010 was like the second American Revolution that led to the assassination of former President Abraham Lincoln in 1863 for ending African slavery and slave trade. The most painful thing that the majority of Americans ever experienced before he assassination of Abraham Lincoln was the push to become independent as opposed to using African as oxen in their agricultural farmlands while they sat down idle and a sign of mental disorders. Many educational institutions like Capella University Online could hate patriotic students to death for even attempting to perform theses or dissertation research studies on anything to do with or in support of health insurance for the weak, oppressed minorities, or more precisely the Obamacare as it is called today. One wonders what their goal could be apart from even describing itself as an educational institution to start with. As mentioned previously, such Universities serve as the best examples as to how Africans are being ripped money in the form of selective education, colonialism, and slavery without actually learning anything other than a burial of the African cultural past at the expense of a rigged civilization system as Elizabeth Warren termed it. Instead of wasting money with such institutions, Africans should simply concentrate on material science exploration and writing publications of their own books of interest to rescue the African dream from becoming extinct. Some politicians could even sue President Obama for extending such healthcare act to all Americans including those who have never ever had health insurance.

If financial institutions cannot afford to respect other cultures and negotiate on merging their financial principles so as to realize profitability on both sides, then financial independence is a call in waiting in all countries. That was why it was recently noted on the news that people in Mombasa township in Kenya were printing their own money because they couldn't afford to keep searching for money printed in Britain that is designed to benefit only a few who can access it or claim to be fortunate to have it and own it at the expense of the poor in the whole African continent. Elsewhere, the new world order encounters a new rival in the banking industry with a new name of BRICS. **BRICS** is the acronym for an association of five major countries that include: **Brazil, Russia, India, China, and South Africa.** The grouping was originally known as Bric before the inclusion of South Africa in 2010. The BRICS members are all countries, but they are distinguished by their large, fast-growing economies and significant influence on regional and global affairs.

As of the writing of this book in 2014, the five BRICS countries represent almost 3 billion people which are 40% of the world population, with a combined nominal of US$16.039 trillion (20% world GDP) and an estimated US$4 trillion in combined foreign reserves. As of 2014, the BRICS nations represented 18 percent of the world economy. All these developments were as a result of disparities and most of which were exposed on the fight against Obamacare (ACA) or the greatest political fight of the new millennium. Thus, it is imperative to note that more concentration is focused on the impact of financial health care systems on living disparities and public policy developments especially among minorities and Africans. There is no way a health financial system can become workable if one group of people and Africans for that matter is made to survive on rugs and one group assigns itself with all banks ownership to impose the prevailing disparities on everything. While the democrats want to see something close to that happening, the republicans don't even want to hear about it even when the repercussions are feasible in the future.

When most world governments foresee a collapse of the current banking civilization they always think about saving the owners by bailouts to the collapsing banks attached with stimulus packages. However, the fact is that when the elephants fight, it is the grass which suffers much the same way as when they make love. Consequently, it is the Africans who still suffer the disparities which may range from credit scores which die in that midst and head on to homelessness or racial disqualifications on themselves as usual. For one, a person or professional like Madoff would have a credit score as perfect as 800, but a chemist or nurse could be denied a mortgage loan if one of the credits payment is simply one day late. This is all based on the original methods of suppression dating back to the times of creating the slave in the name of civilization and voyages of exploration. This has to continue so long as the Africans don't own any financial institutions, banks or even standing as employers in corporate terms in development. Thus, the idea of creating ones resume and background checks is not meant for all people, but minorities and Africans in particular when residing outside Africa. The question as to how it really works is something that requires deep understanding because it can follow any professional all throughout their lives and whether in the East or Western countries.

The answer to the above question starts with employment and discrimination itself attached with daily harassments on a given simple job. In such a condition, the resolution becomes difficult and challenging because one factor is cause by another factor to create a chain of similar consequences to be used as weapons of minority or African destruction. Respectively, if a racist boss terminates somebody because of his skin color, they struggle to create a fake case against that individual so that it continually affects the jobseekers all their lives. That is basically worsened by the credit score which was knocked down by the termination of the employment and failure to make the credit card payments. The suffering becomes a double sword against minorities and particularly Africans because the next thing is premature death that the racists could describe with joy as something caused by laziness while some were just made the greatest of the banks by the failures of the rigged systems. A probable resolution is a blend of financial institutions so that the poor countries like South Africa's monetary value can be acculturated with rich ones as in the case the creation of BRICS as mentioned above. That has to start with healthcare insurance as it has recently demonstrated the greatest fight of the century against minorities of Africans in that sense. The merging of such financial institutions could enhance the development of a workable blend that can open the avenues of equality in lending and overall equal opportunities in the system.

The current chapter is based on the principle of mergers from a healthcare financial impacts analysis point of view for policy reform development on such minorities as the African immigrants. For the past half of the last century, no other study has superseded the financial impacts of health policy developments as displayed by the cases with the health insurance reforms in both the developed and the developing countries. Some of those impacts studied have been experienced within the frequently emerging consolidated systems displayed through hospital mergers and other healthcare institutions like the pharmaceutical industries. While the impacts of many of those studies are felt in daily practices, not much has been done in terms of analyzing the effects of financial implications among certain groups of people and particularly the minorities. The impacts within the African immigrants tend to serve as the plausible example. An analysis of such impacts would be the target of this module in both theory and the practical perspectives.

The term merger can be well understood from the practical perspectives of such simple terms as the traffic lanes merging to become one lane in the busy driving highways in the metropolitan modern world. In such a process there are advantages and disadvantages to all the parties involved and probably beyond. Since the focus of this module is based on minorities and particularly the Africans, some applicable inferences might be mentioned in context. Thus, in some African perspectives, the term merge can be inferred from the saying that talks about the effects of two merging elephants with one or two types of interests in the African grassland in arena. The saying states that "when two elephants merge in terms of peace or conflict, it is always the grass that suffers or gets destroyed" in the grassland. Within that context, the best interpretive examples are the large elephant size healthcare institutions like the pharmaceutical industries which have accelerated their merging movements in the last few years where they suffered minimal damages, but the weakest or poor employees remained the victims of downsizing. Thus, as a burning essential in the financial healthcare system, it is not only in the clinical and social worlds that rationality must be questioned, but also in the managerial world where even immigrants experience the heaviest impact in the financial healthcare mergers. Respectively, several studies have explored the processes and impacts of mergers between certain trusts based on interviews with 96 board members, clinicians, service managers, and other health officers. They aimed to identify the "stated" and "unstated" (not publicly stated) objectives of each merger.

One aim of a merger is to achieve economic gains by taking advantage of economies of scale and scope (especially with regard to management costs) and as a result of rationalizing the provision of services. It is also argued that trusts with a single focus can provide higher quality services. Other publicly stated reasons include: "invest savings into services for patients, safeguard specialist units, and ensuring that quality and amount of services provided were maintained". The unstated drivers were concerned with specific local issues. These included a need to impose new management regimes on trusts perceived by health authorities or regional office as "undermanaged" or "lacking control", and to negotiate reductions in accumulated deficits of one of the constituent trusts.

All four cases of merger studied by the research team showed that the mergers had a negative effect on the delivery and development of services. Senior management had underestimated the timescale and effort involved in the mergers. There were some positive effects on service development, for example, that there would be more clinicians in small services to run them effectively. The creation of large trusts means that there is a larger pool of professional staff. But merger also means that senior managers had become remote, and service managers felt cut off from the services they were managing. Management lost their focus on the service and people who had been used to relating directly to senior management came to a level where they had to deal mainly with middle management which, some felt, compromised strategic developments. Management structures after the merger tended to consist predominantly of staff from one of the constituent trusts that created the impression of a 'takeover' for many employees.

While there were savings in management costs, these were not to the degree anticipated. The low savings in management costs achieved particularly in the first year after the merger suggests that the implementation of mergers needed more management support than had been anticipated. Merged organizations thus need to set realistic objectives in terms of savings in management costs by taking into account the amount of managerial input needed to implement the merger.

Far from suggesting that cost is unimportant or that great care should not be taken with the allocation of precious resources, this scan has put together a number of sources that suggest economic rationality is not the dominant mindset for patients, clinicians, or managers and therefore it should not be assumed that the future of the National Health Service can be shaped by economic rationality alone. The National Health Service needs to better understand different ways of thinking. It is unlikely to meet the needs of the public and fulfill its expectations through economic proxies. The vision of a National Health Service that moves resources closer to patients, plans care more around their individual needs, and involves patients at every stage will fail if economic rationality alone is employed to shape behavior.

It is not known how deep the analysis of the financial impacts of healthcare mergers on insurance policy reforms affects African immigrants in America. The suspected burden that undocumented immigrants may place on the U.S. health care system has been a flashpoint in health care and immigration reform debates. An examination of health care spending during 1999–2006 for adult naturalized citizens and immigrant noncitizens (which includes some undocumented immigrants) finds that the cost of providing health care to immigrants is lower than that of providing care to U.S. natives and that immigrants are not contributing disproportionately to high health care costs in public programs such as Medicaid. However, noncitizen immigrants were found to be more likely than U.S. natives to have a health care visit classified as uncompensated care. Thus, to deepen such an understanding and fill any prevailing gap, the impact of such classifications and their consequences on health insurance policy reforms was selected for this publication and book. In that respect, the approach to analyze the selected topic from the related studies is quite imperative for further understanding.

One of the most outstanding dilemmas in the universal healthcare policy development is the determination of the fair financial accountability for equality and the validation of the coverage issues in the medical care services as well as their incorporations into the related administrative programs. Previous research has shown that provider patient communication is linked to patient satisfaction, adherence to medical instructions, and health outcomes. On the same account financially poorer related health outcomes may result when socio-cultural differences between patients and providers are not reconciled in the clinical encounter. That may therefore seem to be consistent with the above saying on the two elephants' effects. In that perspective, the impacts of healthcare mergers have been the most challenging in the healthcare financial analyses in industrial development and particularly within the African immigrant context. Among the public health associations, the American Psychiatric Association has long supported principles of fairness, including equity, parity and non-discrimination. Professionals in other health and mental health disciplines, including psychology and social work, have taken that one step further by declaring strong positions against the negative impacts of healthcare mergers effects.

The foremost theoretical considerations in financial analysis include those pertaining to the policy process in health promotion with respect to research which can be extended to the universal insurance developments within the looming minority disparities. Likewise, the literal use of 'critical theory' as an agent to describe any theory founded upon it explains why injustice and disparities in healthcare financial systems are based on financial status quo structural features in the applicable spectrum. According to the critical theory, the issues of power and justice with respect to minorities are applicable in the imbalances experienced in policy developments on the basis of the prevailing financial insurance system. In that respect the knowledge that best reveals the context of the phenomenon is called the critical theory. As with positivism its ontology is a critical realist where truth is still expected to be really there but hidden by more superficial or transient truths in the financial system. In such a sense the researcher considers different perspectives and meanings that are not immediately obvious. Its epistemology is subjectivist in that critical theory values what people know from experience as in this financial analysis. Its methodology is dialogically negotiable where people of different perspectives debate the rights and wrongs of different versions of the truth to remove false consciousness and arrive at a better version of the financial or general truth. This approach uses research methods, such as case studies that focus on a contemporary phenomenon within some real-life context. Validity requires harmonic agreement between different perceptions that pinpoints the so-called real truth. The origins of critical theory are attributed to the German philosopher Jurgen Habermas, who maintained that our understandings of the world are distorted because we are blind towards much of what is relevant. That is probably what the 2016 American presidential candidate Bernie Sanders tries to explain on his running proposal when he says that American has to guarantee healthcare and education to all its citizens like other countries such as Germany and Canada. In that respect, contemporary application of the critical theory is concerned in particular with issues of power and justice and the ways that the economy grows, matters of race, class and gender, ideologies, discourses, education, religion and other social institutions, and how cultural dynamics interact to construct a social system.

The next base is the immigration theory which hints a lot on the financial analytical impact of healthcare mergers when it talks about the importance of immigrants in research and development as well as other desirable areas. Yet immigrants and minorities are the first victims of merger processes.

According to social disorganization theory, instability makes it difficult for residents to establish strong social ties, which undermines informal social control. The social disorganization theory identifies neighborhood disadvantage on analytical insurance functional disparities as one of the strongest predictors of community violence and policy reform development. Yet the evidence suggests that the link between disadvantage and violence may be less pernicious for Latinos than for Africans. Recently, many studies found that neighborhood disadvantage is a stronger predictor of African than Latino homicide victimization. Such a disparity can be a victim of downsizing within the financial mergers under the previous descriptive inter-racial terms and respective processes.

The main assumption is that the analytical focus is based on the predictability of the financial impacts of healthcare mergers on insurance policy reforms among African immigrants in America. The prevailing impacts are closely and firmly related on the issues of disparities in the given perspective. The suspected burden that undocumented immigrants may place on the U.S. health care system has been a flashpoint in health care and immigration reform debates. A financial analysis of health care spending during 1999–2006 for adult naturalized citizens and immigrant noncitizens (which includes some undocumented immigrants) finds that the cost of providing health care to immigrants is lower than that of providing care to U.S. natives and that immigrants are not contributing disproportionately to high health care costs in public programs such as Medicaid. However, noncitizen immigrants were found to be more likely than U.S. natives to have a health care visit classified as uncompensated care in that analysis. Thus, the impact of such classifications and their consequences on health insurance policy reforms cannot be over-emphasized. In that respect, the approach to analyze the financial impacts of mergers from the related studies would be based on financially related disparities in healthcare.

For the past few years the global financial systems have greatly impacted healthcare institutions in terms of accessibility and affordability of the necessary medical life services. In retrospect, it was during 2008 and 2009 that the insurance industry experienced unprecedented volatility in its functionality that now seems to call for more research work on analysis and accountability. The large swings in the insurance market valuations, and the significant role that financial reporting played in the uncertainty surrounding insurance companies during that period, translate a lot to highlight the importance of understanding insurance financial information and its implications for the current and the future generations. Thus, the rationale is depicted in terms of the risk and value of insurance companies and the related mergers in healthcare organizations such as the pharmaceutical industries and hospitals that would seem to be greatly impacting on the immigrants and particularly of the African origins. Consequently, it is plausible and imperative to analyze such impacts so as to offer alternative proposals to resolve the current dilemmas on health insurance coverage within the United States and serve as possible model for the rest of the financial world systems.

According to conventional theory, insurance premiums should be informational for efficient predictors of the present financial value of policy claims and expenses. Respectively, some studies reveal such validity and try to develop an alternative theory of insurance market dynamics based on two assumptions. First, insured risks are dependent. Under this assumption, insurers' net worth determines the market capacity since it is necessary to back the contractual promises to pay claims. Second, is that in raising net worth, external equity is more costly than internal equity? The theory explains the variation in premiums and insurance contracts over the "insurance cycle" and is supported by tests on postwar data. Along the same understanding, it is encountered that traditional life policies provide primarily death benefits, although many contracts have significant saving elements or contain living benefit clauses. The products offered by life insurers also include life-contingent annuities as well as pure investment contracts. Health insurance contracts provide reimbursements for medical expenses or income in the case of disability. According to the Insurance Information Institute, direct premium written in the life health insurance sub-industry were approximately $684 billion in 2008 fiscal year. About 51% were paid for annuities (32% ordinary individual, 19% group), 25% for life (20% ordinary, 5% group), and 24% for accident and health (13% group,

11% other). Approximately 60% of the individual annuities' premiums paid in 2008 were for variable products including direct services to consumers.

The above information is the analytical figure which presents a reasonable cause to such a complexity of accounts in the financial aspects of health insurance. The specifics are not well defined as impacted among the minorities. Thus, there seems to be no doubt that within such a gap more research in the financial analytical systems in healthcare development is an unavoidable administrative instrumentation in the modern medical business world.

While conceding that the above statements are quite imperative, it is relevant to point out that the foremost analytical study falls within the trends of the current system. One method for analyzing the impact of hospital mergers is to evaluate how costs and prices change following a merger and how changes compare with those of non-merging hospitals with similar characteristics. It is important to evaluate how these changes vary by characteristics of institutions and markets, to help antitrust enforcers identify situations in which hospital mergers are more or less likely to be harmful to consumers. This approach is consistent with the current interpretation of rule-of-reason analysis of horizontal consolidations in healthcare financial analysis.

As much as the effect of mergers continues to be felt, the process usually leads to the closure of certain holdings. In that respect, the effect of closure of a local safety-net hospital on primary care physicians' perceptions of their role in patient reveal that that group of physicians in South Los Angeles after the closure of Martin L. King (MLK) Hospital provides important insights into how the roles and practices of primary care physicians change after a local safety-net hospital closes. A majority of the physicians from both underserved and non-underserved practice settings acknowledged an effect in the year after hospital closure. More than half of the physicians interviewed reported widespread and noteworthy effects of the hospital's closure on their practices. Although health care reform may extend insurance coverage, it may still leave out certain populations such as the African immigrants, particularly in states with large numbers of them undocumented. Safety-net hospitals will hence continue to serve a vital stop-gap role for those who do not meet coverage criteria for Medicaid, Medicare, and other targeted programs in that analysis.

Another merger effect was witnessed on the analysis of the market and capital investment strategy at Catholic Healthcare West between 1996 and 2005 to illuminate the strengths and weaknesses of chain organization. Abandoning its worthwhile focus on integrated delivery and growth for growth's sake in favor of selective divestments and investments, Catholic Healthcare West achieved a remarkable turnaround in operating earnings and financial asset strength. As a nonprofit organization with religious sponsorship, however, Catholic Healthcare West also developed a strategic approach on how to balance the financial investment and divestment priorities with those stemming from its charitable mission. The study illustrated Catholic Healthcare West's strategy to distribute capital investments across the system's forty hospitals in terms of each facility's profitability, the economic prospects of the market in which it is located, the extent to which it provides charitable services and the social and health needs of its community. The study revealed that hospital consolidation, by way of hospital systems acquiring other hospitals, far outstripped the competitive transformation achieved through mergers.

Various related mergers studies have continued to be conducted and exemplary supportive results were encountered in a correlative investigation with that revisited the research on the relationship between Managed Care and Hospital Consolidation. In that study, it was widely believed that the rise of managed care caused the hospital consolidation wave of the 1990s. The study tested the proposition using data on managed care penetration and hospital consolidation from 1990 to 2000. The results suggested that the common wisdom is that false managed care penetration is not significantly related to hospital consolidation. That finding is robust to different specifications, time frames, and sample selection criteria. Furthermore, the analysis does not find other correlates of hospital consolidation leaving the question of what caused the hospital merger wave an open one. The financial impact resulting from the rising healthcare costs led to the consolidation which in turn victimized the minorities due to the inability to afford the related expenses.

Further research on the analysis of financial mergers impacts on health insurance was noted in a study with a Taiwanese institution. In that study, the impact of universal National Health Insurance on population health was analyzed within an experience based in Taiwan.

In that study it was stated that Taiwan established a system of universal National Health Insurance in 1995. The study assessed changes in amenable mortality before and after implementation of universal health insurance coverage in Taiwan. The introduction of National Health Insurance was found to be associated with a significant acceleration in the rate of decline of causes of death considered amenable to health care. In one way such nationalization would be similar to the United States Affordable Care Act of 2010 on health insurance if a similar background in the financial analysis is employed in consequence. However, in contrast, there was no clear change in the trend of mortality from conditions not considered amenable to health care that could be associated with the introduction of National Health Insurance. Those findings are in general consistent with other hypotheses and with studies reviewed by Levy and Meltzer which, while noting methodological limitations, found that improved health insurance coverage was associated with improved health. In many financial analyses in perspective, the impact of such a deal would be positive for the minorities such as the Africans or immigrants, but actually negative for the mergers corporate holdings.

The impact of mergers can be visualized from the perspective of performance on resource management of the non-profit organizations. The idea of mergers could always emerge whenever the economy of a nation experiences stagnation as to display recession in combination with severe joblessness to compensate for lack of revenue generation. One of such experiences may be detected in religious organizations where several performed features over the years do illuminate the strengths and weaknesses of chain organization after merging on big projects. Consequential analysis indicated that abandoning its erstwhile focus on integrated delivery and growth for growth's sake in favor of selective divestments and investments, the organization achieved a remarkable turnaround in operating earnings and financial asset strengths. The example illustrates the organizations' strategy that was aimed at distributing capital investments across the system's forty hospitals in terms of each facility's profitability. Such an economic distribution demonstrated an extended impact on the economic prospects of the market in which it is located, the extent to which it provides charitable services and the social and health needs of its community. Thus, the idea of the merging in the underlying context cannot be over-emphasized because the study seems to imply that hospital consolidation, by way of hospital systems acquiring other hospitals, tends to outstrip the competitive transformation achieved through mergers. However, it is not clear as to how much can be really gained in terms of employment under the diversity policies towards the healing of inter-racial tensions.

Part of the answer to the above question resides on the extent of a diversified evolution in healthcare management in such or the related institutions. In retrospect, the management analyzed in the above description was a diversified evolution of a modern capital investment economics at the non-profit hospital organization. In so doing so as to accomplish the process the forty-hospital system actually reversed its financial losses and diversified into ambulatory services and high-growth markets. While it may not present the whole answer towards the healing of the inter-racial tensions in the given healthcare industry and the related financial systems, it is true that it forms part of the solution. In the given example, the system developed a formal process for allocating capital among profitable facilities and those providing charitable services in communities with high social needs. Under the same class of development, weak capital investments were transformed tremendously for which others can read as examples of inspiration towards other projects. As a consequence, related investments as to those attached to mission development were actually made to maintain sustainable operations without expanding the system's presence in low-income communities and beyond in various merging prospects. For minorities, their strength and survival could be open ended and the choice between mergers and acquisitions could only be depending on the high level management and administrative decisions. Whether the low-income members of the community are vulnerable to any defects of the revolving decisions is a question that actually matters less in the given perspective.

Future recommendations would use the above example to support acquisitions more than simple mergers according to the evidence and reasons indicated. While that may be true, it is also a common encounter that in either case the first victims of merging or acquiring another investment are the weak or the low-income prejudiced members of any organization who present popular chronic disorders such as diabetes that heavily impacts them severely in the United States while struggling without health insurance. In such struggles other issues usually develop unconsciously on the area of compliance and adherence as the conditions keep on deteriorating. Thus, in a related study, the subject of compliance and its deteriorating effects was explored with the question as to whether medication adherence does lower health financial spending among patients with diabetes. The study involved Stuart and colleagues who examined persistently the cases of the low-cost Medicare beneficiaries and determined the extent to which health behavior, preventive services, race, and socioeconomic status are related to low spending. The objective of the project was to identify which disease states and beneficiary segments show the greatest promise for improved compliance and persistency in use of preventive therapies. In the process, Stuart and colleagues' analyses explored the role of health behaviors in combination with medication compliance to control clinical costing and financial re-imbursement structures. From that study, they concluded that higher medication adherence among diabetic Medicare beneficiaries resulted in lower medical spending. On the basis of the overall evaluation they concluded that Medicare savings exceed the cost of the drugs in the given scenario. In the given perspective, it is reasonable to conclude that those types of savings can be linked into the results obtained from the hospital closures or mergers with consolidated financial health insurance holdings that impact the minorities in the policy reform processes. The significance is going to resonate around the strategies of selective diversification as opposed to integrated delivery to uplift the victims of inter-racial tensions and keep hope alive.

One of the foremost fundamental assumptions of selective diversification is that some investments are deeply profitable while others are non-profitable at all. That is because of the fact that health care services are twofold on their future prospects, and that organizational success is determined by a judicious choice as to which to provide and which to avoid. Many people tend to think that health care administration as it stands will be segregated into bundles of physician, pharmaceutical, hospital, and ancillary services that are priced and purchased per member per month and probably from year to year. Thus, in such cases as indicated and especially where the relation between marginal cost and marginal revenue for each individual service is indicated seems to be non-existent or irrelevant. Hospitals compete with each other not for the entire clinical continuum but for each service separately, and hence the decision of which services to avoid is as important as the decision of which to provide financial implications or monetary values in healthcare.

On another perspective, the principles of selective diversification have resulted in the expansion of segregation activities in various financial healthcare systems in many communities. However, some communities have displayed a vast amount of development because they have been relatively advantageous with a growing and probably very prosperous population. In another hand and in comparatively weak competitive environment, several others have been affected by small or minority communities who are struggling with discriminate financial privileges, or very smart challengers.

In any level, the financial analytical challenge facing the healthcare systems is that each additional institution is not only a competitor but another mouth to feed, standing hungry for renovated structures to match current technologies or upgrades that would focus on maximum savings and better revenues.

On the basis of the above analysis, it seems that the hospital competitive landscape has endured often convulsive transformation during the past decade as much as the various acquisitions and mergers have demonstrated. The industry has been buffeted by conflicting forces, hampering its health as a sector and influencing the strength of its competitive posture with respect to other components of the health care delivery system. Such factors have, at various times, included persistent overcapacity, misallocation of institutional assets and resources, low payment rates, aggressive competition from physician-owned entities and specialty hospitals, and the increasing burden of uncompensated care in the financial arena.

With respect to the conventional competitive financial wisdom that size begets strength, the exemplary market forces have sparked a trend toward rapid and aggressive hospital mergers and the ascendancy of hospital systems operating as integrated delivery systems. As learned from studies in Health Affairs' 2003 thematic issue on hospitals, hospital consolidation, by way of hospital systems acquiring other hospitals, far outstripped the competitive transformation achieved through mergers.

Nevertheless, as far as this presentation is concerned and with every significance, the unintended consequences need to be accounted for when mergers are planned while other organizations undergoing restructuring operations need to take the related inter-racial findings into account as well. That would make the analyses more comprehensive for the betterment of policy reform developments in universal healthcare education in administration.

CHAPTER V

NEW WORLD ORDER BY IMMIGRATION AND WORKPLACE DIVERSITY BASES:

According to many expert views, America is a country of immigrants even when it is clearly known to belong to the Native Americans so called the Red Indians. To lead the world in the right global order or direction a demonstration and display of the due respect for newer immigrants by the older ones is strongly recommended and very mandatory. There is no possibility of achieving a new world order by America and easily for that matter unless immigration is viewed as a beneficial institution where honesty with respect to one another on a global perspective is more than welcome and necessary. Second to that is that for a new world order to work without an eminent third world war, all nations have to initiate a tribal-blind formula in their own localities or countrywide communities especially where immigrants are the basis of the economic powerhouse. The impact of the historical patterns of immigration around the world and particularly to the American continent quite truly surpasses any others as the roots of diversity in development. In that respect, the United States as a sovereign nation presents a powerful immigration case than with any other country in the world. Patterns in each generation witnessed very specific trends of immigration from varying countries of origin. The underlying cyclical fashion would result in the federal government reacting to the varying trends with legislative initiatives particularly in the workplace.

While the legislators, presidents, and the general populace often attempted to maintain the social make-up of the United States, the influx of immigrants from all over the world would come to create the multi-cultural country that grew with every decade towards a global diverse institution. In that regard, the workplace is the central melting point of diversity impacts around the world. However, it still falls short of attaining a tribal-blind formula for a truly valid diversity desired by the place sometimes called the land of opportunities in the land of immigrants. The tribal-blind formula is particularly necessary in the African countries where tribal wars have been utilized by foreigners as the major weapon of mass destruction. While some have counted it off when I proposed the original tribal-blind formula, many have not been able to offer anything better to serve as an alternative remedy for the underlying problems based on ethnicity and tribalism. My formula was backed by some prevailing prove as it will be noted in this writing because it based on the previously proposed theory of permittivity under the crisis politics of identity.

According to the foundations of the tribal-blind formula, the hypothesis takes into account the fact that basic structure of a human being is the same for everyone when considering the functional assembly of the dust from which we originate or grow and develop. Consequently, any differences that may be detected in life are only due to the environmental pressures that impact various systems and localities. In that respect the difference in skin color may be due to the differences in the nature and amount of heat absorbed as well as the type of other environmental conditions in geographical and solar changes. The prove of the tribal-blind formula is that if all African Americans could become tribe-blind by adopting to the enforced slave names, then most tribalism or ethnic wars can end in Africa. That can be accomplished by utilizing a similar principle in a different capacity of the same formula without slavish enforcements. That is because all African Americans see themselves as one even though they originally came from all parts of Africa as slaves representing almost five thousand tribes of the whole African continent. They are truly tribal-blind among themselves because their only identity is Black or African Americans all across America and the world. The question is whether Africa with the common ethnic pride can ever achieve that kind of great tribal blindness as much as we want the world to achieve skin color blindness if a workable new world order is expected to be validated as such.

Part of the answer to the above question resides on the understanding of the current world order and identity crises as previously illustrated in the first chapter. As supported by some great thinkers from Africa professor Kivutha Kibwana and doctor Matunda Nyanchama both of Kenyan origins, the understanding has to get into the grass roots and grow upwards other than from top down. Once the literate and illiterate develop that the cultural identity crisis is the cause of all other crises, then planting a new seed at that level will work the same way as the current African Americans whose identity was resolved by adapting to a uniform terminology. If the Africans were capable of being easily transformed from the original identities to the currently used European names, it should not be impossible to do likewise to utilize Kiswahili names which is actually composed of some tribal names in a match. Thus, some names like Uhuru Kenyatta, Uhuru Maneno or Uhuru Odinga should be better than Uhuru Washington or Washington Kenyatta and so good that every African should name one of their male children. Eventually that seed in principle could grow into pure Kiswahili names as Uhuru Matata or Uhuru Munene and get carried from generation to generation to a complete tribal-blind regional or continental Africa. It is quite conceivable that such an adaptation is possible because after a long campaign on formulating a common language of African communication, it was eventually agreed that Kiswahili had to become the official African language in only about ten years ago at the writing of this book.

As the world becomes more and more unified or globalized for modern mankind prosperity, the challenges of diversity in the workplaces are gaining more focus in terms of the prospective management solutions. That is particularly true within a country of immigrants like the United States of America with an emphasis on those originating from Africa and attached with several cultural differences. While the impact is well noted in terms of brain drain, it is even more so as a brain gain in such areas as health care nursing around the western world. Consequently, for the past few years, it is has been getting clearer that organizations are beginning to pursue workforce diversity as a competitive necessity in corporate development in many perspectives. In that respect, it is not only happening in order to avoid the heavy costs of litigation which often involve real equal employment opportunity legislation, but to value and pursue workforce diversity evenly so that organizations could attract, retain and encourage the contribution from a diverse population of employees to serve diverse range of customers, work effectively with business partners and suppliers, and satisfy shareholders in the long route. The whole message is based on the confrontations of the growing multiculturalism of workforce and market places around the world.

The new concept of diversity goes well beyond the traditional equal employment opportunity. It calls for recognition of contributions of the individuals with diverse backgrounds. Likewise, it calls for management of organizations to embrace difference and inclusiveness, not just tolerating those who are different but celebrating those differences as well as for the opening of work opportunities to the men and women of different colors, races, nationalities, and religions. Even further, it calls for diversity beyond gender, values, or social norms that each individual lives with. In that regard, the study of the African immigrant impacts on diversity needs a new scope of analysis for better resourceful explorations. Such a proposal is quite prominent for a more standardized accountability on global diversity in the workplaces.

Part of the answer to the above challenges resides on the development of grass root beliefs on addressing the idea that workforce diversity is no longer just about anti-discrimination in legal compliance as traditionally encrypted. It is rather the spotlight of concept of workforce diversity on the basis of the impact of inclusion and corporate performance. In that respect, many modern corporations view diversity as a competitive advantage that brings economic benefits when it is realigned to the strategic business goals of the respective organizations.

There are various ways by which diversity can be viewed and analyzed. The prominent methodologies are based on two theoretical frameworks that encompass the social identity theory and self-categorization theory. The social identity theory can be described as a theory of group membership and behavior. It is developed with the purpose of understanding how individuals make sense of themselves and other people in the social environment. Self-categorization exists when people stereotype themselves by attributing to themselves the attitudes, behaviors and other attributes they associate with membership in a particular group. According to some professionals, social identity theory and self-categorization theory are complementary theories explaining social identity, in terms of its elements and processes. Through self-categorization and group membership, individuals develop a social identity, which serves as a social-cognitive schema (norms, values, and beliefs) for their group-related behavior. Thus, it seems that stereotyping, prejudice, and conflict are critical consequences of human social identity and self-categorization.

As far as the theory of social identify is concerned, it could provide a conceptual foundation for various researchers in the examination of diversity. However, it tends to lead diversity researchers to the study of power and inequality that is usually referred to as the "minimal inter-group paradigm". This paradigm suggests that all identity groups at all times engage in in-group bias and the bias is stronger in a high status group than a low status group. Furthermore, in-group bias practiced by highly privileged groups; it is likely to be decidedly more costly to historically disadvantaged groups than the reverse could ever be. That is a valuable element in the workplace diversity development.

A review of the literature of workforce diversity in terms of the impact of the African immigrants on workplace diversity from a global perspective can be illustrated in several levels. Such a review can be accomplished with prevailing identifications of an elaborate overview of a specific group of people under the study in consideration, the theoretical analysis, and the analysis of the best practices and recommendations. In such a perspective, the review would include the definition of workforce diversity, the benefits of workforce diversity in organizational development, the impact of African immigrants on workforce diversity developments, the practices that most management can do to enhance work force diversity in organizations and especially those that would include African immigrants with a unified conclusive evaluation.

The impact of African immigrants on the workforce diversity is a primary concern for most of the local and international organizations and particularly those in the developed world. The alienation of the African from his cultural past to the present has been one of the most controversial issues in several research institutions around the world that extends more into the workplace environments. The estrangement from within the continent caused by the explosive political and economic atmospheres has added more inspiration to the issue as it affects the whole workplace performances. That has impacted today's organizational needs so as to recognize and manage workforce diversity more effectively. Many articles have been written on that topic, but there is not much on the specific definition of workforce diversity that is well focused with more concentration on the African immigrants.

Consequently, it would be reasonable to review the literature of workforce diversity in terms of the impact of the African immigrants on workforce diversity from a global perspective. Such a review would include some of the following questions: How can workforce diversity be defined? What are the benefits of workforce diversity in organizational development? What is the impact of African immigrants on workforce diversity developments? What can most management programs do in order to enhance work force diversity in organizations and especially those that would include African immigrants within the bigger picture that focuses mainly on Latin America?

A Partial answer to the above questions resides on the review of literature that would address the underlying issues from a wide perspective including the brain drain or brain gain that is being debated most on both sides of the immigration context on Africans. That would include analysis and applications of related research as well as the inclusion theories. It sounded like a new revolution back in the 1990s when the world marked the development of a new trend in manpower development in the form of workforce diversity mainly because of the liberalization and globalization of markets around the world. At the same time the liberalization of economies and structural adjustment policies brought about by such institutions as the Brentwood, opened the doors to free market economies especially in Africa which accelerated immigration tactics to various parts of the world particularly the United States and China. Those free market economies brought in the free movement of labor as a commodity which has resulted in the diverse workforce development across the continent as well as the world at large.

Workforce diversity is a complex phenomenon to manage in an organization. According to some researchers, there is no one definitive definition of diversity. In that regard, diversity is a complex, multidimensional concept as a whole with various ways by which it can be viewed and analyzed. The prominent ways can be based on two theoretical frameworks that encompass the social identity theory and self-categorization theory. Identity and self-categorization are the basic elements of immigration.

With respect to the above underlying theories of inclusion along with the common human living structures, it is quite convincing that African immigrants are arguably the most underserved subgroup within the United States. They have to date been largely ignored by researchers and public health agencies. While the number of African immigrants is relatively small, they are one of the fastest growing groups in the United States and are likely to change the demographic makeup of the black American population. Even though there has been growing interest in African immigrant groups, existing literature does not recognize the heterogeneity within this diverse population. In that regard, the result is an incomplete understanding of the factors that influence their manpower potential in such areas as health, access, and utilization of services among African immigrant groups. It is important to state that although the African population is diverse, there is limited information on African immigrants as a whole with even fewer studies that distinguish between national, ethnic or religious African communities. Literature review on the subject revealed that existing research does not distinguish by country-of-origin or ethnicity which makes it impossible to provide details along national or ethnic lines. For that reason a general analysis of African immigrants' impact in the United States is given rather than specific data on national and ethnic African groups.

As the United States policy on immigration continues to change and civil unrest forces more Africans to emigrate, public health agencies, health care providers and school administrators in the host society have been forced to launch preparations designed to address the needs of the respective communities. If those individuals, refugees in particular, are not adequately acclimated in an inclusive manner, they are at risk of downward talent assimilation with limited diversity channels. The result would be increased strain on manpower talent acquisition such as health and human service agencies as well as on public school system that would add to negative diversity developments in the workforce arena around the world.

In view of the above, it is noted with interest that the impact of African immigrants into the United States in particular can be strengthened by the consideration of their grass root historical and cultural perspectives in addition to other factors. In general foreign-born blacks are a growing subgroup within the United States black population. Those of African origin represent the largest segment of foreign-born blacks after Caribbean immigrants. Foreign-born black Africans generally have higher levels of education, income and employment rates than their American counterparts. Out of every eleven people of those who immigrate to the United States from Africa, approximately 88 percent of the adult population has a high school education or higher as compared to only 77 percent among native-born American adults regardless of race. Additionally, with one-quarter of the African immigrant population holding an advanced degree, they are one of the most highly educated groups in the United States. Nonetheless, 50 percent of all United States immigrants including Africans experience occupational downgrade upon arrival. In general, foreign degrees and experience are undervalued by United States employers and accrediting bodies, which existing literature suggests is a contributing factor for high rates of "self-employed" among certain segments of the immigrant population. It also results in the creation of ethnic enclaves that provide an economic niche in low-paying labor markets and in creating businesses that cater to ethnic communities. In that respect, individuals who are self-employed are less likely to have health care coverage than wage employees, and immigrants have greater likelihood of being self-employed than native-born Americans which means they are at greater risk of being uninsured.

An important note is that the vast majority of the African immigrants in the United States are from previously British held territories like Nigeria, Kenya, Egypt and Ghana. Common continental heritage notwithstanding, these groups are divided along linguistic, cultural, ethnic, class, nationality and educational lines. Strongly kinship-oriented, many Africans maintain strong ties with family members back home and often send remittance in order to share whatever economic prosperity they have gained in the US. That positively impacts workforce diversity in many areas of development.

Given the United States social context, the notion of a cultural and social melting pot is not representative of reality. Different groups and individuals experience varying degrees of incorporation. In the same line, immigrant groups do not uniformly undergo the same process of incorporation into American society. The question here is not whether or not the current stock of immigrants from the African continent will be incorporated, but rather into what stratum of American society will they be fitted into. Will they enter mainstream Middle America or will they join the multitude of racial groups and disenfranchised individuals at the bottom of the social ladder and economic status. There are several factors that affect the pattern of immigrant incorporation into the American society. They include race, economics and residential settlement. Incorporation is still a timeline challenge in many if not all workplaces.

By far the most impacted feature of the African immigrant in the workplace diversity development is the health care institution. The foremost structure is the brain gain that is often translated as the brain drain in the African arena. The brain gain has resulted in the recruitment of many health care African immigrants particularly in the nursing homes or assisted living institutions as well in the medical research hospitals. Such recruitments have directly impacted on workplaces diversity in terms of reducing the racial and ethnic discrimination on black or African employment in the United States workplace in particular.

While the health disparities are still an enormous concern in the United States, the impact of African immigrants on health care disparities cannot be overlooked. Systemic causes of health disparities are due in part to previous patterns of behavior and beliefs founded upon racial and ethnic stereotypes that continue to impact the level of services provided to visible minorities, in particular those of African ancestry. It has been well documented that racial minorities receive lower quality of care regardless of insurance. Noticeable impacts are that black Americans in particular have been found to receive lower quality prenatal care, are less likely to receive counseling regarding smoking and alcohol cessation as well diet and exercise, are also more likely to receive fewer pediatric prescriptions, fewer and lower quality care for hospital admissions for chest pain, and inferior management of congestive heart, and are less likely to receive access to advance therapeutic health care services including access to particular treatment for HIV/AIDS as well as differentials in mental health services. The perception of all these factors has impacted a lot on the African immigrants in the development of diversity in the workplace environment.

Further research shows an improvement of diversity in the workplace on health status stereotypes for which the African immigrant has clearly impacted. Studies of immigrant populations and regardless of country origin indicate that immigrants are generally in better health than the American born population yet they are perceived to be coming from a poor environment. Foreign born African immigrants have a life expectancy that is seven to nine years longer than their African

American counterparts. Further, foreign born black Africans over the age of 25 have the lowest age adjusted mortality rates of any immigrant group in the United States. Overall, foreign born blacks have a lower mortality rate than black Americans and white Americans. However, the black foreign born populations vary significantly among themselves. For example, of all black immigrant groups, African immigrants have the best health status, followed by Caribbean and lastly, Europeans. All these are factual impacts that have lessened most of the negative attitudes for the better workforce diversity in development.

In view of the above, it is interesting to note that an extended impact in the workplace diversity development would be the health care policies. For one, the United States immigration policy is such that a selective process is employed where by only the healthiest are permitted legal entry. In other words, only those who are more likely to be successful and contribute to the United States economy are permitted to emigrate. Consequently, if the African immigrants are proven to be the highest in terms of holding the best status in healthful living, then their impact on the American workforce would be a more developed diversity program for the betterment of the overall economy. Thus, the wages would be neutralized in the impact as the workers would be expanded as well as the respective consumers. In that respect, appropriate numbers of African immigrants and their descendants can have a significant impact on the cultural, political, and economic situation in their new country such as the United States.

Another impact that can be felt based on the African immigrant in the workplace diversity is the training base. That is the learning challenge as to how a diverse workforce in organization can be managed for global businesses. It is very likely that diverse consumers can be created through diverse education at all levels of corporate administration. Companies can succeed at diversity if the initiative to create, manage and value the diverse workforce has the full support of the top management. The rationale for diversity training programs for African immigrants is often misunderstood at all levels. So it is important to first communicate what diversity is and what an organization hopes to achieve by managing it more effectively.

A high level impact of the African immigrant is based on the employment benefits in the workplace and better understanding of customer needs. Benefits in particular such as the health insurance can be greatly appreciated as managing diversity can create a competitive advantage. Potential benefits of this diversity include better decision making, higher creativity and innovation, greater success in marketing to foreign and domestic ethnic minority communities, and a better distribution of economic opportunity. In that respect and according to one study, culturally diverse groups relative to homogeneous groups are more effective both in the interaction process and job performance. These benefits occur after a diverse group has been together for a period of time. The maintenance of diversity in organizations may be important, however, for creativity, and for improving representation and access to power in view of the demographic changes in the workforce and equal opportunity, employment equity or affirmative action, and human rights legislation. Organizations with a diverse workforce can provide superior services because they can better understand customers' needs locally or globally. In that respect, the recruitment of African immigrants has impacted a lot in the hiring minorities, women, disabled people and many more in other areas as religious institutions. Such an impact helps organizations to tap those niche markets and diversified market segments for better diversity. By the fact that all the segments of society have a stake in the development and prosperity of society as a whole, creating and managing a diverse workforce should be seen as a social and moral imperative for all mankind. As the economies are shifting from manufacturing to service economies, diversity issues will gain significant impact because in service economies, effective interactions and communications between people are essential to business success. As globalization is increasing, diversity and especially with the inclusion of the African immigrant will help organizations to enter the international arena. In that respect, some studies have indicated that diversity enhances creativity and innovation, and hence capable of producing competitive advantages. In retrospect, diverse teams make it possible to enhance flexibility and rapid response and adaptation to change. On the address of legal concerns, general legislation is to promote gender equality in the workplace. Thus, managing a diverse workforce helps in addressing concerns against discrimination that is illegal in the working situations so as to improve human rights practices around the world. That pinpoints to greater developments because it leads to a wider range of ideas and abilities, offering greater scope for innovation and competitive performance in the future and therefore enriching an organization's human capital from a global perspective.

The impact of competition in the workplace diversity is often based on the view that immigrants are generally better employees. While many employers are stereotyped to utilize one visual lens on a black skinned person, there is certainly a lot of anecdotal evidence and some systematic impression that immigrants including the African immigrants are seen as better workers by some employers, especially in comparison to native-born African Americans. It is certainly not uncommon to find small businessmen and women who will admit that they prefer Hispanic or Asian immigrants over native-born blacks. This is especially true of Hispanic and Asian employers, who often prefer to hire from within their own communities. We would expect this preference to result in lower wages and higher unemployment for those natives who are seen as less desirable. In that respect, a study of the Harlem labor market provides some systematic evidence that employers prefer immigrants to native-born blacks. Their study found that although immigrants were only 11 percent of the job candidates in their sample, they represented 26.4 percent of those hired. Moreover, 41 percent of the immigrants in the sample were able to find employment within one year, in contrast to only 14 percent of native-born blacks. The authors concluded that immigrants fare better in the low-wage labor market because employers see immigrants as more desirable employees than native-born African-Americans. Physical and personal literature reveals with some evidence that, in comparison to whites, there is an added negative effect for being black and in competition with immigrants. That is a challenge that researchers are still trying to unfold.

By far the most important impact that the African immigrants have on the workforce diversity is that it increases the supply of labor. Based on the March 2005 Current and whole immigration Population Survey, there were almost 21 million adult immigrants holding jobs in the United States. However, they are not distributed evenly across occupations and the African immigrants formed a lower percentage in that survey. For the most part, related literature generally indicates that a few years after arrival immigrant wages are very similar to those of natives in the same occupation with the same demographic characteristics. This may not be true in all places and at all times, but in general it seems that only newly arrived immigrants undercut native wages. This is probably true of illegal aliens as well. While immigrants as a group and illegal aliens in particular do earn less than native-born workers, this is generally due to their much lower levels of education. In other words, immigrants are poorer than natives, but they generally earn wages commensurate with their skills, which as a group tend to be much lower than natives.

Further research in literature indicates the presence of a big impact of the African immigrant on the incorporation processes in the workplace diversity development. The particular experience of an immigrant group or an individual is determined by social forces that predate their arrival to the United States. The social context, while ever-changing, is rooted in history of racial hierarchy that has the potential to impact opportunities for upward mobility. Issues of discrimination cannot be overstated as they are relevant factors that persons of African origin must contend with on a daily basis. American racial constructs help to define how African immigrants are perceived and self-identified within the United States social framework. For blacks in general, discrimination, systemic or overt, dramatically affects access to a wide range of resources including health care services. The social barriers created by discrimination or past discriminatory patterns of behavior continue to influence the lives and health outcomes of all persons of African ancestry even when they impact negatively on diversity developments. Racism and discrimination do largely impact on the psychological and ultimately on the physiological state of anyone exposed to this treatment. Workplace diversity consequences of exposure to racial perception and discrimination include induced stress, internalized oppression, health care barriers and structural disadvantages on all parties involved. Quite frequently, covert discrimination may take the form of systemic organizational practices and discrete life events or overt observable stressors. It may be expressed through daily hassles or sporadic irritants like single incidents of discrimination. These instances may be interrelated or independent of one another.

The major characteristics of stressful experiences in impact include "the domain in which the event occurs, the magnitude of the event, the temporal characteristics of the event, and the nature of the relationship between the stressor in question and other race-related and non-race related stressors". The consequences of racism and discrimination become increasingly more important as immigrant groups become assimilated. Existing literature states that in time foreign-born persons begin to resemble their United States counterparts in terms perceptions and lifestyle habits that include an increase in foods high in fat, smoking and living a more sedentary lifestyle. The impact of resemblance struggles is quite phenomenal. First and foremost, immigrants can escape some of the harmful effects associated with discrimination by insulating themselves within their ethnic community. Yet, successive generations that will have become increasingly more Americanized and further removed from their ethnic community will not have that benefit. Since discrimination has been identified as a catalyst for stress induced negative health outcomes, and that increased residency increases exposure, it is likely that the health of second generation and potentially African immigrants will be impacted. That is likely to extend the impact to diversity development in the workplace environment.

The impact of the African immigrant has affected workplace diversity in terms of recent political changes in the United States of electing the first African president fathered by a Kenyan African immigrant. Such an impact is greatly being felt because of the historical inequities that have produced systemic barriers to access in the past. There is a creation of additional sources of stress for which risk-taking behaviors are used as coping mechanisms on diversity developments in the workplace. Persons of African ancestry entering the United States require additional public health efforts that address the unique combination of both recent immigrant status and racial marginalization. While there is a substantial amount of literature discussing the topic of discrimination and health, few studies examine the impact of discrimination on immigrant minorities in areas where there numbers are relatively small. Of the studies conducted on the subject, few have employed psychometric tools in the design, administration, and interpretation of quantitative tests for measures of psychological variables and data in measures of discrimination.

In view of the above, identity becomes the next major impact in the development of diversity in the workplace. Identity and identity formation is the result and processes of multiple factors working on different levels. It is shaped through interactions with individuals, communities and society. People are dynamic and complex and depending on their social surroundings, certain identities may become more prominent within a particular context. The question with regards to Africans is, "to what extent is race salient?" since they have not historically been a part of the "African-American" diaspora. For a considerable portion of the first and second generation African immigrants, the adoption of a black American identity is relatively natural as they undergo "Americanization". A common racial identity within the United States social context, and close residential concentration makes it easier for the African immigrants to more readily incorporate into the popular black American culture. African immigrants would sometimes emulate black American styles of dress, popular music and use black American vernacular English to impact diversity.

The review of literature suggests that racial identification occurs through the reactive, selective, and symbolic identification processes. Reactive identification is the result of exposure to experiences related to discrimination and is associated with individuals in a lower socioeconomic position. This form of identification would represent minority groups who may feel socially and economically disenfranchised and overlooked by policy makers in the workplace. Racial and ethnic identities are reinforced by social and economic exclusions. The result is a strong ethnic identification necessitated in part by economic and social needs that foster networks to address these matters. An example of reactive identification would include pan-ethnic identification used to lobby for increased services that address collective racial or ethnic community needs. Selective ethnic identification occurs among the more affluent members of society. It is used to facilitate opportunities for advancement through social networks in which case ethnic identification is advantageous. Symbolic identification, which occurs among ethnic groups that have already been incorporated basically on economic terms, ethnicity is used as an outlet of personal expression. Like selective identification, it too is most common among those in higher socioeconomic positions. The impact of racialization can have long lasting effects as an exposure element. For immigrants it compounds an already stressful situation caused by the immigration processes and struggles with identity. In addition to facing prejudices from mainstream society, Africans also perceive their being African as a source of prejudice for employment or workplace diversity. In light of the media's portrayal of Africa only in times of political, environmental or social upheaval, Africa is often perceived as antiquated and chronically impoverished. The related natural feelings on the above basis can have tremendous impacts on workforce diversity development.

On the basis of the underlying review, literature research indicates that there are several methods that can be employed in practice to enhance the development of diversity in the workplace and hence offer solutions towards the healing of inter-racial tensions in healthcare and other practices. While we still lack a specific theory on which the genetic defects that cause inter-racial tensions can be tackled, there is one of the old useful theories that can be selected in such a perspective called the social bonding theory. The Social Bonding theory provides practical and appropriate constructs in facilitating better incorporation and management of various identities among the same species as the current human cases. While the theory was originally formulated as a tool geared towards the prevention of adolescent delinquent behavior, it turns out that the collective subscription on the premise behind the theory is that individuals become delinquent because they mostly fail to establish or maintain strong ties with current or prevailing societies which are exponentially becoming more and more diversified. The four constructs to that theory include attachment, commitment, involvement, and beliefs.

- The attachment part refers to the factorial development between an individual and the surrounding diversity for a given community. In this case the factorial development refers to affective relations that some people establish with others in significance where the family is the primary source of attachment, and parents are the primary models.
- The Commitment part refers to the cultural competence as encountered in society that is associated with ambition to attain a specific desired goal like attending higher education institutions like college or university into becoming professionally successful within the diversified community.

On the basis of those two constructs, it is highly conceivable that the above literature in review is quite consistent with the practical impact of the African immigrant on the development of diversity in the workplace environment. In that consideration, it is noted that the extent to which managers recognize diversity and its potential advantages and disadvantages many people can successfully define an organization's approach towards better management and implementation of the diversity related programs in a given community. Consequently, it becomes relatively true that no organization in the current world of globalization could survive without workforce diversity in their product developments. Thus, it is the duty of the respective managements to critically evaluate the benefits of workforce diversity in their organizations. That could be true if the healing of the burning inter-racial tensions is anything to ponder about by such managements. On the other hand the management should put in place conditions which would enhance the workforce diversity in their organizations, more especially in their strategic formulation on the diversity of the manpower development. Hence, with the diversity of the workforce, the organization would be internally and externally competitive. On a closer examination, it seems reasonable to speculate that the process of diversification of organizations could constitute six stages that include self-tolerance or denial; symbolic recognition; Unanimous acceptance; compassionate appreciation; substantial valuing; and active utilization. In such an examination the background review could seem to be in support of the belief that organizations should put in place strategies that enhance workforce diversity as part of the deal for the healing of inter-racial tensions in all applicable private and public business sectors. Thus, in such an understanding it implies that managing diversity in organizations is absolutely dependent upon the acceptance of some primary objectives to which employees are willing to commit, such as the survival of the residual community. Consequently, in today's fast-paced work environment, a successful organization is one where diversity is the norm and not the exception. Nevertheless, the above cited literature confirms that the impact of the African immigrant has been felt under in certain precincts of the terms in the given illustration. In that respect, it could be worthwhile to call for more work to expand the same research in literature so as to understand more in terms of the impacts of the diverse immigrants in the modern industries to boost the workplace diversity developments and accommodate the co-existence of Black and white people.

From the practical point of view along with the above cited literature, it is noted that the management of workplace diversity is faced with a number of challenges in order to accomplish the appropriate universal goals that are contained in various written policies and procedures in many organizations. That preview alone is a challenge that is still being explored in research for better organizational developments in diversity.

According to some analytical experiences, there is no one specific definition of diversity that can be solely applied for all practices and one that can stick together quite consistently within a given environment. In that regard, diversity is a complex, multidimensional concept as a whole. That is quite in agreement with other professionals some of whom do agree that diversity is a plural term which may depict different perceptions in different organizations, societies and national cultures without any unitary meaning. A further definition by some professionals is based on lack of a specific formula that can integrate diversity and corporate changes. Thus, they do argue that employee diversity and organizational change are inextricably linked so much so that these two elements have rarely been integrated sufficiently to meet the demands of today's fast-paced economic development towards the healing of inter-racial tensions in the United States and other affected areas of the world.

In view of the above, some professionals have noted that the management of diversity initiatives have moved beyond legal compliance with equality legislations to accepting and valuing differences. An analytical challenge is one that can explain why there are many policies and procedures still staying far from implementation. While walking the talk in that perspective is quite difficult, it is often noted that organizations react to resist change due to diversity by maintaining the status quo in the absence of any pressures to increase diversity. That retards the real root-based solutions of the inter-racial healing phenomenon that is being pursued by many administrations. As far as equal opportunity legislation is concerned, the Discrimination-and-fairness Paradigm Organizations seem to embark their focus on equal opportunities and fair treatment through legislative actions and by treating everybody the same. Such a behavior is a strict requirement that may be a bitter pill to swallow, but is being demonstrated by feasible concentrations on staff recruitment by various companies as a means of increasing the numbers of employees belonging to disadvantaged groups as in the case of African Americans.

In another perspective, there are still hurdles to be cleared in terms o inter-racial healing on the current tensions because many do not focus on the search for business benefits and the maximizing of every individual's potential as a source of competitiveness. Even with that it is rarely addressed in various organizations while a mention of diversity is non-existent. It is a solvable case as it is simply due to lack of cultural awareness on diversity which is consistent with the studies that aim at creating a culture and environment of respect. Along the same line, it is noted that the egalitarian organizational culture is often considered as a means towards the achievement of higher standards of performance and in which employees in various workplaces are viewed as valuable resource materials, strategic assets and as future prospective investments.

As far the management of diversity is concerned, there are various approaches that are utilized in order to provide insights and rationale into the importance of incorporating diversity management as part of strategic goals and objectives of the organizations. A respective approach in that context is one based on business case logic. That is to argue in favor of diversity management because of its positive impact on performance, effectiveness, as well as the anticipated economic benefits. In another similar citation, it is argued that there is an increasing shortage of qualified and talented staff and therefore organizations must exhaust all possible segments of the labor market, including minority employees where African immigrants are among the most qualified.

Another viable practice that can support organizational diversity is the utilization of the critical approach with the freedom of flexibility on proposals or suggestions related to its business expansion strategies. In the critical approach, it sometimes raises a complaint that much of the management literature on workplace diversity tends to ignore or gloss over those dilemmas that do exist while continuing to stress the potency of workshops and training to accomplish the goals of its central focus. The discipline of diversity management is inadequately theorized and characterized by political ammunition differences in approaches and Universalist frameworks. The result is that it ends up in the possibility of establishing an inadequate understanding of inequality and discrimination in the workplace that tends to be problematic. In eventuality, the whole scenario actually hinders the development of diversity and particularly in the precincts where it is needed most as within the African immigrant paradigm. On such an understanding the aims of healing inter-racial differences is slightly distracted in the process.

According to some politicians on research diversity management in terms of a postcolonial argument, they argue that the study of "inclusions" to symbolize others as well as in diversity in a globalized environment, there is an involvement towards paying attention to "the chronology of shifting identities and alignments that are brought together in the process of constituting the "other", and the current ideological realities and global integrations that mediate the formation of identity accommodations in organizational and institutional locations". It may be pointed out that neo-colonial and neo-imperial discourses of otherness continue to exist in diverse organizational environments, and that those discourses are produced both within and by organizations. In that respect, training programs that intend to assist organizational members in appreciating internal and external cultural differences may turn into symbolic sites that could be good for the systematic and problematic production of otherness in the development of diversity. In order to leverage the full potential benefits of diverse workforce on minorities or African immigrants for that matter, organizations should be urged to realign the diversity management strategy to the overall business strategy and objectives of the organization.

In view of the above information, human resource diversity leaders should develop challenging yet realistic goals for diversity interventions. Organization commitments need to be demonstrated through the appointment of senior diverse and particularly African immigrant executives to diversity task forces for succession planning, education and training initiatives. That could extend through other systems as to recruit diversity candidates for senior leadership positions; establish diversity goals and objectives for all leadership levels in the performance management process and reward programs. In another study, it is stated that accountability for the results of diversity programs is an attribute of diversity best practice organizations. With respective agreement, accountability is determined through the use of metrics, surveys, focus groups, customer surveys, management and employee evaluations, and training and education evaluations. Diversity competencies may be incorporated into management systems so that organizations can determine how employees deal with people of different cultures and styles, support workplace diversity, include diverse people in work teams, and understand the impact of diversity on business relationships. In the best effort to achieve the goals of diversity, organizations must use measurable criteria to evaluate the progress of the initiative without ruling the scientific medical aspects such as those that are related to the gene therapy theories for various incurable diseases or disorders.

It is generally true that organizational diversity initiatives and diversity programs pose serious challenges to the human resource practitioners in terms of new programming for African immigrants. In order to meet such challenges, it is essential to acquire top management commitment, the skilled training and breadth of organizational knowledge human resource possesses, and a shared understanding that managing diversity is not an isolated problem to be solved but an ongoing and lengthy process. All three of these elements are needed to sustain people's willingness to work together when they do not share values, experiences, culture, and ways of interpreting meaning and solving problems.

In the process of developing a strong diversity workplace in the underlying challenges, global diversity management should be defined to relate to the management of workforces of citizens and immigrants in different countries according to some experiences. It is management discipline that offers high concern as to how effectively a global workforce can be managed in achieving competitive advantage and business benefits, while being influenced to a large extent by organizational strategies and pressures from local labor and the product market developments. In that regard, the author recognizes that the cultural dimension of diversity program has strong sensitivity when corporations are faced with different types of customers and markets and it could be used to solve problems related to multicultural teams, gaining new market shares and product development. Thus, effectively managing a global workforce is considered to be critical in achieving benefits for business and in sustaining international competitive advantage as well as workforce mobilization where universality means all available cultures.

Nevertheless, the collective similarities between domestic and international diversity initiative designs identified above still arguably represent distinctly some of today's approaches towards conceptualizing and managing the diversity of a global workforce in development.

A valuable modern style of improvement consists of some workplace inspiration that can be developed towards the attitude of seeking for actions that make a difference. Such an attitude can be accomplished by making time to talk privately with each of the workplace employees on a regular basis. For example, if they have ten employees, then provide each with thirty minutes every two weeks where they have the opportunity to share with others or in management whatever they wish. They can ask any questions, give ideas, and have the opportunity to get to know them personally and coach and counsel them as necessary.

Another method could be to ask about employee concerns, individually, as to how they would prefer to be managed and how they would prefer to be rewarded. While many organizations often assume that money is what everyone wants, it is not necessarily true. Using learning assessments such as the Personal Profile or other tools to better understand communication styles and ingredients for the most motivating environments for different styles can be very helpful for workplace diversity developments.

A further improvement model is developing relations beyond the internalized workplace such as taking related staff to lunch every now and then, just to chat. The more actions taken to demonstrate sincere interest in the individual, the more likely the staff will want to "go the extra mile." The challenge is to be able to make the time. However, once done, they will more likely see the real person, instead of just their "packaging." Their differences will then be an asset instead of a barrier to workplace diversity development and overall productivity.

While the above evaluation may not include everything, it is acceptable that there is no "best way" to manage diversity. The execution of the workforce diversity concept could be vastly different from company to company and country to country. The very success of its implementation is dependent on business needs and workforce issues as well as situational factors, such as the organizational culture and workplace environment on its training and educational patterns. While a broad range of issues is covered, it should be noted that "one size does not fit all" as organizations are in different stages of development regarding workplace diversity. Ultimately, the strength of commitment by the chief executive officer, senior management and human resource leadership will determine whether the organization successfully leverages workforce diversity, in achieving a cultural competitive advantage.

On the basis of the above evaluation, it should be considerably necessary to assess the related issues in diversity development to determine the best way possible for the future. For the past half a century, there has been a continuous trend of immigration of the Africans from the African continent that is still popular and often presented as one of the most controversial issues in the major workplaces around the world. That is true in both the developed and developing countries within the respective diversity developing organizations. As much as it would be debated and offered in analytical evaluations, such a controversy could be affected by many factors that could trigger relevant solutions to the related issue. The greatest issue-based factor is that of education in relation to the gains and loses along the industrial developments on both sides of the diverse workplaces. The transference of the highly skilled and educated African immigrants from their home countries in the past few years has presented the greatest impact in the underlying controversy. Consequently, there is a challenging dilemma as to how the development of diversity in corporate workplaces should be treated for the best results in the future administrative global business of the world.

Part of the answer to the above question resides on the recognition of the fact that both the developing and the developed countries have been affected by the global immigration impact in various sectors of work even though the percentages may differ in that perspective. By so doing, many professionals and leaders on the two sides would be challenged to offer hypothetical recommendations that may eventually yield long lasting and fair solutions in global workforce development in diversity.

A diverse workplace includes all types of employees such as those of various races, genders, sexual orientations, ages, disabilities, with various religious and political beliefs. Employees in a diverse workplace must be willing to work with other employees who are not the same. When diversity is not present in the workplace, issues arise around discrimination, fair pay and affirmative action. To prevent diversity issues in the workplace, diversity training and seminars can be given to employees.

Workplace diversity development can be argued on the basis of disparity issues as Bernie Sanders points out and of which the most notable is concentrated in health care that still lacks the best plausible universal policy from a local and international perspective. A workplace strategy on diversity development would certainly fit the critical theory framework for further analysis as immigration of the skilled Africans creates a developmental gap in their country of origin while the same amount is added to the new country of residence. That is an inequity gap that can be illustrated by the critical theory. The critical theory focuses on political, cultural, economic, and social relationships within a culture; particularly as they are related to what groups have power and which do not as in the cases between democrats, republicans and independents. A critical theorist, for example, might do an analysis of the ways education or schools are funded and point out that children from poor families tend to go to schools that are poorly funded while children of well-to-do parents go to schools with better funding. Critical theory also argues that workplace information technology, or technology in general, is not value free. Critical theorists view information technology as another means of production and as such it has to be viewed in the context of the political, ideological and cultural assumptions of the society that has given rise to it. Critical theorists are critical of behavioral models of instruction because they are based on capitalist "efficiency" models of factory workplaces that demean the laborer and produce undesirable outcomes including negative diversity as commonly seen on immigrants notably of the African and Latino origins. Critical theorists also criticize educational software that portrays boys and men as the "movers and shakers" while portraying girls and women as "second class" participants. The critical theorists have been much more active as critics of what has been done than they have been as creators and developers of models of what can be. It is true that some of the studies by professional immigrants are good examples. However, critical theorists do make some important points, particularly concerning equity issues such as equal access to technology resources in rich and poor schools and in regard to cultural and gender biases in some educational instruments.

Another similar framework in relation to the current issue is the social identity theory that can also be considered for further improvements of the workplace diversity development. It can be described as a theory of group membership and behavior. It is developed with the purpose of understanding how individuals make sense of themselves and other people in the social environment as in the current immigration debate in the 2016 presidential race that impacts everybody in one way or another.

In view of the above analysis and with respect to the global manpower development in workplace diversity, the health care sector seems to have taken the lead on the immigrant impact and suffered the most when it is closely examined in terms of both the positive and negative effects. In that perspective and on the basis of the previously conducted practices in health care institutions, it is quite convincing that the same area can serve as the model of workplace diversity development towards immigrant inclusion and particularly on the Africans. Consequently, there is a proposal from some quarters of the world for the initiation and implementation of policies that would restrict the immigration of highly skilled professionals from developing countries and mainly in health care as the best example. Such policies may not be effective in the health sector and for which reason there is a need for innovative solutions in all diverse workplaces. According to some studies, the effectiveness of controls on the recruitment of health professionals or the so-called "ethical recruitment" policy as advocated by the United Kingdom has been limited in several cases. There have been continuing inflows of nurses from some of the poorest countries in Sub-Saharan Africa such as Malawi and Swaziland, which are prohibited by the United Kingdom's code of practice. Also, requiring graduate students to refund the cost of training if they emigrate has been ineffective, and discouraged return in such places as Ghana, Trinidad and Tobago just to name a few examples. Some promising schemes include establishing occupational categories that do not require huge investments in building specialized skills, such as "health surveillance assistants" in Malawi, who require two weeks of training.

The rationale for increasing diversity in the health workforce is evident for the overall educational development. As popular as education is in general terms, the foundations of any ancient or modern developments is based on the roots of an educational system and in this case towards a more diverse workplace. In that limelight, health care education and research remains the outstanding foundation for all other workforce diversity developments. Thus, increased diversity would improve the overall health and education of a nation especially when a policy like the popular affirmative action is utilized and expanded with enforcement even to a universal level in that perspective. That is true not only for members of racial and ethnic minority groups, but also for an entire population that would benefit from a health workforce that is culturally sensitive and focused on patient care. Diversity in the health workforce would most visibly strengthen cultural competence throughout the health system. Cultural competence profoundly influences how health professionals deliver health care. Language is a critical component of the workplace educational development, with two out of ten Americans speaking a language at home other than English. The cultural challenges posed by shifting patient demographics can best be addressed by health professionals educated and trained in a culturally dynamic environment affected by globalization. That is just an example of what is prevailing in the general workplace diversity development as globalization dictates all nations.

Nevertheless, historically, racial and ethnic minorities have always been underrepresented in the health professions in America, just as members of these populations have always been more likely to receive a lower quality of care, experience higher rates of illness and disability, and die at earlier ages than members of the white population.

The likely policy goals are those that would guide the balancing of the equation that is believed to be causing gaps on the two sides even though one side may be gaining more than the other in terms of manpower development in workplace diversity. In that respect, it is pertinent to give a brief summary of those options.

Establishing best practices on the employment of foreign workers.

Safety and Protection of foreign workers in the developed economies is the right thing to do and integral to protecting the domestic labor force.

International migration policies:

There is broad agreement that in an ideal world both migrant receiving and source countries would be working from the same script on high skill mobility.

Boosting developing countries. Trade in services.

In another scope, information could make several suggestions for Global Association of Trade Services that would benefit developing countries: expanding and standardizing the definitions of occupations; specifying standard timeframes for stays and extensions to make a clear distinction between temporary transfers and permanent migration; creating a new category for small teams and self-employed foreign specialists.

Migration policies to facilitate and protect in a global economy

Migration policies that respond to the demands of a modern economy can benefit both receiving countries and developing countries. The balancing act is in devising policies that facilitate not by making everything easy to do but by managing the process in a way that protects domestic labor markets and the economic interests of developing countries.

Facilitating means flexible, efficient, and transparent policies.

This means migration policies that are flexible, efficient, and transparent. Flexible migration policy permits increased supplies of foreign workers when demand is hot, but restricts access to foreign workers when demand is down. It protects domestic labor markets. Transparency protects the conditions of employment and human expectations.

Migration policies to help protect the interests of developing countries

There are a number of policy options open to developed countries that could help to protect the interests of developing countries and in research. Primary among these is the encouragement of return migration, but there are complementary options including restrictions on recruitment, establishing good practices, and regulating recruitment agencies.

Today, talented minority students are among the most sought-after applicants at some leading universities and professional schools that would proceed to diverse workplaces. Consequently, strong steps must be taken to expedite inclusion of underrepresented minority groups among the various health professions. According to the above analysis, an organization had been established that was named the Sullivan Commission which presented the following recommendations to set up a universal example on the development of workplace diversity:

* The complementary strategies of increasing diversity and ensuring cultural competence at all levels of the health

workforce should be endorsed by all in our society, with leadership from the key stakeholders in the health care system.
* There should be increased recognition of underrepresented minority health professionals as a unique resource for the design, implementation, and evaluation of cultural competence programs, curriculums, and initiatives.
* Public and private funding entities, including U.S. Public Health Service agencies, foundations, and corporations, should increase funding for research about racial disparities in health care and health status, including, but not limited to: research on culturally competent care, how to measure and eliminate racial bias and stereotyping, and strategies for increasing positive health behaviors among racial and ethnic groups.
* Health systems should set measurable goals for having multilingual staff and should provide incentives for improving the language skills of all health care providers.
* Health professions schools should work to increase the number of multilingual students, and health systems should provide language training to health professionals.
* Key stakeholders in the health system should promote training in diversity and cultural competence for health professions students, faculty, and providers.

All of the above recommendations are a representative of the gaps that do exist in the general initiatives in the development of workplace diversity. While health care is the dominant educational foundation of universal diversity development, the future priority is one that requires policy establishments and implementations through research expansion. That is consistent with the International Labor Organization.

The development of workplace diversity is a challenge that seems to require cooperation between the developed and the developing nations for the best way forward in terms of recommendations for improvements. The impact of the African immigrants in that perspective seems to fit into that loop of description in the mentioned training and educational programs. The effect of the accelerated globalization has many complex effects, which will directly influence future trends in skilled migration from the developing world particularly in Africa. First is the increasing importance of the global organization of production and service activity. Demographic and economic trends in the developed countries will probably lead to increased numbers of skilled immigrant admissions. In fact, it is likely that various national policies will combine to further the movement of highly skilled workers from developing to developed countries. One thing which is most likely agreeable is that developed countries stand to benefit from the contribution of highly educated foreign workers like the African immigrants for the development of workplace diversity and culture in competency. Having accepted the principle of opening markets to trade, and the belief that all parties win in an open regime, policy makers are more likely than in the past to listen to those who urge more liberal regimes of international mobility. Nevertheless, developed countries can help develop human capital with targeted policies on education and training, academic exchange, and integration in advanced information, communications, and technology for the betterment of diversity in the workplace.

CHAPTER VI

NEW WORLD ORDER PILLAR?

American and Minority Dreams – What are the two Dreams lacking that can prevent the 3rd World War?!

When Russia described Africa as the pillar of the new World Order in the year 2014, it was both inspiring and a serious business matter in ideology that only takes a lot of intelligence to understand. The same as when China was declared the number one world economic power in late 2014 to knock America to number two, but not as much as when the Clinton's apology on slavery took place in the last century. Even though it has been pointed out in the previous chapter that the future world order is about sparring partners between Western and Eastern nations on civilization superiority, it is also indicated in a lot of research that real civilization started in the African continent before spreading outwards to other nations which later surpassed Africa. Thus, the American and African civilizations are rivals of one another while the eastern bloc may tend to take sides and bend towards Africa because of on non-competition or enmity. Africa so called the foundation of modern civilization is still far from realizing its God given fruits despite the several plots through many revolutions of various magnitudes. From generation to generation dreams keep developing into bear desolate pipes leaving many to wonder what the real holding bond or force could be as the poor continue drowning in various ditches of miseries. While America is still struggling to see the need to have everybody insured by health insurance like they do in Canada, Africa is confronted with a chain of failures in most projects because of corruption and lack of cultural competence in all sectorial phases of practical operations. That is why it was stated in the previous article by Jason Riley that 'Blacks

Ultimately Must Help Themselves' However, is probably the only large massive area that has failed to recognize what it is really lacking in order to begin running the same race that is run by the rest of the world. Jason's statement is more of a question than an answer because it does not actually specify the real force that is still holding the poor masses of people from attaining the intended goals of better living standards.

To answer the above question, it is important to know that there is definitely a large number of poor people and particularly Africans who are still far from understanding what the real central force is that keeps holding the affected groups of their own people from attaining the same standards as everyone else does. Many still believe that the alienation of the African from his cultural past is basically the most controversial issue that is yet to be treated and resolved exponentially even into the highest learning institutions. However, as much as the song goes as exemplified by Michael Jackson on "We Are The World" it becomes indisputable a fact that without the realization of the African Dream, the world will never be at peace as escalation of disease and poverty would continue to infect everyone at some point. It is a big question that requires a unified solution as initiated in this authorship. Intelligent people do agree that disease and poverty are preventable by smart leaders. However, if not then they remain as biological weapons of mass destructions where anybody can be a launcher, but everybody remains a target.

Part of the answer to the above question is based on the theory indicated on the first chapter that resides on the status of the schooling textbooks that are largely utilized in many if not all institutions right from elementary through the university levels. The textbooks status is based on the previously proposed and mentioned theory of consumerism where Africa still stands as the only continent that sends their children to learn more about neighbors than themselves and pay so much for that education that later turns out to be worthless as seen in most cases of joblessness and brain drains. That begins creating the sense in attitude that we are actually inferior to our neighbor foreigners and right from the first textbook of the first grade in school. Consequently, the initial textbook which is supposed to be the mother tongue or the language called Lugha Ya Kiswahili as the one that was officially accepted as the African language by all countries in Africa is actually replaced by one designed in a foreign country like France or Britain. That is only happening in Africa where it is designed to teach that the human learning alphabet clearly originates from a neighbor or foreigner or along that combination. Thereafter the next textbook would definitely get into a slightly more advanced stage of the making to create something close to a modified instinct. The next thing is to advance the repeat process through university and then through life for generations as it is today where several victims ask about the origin of the problem where rain is actually beating us without knowing when it started. If we knew when and how the rain started beating us then the question of what kind of repair mechanism is needed will be easy to formulate just like we do with drug development once we figure out how the disease kills people.

A recent professional asked this big question, does African American child have an American dream as indicated in the article below in addition to the frustrations of the murdering of the 9 church members in South Carolina in 2015 in the United States of America:

The death of the nine church members in South Carolina is not even comparable to the Fergusson incidents of the previous year of 2014. The particular events that took place in in Ferguson, Missouri, have once again made a lighted world about the foundations of American systems as the nation began to consider the durability of racial injustice as a defining factor of the American experience. Because of what someone recently call Caucasian privilege, African children tend to experience significantly less mobility than whites and are far more likely to be incarcerated for nonviolent crimes when there is completely no tangible evidence. The American Dream has always been defined by upward mobility, but for black Americans, it's harder to get into the middle class, and a middle-class lifestyle is more precarious than previously thought.

There are numerous factors that help explain why blacks have lower levels of upward mobility, but a surprisingly unpersuasive one is family structure. It is the conservatives of the research of Raj Chetty and others who find that, "The fraction of children living in single-parent households is the single strongest correlate of upward income mobility among all the variables that was studied and explored to turn things around." But this observation comes with a caveat where children in two-parent households fare worse in areas with large numbers of single parents. There is reason to believe the causation is reversed. Rather than single-parent households causing low upward mobility, low upward mobility and rampant poverty lead to single-parenthood.

Honest research is pretty to read. Respectively, two researchers from the National Bureau of Economic Research whose names were Melissa Schettini Kearney and Phillip B. Levine conducted studies and confirmed that single motherhood is largely driven by poverty and inequality other than the other way around. Thus, the conclusion of inequality is achieved by combination of being poor and living in a more unequal environment. In a valid example, like the United States, leads young women on making early choices and a childbearing at elevated rates before marriage. All these happen because these women expect to encounter a lot of hardships in their future economic successes.

As mentioned early there is a big loophole in the education system among different groups of people. In a recent report by the British Rowntree Foundation study the above claim was validated by a comparative simultaneous finding. It found that young people born into families in the higher socio-economic classes spend a long time in education and career training with even higher expectations than their own parents. They can postpone marital family lives and family plans of childbearing until they are established as successful adults. Contrary to that scheme of life, women would usually find themselves in the slower channels where they are faced with an atmospheric pattern of unemployment and idleness, low-paid work and training schemes or disparity, rather than ordered, upward career advancement. That puts a lot of question marks on the systems of education because it demonstrates a pattern that is highly truncated in nature.

In a more recent discovery, Bhashkar Mazumder, having been among those groups of people in full life participations between the late 1950s and early 1980s, 50 percent of black children born into the bottom 20 percent of the income scale remained in the same position. At the same time only 26 percent of white children born into the bottom 20 percent of the income scale remained in the same position. His research found that the role of two-parent families for mobility may actually be less important than what the conservatives conceive to be the case. The research also confirmed that while living in a two-parent households increases upward mobility for African Americans, it actually has no effect on upward mobility for white children, nor does it affect downward mobility for either race in a similar condition or circumstances. The question that remains is what the cause could be that is responsible for the lack of upward advancement among African Americans? Some of the defects could range within the following dimensions:

1. Apartheid or residential segregation

In this case, apartheid explains how it's so easy for an African middle class to be deceived and fall back into poverty. Consequently, it resonates into terms in accordance with the sociologist John R. Logan's words. According to the most recent United states census on equal opportunity rights data, it was revealed that on average, black and Hispanic households live in neighborhoods with a ratio of 20% to 30% more of the poverty rate of neighborhoods where the average non-Hispanic white lives. It seems to be a cause that creates a continuation of implications for negative advancement from generation to generation.

While there are a lot of debates including the deliberate stupid that blame Africans themselves for being stuck in poverty, a 2009 study by Patrick Sharkey found that it is actually inherited and continuous in process. Consequently, the study concluded that neighborhood poverty alone accounts for a greater portion of the black-white downward mobility gap than the effects of parental education, occupation, labor force participation, and a range of other family characteristics collectively. That is why the United States should be united in walk more than talk. Essentially, in his study, Sharkley found that if black and white children grew up in similar neighborhoods, the inequality gap would shrink by 25-to-33 percent. When closely examined, the chart below can explain why black children are far more likely to inherit and grow up in high poverty disadvantaged neighborhoods, which is a big factor that makes upward advancement a very tough game.

One particular debate which many Africans agree is that based on compensation for slavery after the great trans-Atlantic slave trade. While most people could support reparations on the Jewish victims after the deadly holocaust in the 1940s, the same group tends to deny that Africans deserve anything closer to that. However, according to the above descriptions, the following charts can provide a summary of the related explanations on the various victims as indicated below:

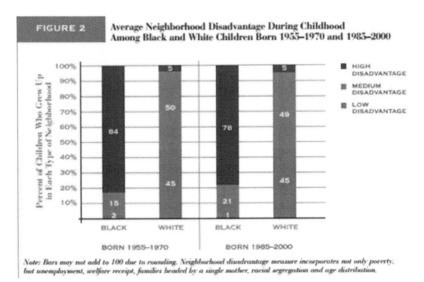

FIGURE 2 Average Neighborhood Disadvantage During Childhood Among Black and White Children Born 1955–1970 and 1985–2000

Note: Bars may not add to 100 due to rounding. Neighborhood disadvantage measure incorporates not only poverty, but unemployment, welfare receipt, families headed by a single mother, racial segregation and age distribution.

2. Business combined with War on drugs and mass victimization

While drugs are controlled for medical purposes, the war on drugs targets people of color quite unfairly and inappropriately. Respectively, one in 12 working-age African-American men is implicated while African-Americans comprise 74 percent of those imprisoned for drug possession and related matters. It is also found that the United States prison population grew to 700 percent between 1970 and 2005, while the general population rose by only 44 percent. It is quite conceivable to note that from these figures on the graph, the effects of incarceration on economic development are very appealing.

On the issue of incarceration, another perspective by Bruce Western it was noted that, "by age 48, the typical former inmate in the above description, will have earned $179,000 less than if he had never been incarcerated." This impact, however, is more conceivable among African Americans. In that study, Western found that while incarceration reduces lifetime earnings for whites by 2 percent, for Hispanics and blacks it was 6 percent and 9 percent, respectively. The implication for all of this is that men who are incarcerated will tend to live a life at the bottom of the graph.

3. Institutionalized employment segregation in all sectors

As Bernie Sanders often states in his series of the 2016 presidential race speeches is that institutionalized racism is still intact and rampant in the form of a cold civil war in America even though a few places are slowly eradicating the evil. Many workplace diversity questions arise when segregation continues on employment opportunities across the board in all sectors. That is revealed by some experts like Harvard sociologist William Julius Wilson who pointed out about important aspects of occupational segregation that contradicts the policies of diversity on employment opportunities. The point is that in comparison commute hardships and complications are twice as expensive for Africans as they are for whites.

An excellent example of occupational segregation is in Silicon Valley, where a claim based on the survey of advocacy groups like Color of Change, suggested that at Facebook, Twitter, LinkedIn, Yahoo, Google and eBay, the issue is so intense that only about 4 percent of workers are black or Hispanic in nature. Such an issue is so institutionalized that it is clearly visible in all professional workforce employment segregation where doctorate scientists are denied opportunities simply because they are Africans in nature. That is why other institutions like Working Partnerships USA upon their research found and confirmed that even though while blacks and Latinos make up only 4 percent of the disclosed companies' core tech workforce, they actually make up 41 percent of all private security guards in the above example at Silicon Valley. They also make up 72 percent of all janitorial and building cleaning workers and 76 percent of all grounds maintenance workers, but almost non-existent in the administrative level in any one company.

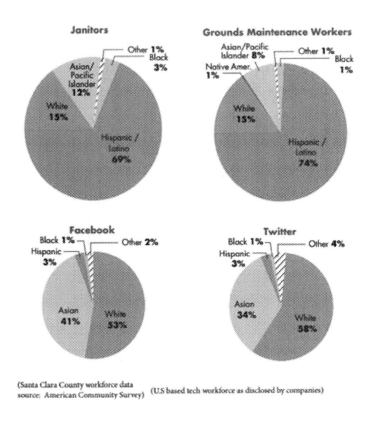

(Santa Clara County workforce data source: American Community Survey) (U.S based tech workforce as disclosed by companies)

On the basis of the above information institutionalized is particularly represented in workplaces while diversity in employment is still the most discussed issue in economic development. A bigger part of the problem seems to be sowed in the social networks. Respectively, a recent research by Nancy DiTomaso revealed that favoritism perpetuates inequality, even in the absence of racial bias. The highly publicized study found that most employees relied on social networks to obtain a majority of the jobs they held in their lifetime. However, social networks are the best tools to advance employment segregation because a prospective candidate can be scanned easily far ahead of time even before a telephone interview is conducted. Consequently, social networks tend to be segregated which fosters occupational segregation. Furthermore,

Miles Corak's study confirmed that many children get their first job through their parents making it even worse for others whose happen to be orphaned or illiterate.

One time I tried to change my name to sound Indian and I was surprised to be called immediately for an interview by Bristol Myers Squibb. However, after giving a seminar during that interview where they found I was African, everything ended and I never got the job or even the next telephone conversation. Likewise, it was quite significant to note that in Marianne Bertrand's study, the changing of the names on resumes to those that are traditionally white or black affects call-backs for jobs. The study confirmed that White-sounding names were 50 percent more likely to get called for an initial interview than Africans or Blacks in general minorities. She also found that whites with better resumes were 30 percent more likely to get a call-back than whites with worse resumes, but for Africans, more experience only increased call-backs by 9 percent. Thus, one of the current and greatest fuels to segregation or barriers to employment is actually the social networks and genetic predisposition. Employers have learned how to segregate by reading a name that is likely to be used by an African which is the exact thing President Obama said on one of his remarks speeches on inequality in America in the year 2015.

4. Economic gaps

Economics is actually based on upward mobility and equality on employment opportunities. Essentially, wealth is an important part of middle-class advancement in various lifestyle mainstreams. Most of the current wealth families were founded more than 100 years ago and in continuous accumulation. Thus, when a family or individual is struck with illness or the loss of a job, the accumulated wealth provides support. When a child attends college or is trying to get on his or her feet, a family with accumulated wealth can help pay the bills. However, that is not usually possible for those groups of people who have never had the chance to accumulate wealth due to segregation dating back to 400 years in history. Thus, the large wealth gaps between black families and white families, then, helps explain why black families have such high levels of downward mobility. It is quite astonishing to note that education rarely counts to anything much if any for most African or Black Americans because while the median white family has a net worth salary of $134,000 the median Hispanic family has a net worth of $14,000 and the median African family has a net worth of $11,000. What else can the worst thing be if this continues to be the case for centuries to come and solely based on the color of the skin other than the content of the character?

Further evidence revealed that between 2007 and 2010, all racial groups lost large amounts of wealth. However, the effects fell disproportionately on Hispanics and African Americans who lost their residential houses and jobs and saw a 44 percent and 31 percent reduction in wealth, compared to an 11 percent drop for whites. The main reason was that blacks and Latinos disproportionately received subprime loans, both because of outright lending discrimination and housing segregation. At about the same time as in the foregoing study, another parallel report by the Institution on Assets and Social Policy came up to confirm that the wealth gap between white families and African-Americans did actually triple between 1984 and 2009. They find five main factors responsible for driving the gap, which together explain 66 percent of the growth in inequality. The factors, in order of importance, are number of years of homeownership, household income, unemployment, college education and financial support or inheritance over the centuries back to 300 to 400 years.

5. Double standard education system without a real one yardstick of measurement

The U.S. increasingly has a double edged gauge for a real standard of educational qualification for job placement, with students of color trapped in underfunded schools and swayed between academic skills and industrial experience. Consequently, a recent study found that schools with 90 percent or more students of color spend a full $733 less per student per year than schools with 90 percent or more white students while job placement is only guaranteed for mostly white students.

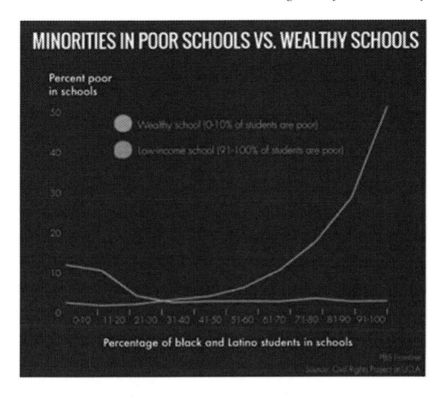

MINORITIES IN POOR SCHOOLS VS. WEALTHY SCHOOLS

The above graph confirms that schools today are more segregated, rather than less segregated as the daily talk may reveal. Just like what is commonly encountered in marriage, the average white student attends a school that is somewhere at 72.5 percent white and 8.3 percent black. In contrary, the average black student in many neighborhoods attends a school that is only 27.6 percent white, but is 48.8 percent black. These schools are underfunded and understaffed while lacking the implementations of diversity policies that later translate into institutionalized racial tensions. In 2001, the American Civil Liberties Union found that more than 18 public schools had literature classes without books. It could be worse if more assessment could be conducted to determine which cultural literature was more supported and why.

In further research on foundations of racial divisions in the American continent and beyond, Mazumder revealed that student scores on the Armed Forces Qualification Test that is often offered as a comprehensive test taken toward the last few years of high school could be helpful in explaining the differences in upward mobility between blacks and whites. He may have good intentions even though not broad enough to contain most issues. In any case, he also found that completing 16 years of education is a very significant analytical element in determining the status of upward mobility even though it matters less among the African or Black American people. At the same, however, it was revealed as short of a guaranteeing point towards any success in crucial life based on employment opportunities that lessen the above illustrated gaps that cause inter-racial tensions in many institutions. Thus, the fact that Armed Forces Qualification Test scores help predict upward mobility is often used by those who argue that racial differences in intelligence largely explain differences in upward mobility. However, since the Armed Forces Qualification Test is taken in high school, a better explanation is that differences in Armed Forces Qualification Test scores represent the combined impacts of poverty, bad schools, wealth gaps, substandard healthcare and segregated employment opportunities working together to reduce long-term mobility in opening the locked barriers that undermine the solutions towards the healing inter-racial tensions in America and the world. It seems to depend on how much one knows from the years in order to cultivate the future positive aspects of the same equation.

The idea that there are biological factors reducing upward mobility for African-Americans is both odious and entirely false because human beings are the same species with different concentrations of melanin or skin complexions. As Nathaniel Hendren reported when discussing his research, we can absolutely reject that theory that human beings are not equal based on skin color both scientifically, spiritually and politically. In order to believe the given theory, you have to believe that the special differences across the U.S. are differences in some kind of transmission of genes. Suppose you move from one area to another and you have a kid. Does your kid pick up the mobility characteristics of the place you go to? Now obviously, your genes don't change when you move. What we find is that kids start to pick up the mobility characteristics of the place they move to, and they do so in the proportion to the amount of time they end up spending in that place. The majority of the differences across places are casual. If people lived in different places, they would have different outcomes. Thus, segregation and racism is a learned entity which we can correct to prevent the possibility of a third world war that will be the worst in human history and a possible end of the world as former Russian President Mikhail Gorbachev concluded recently.

The above discussion all leads to the saddest conclusion of asking whether and if it were not for poorly conceived policies, then could we have had more upward mobility in the United States. While conservatives like to point at cultural factors and throw up their hands, a far more productive solution is to redress our massive public policy problems like the war on drugs and dropout mill schools that are proven to reduce upward mobility. The conservative mind-set is a historical indicator that we are told to throw away the legacy of slavery and segregation to avoid reparations programs and expect blacks to pull themselves up by their own bootstraps, ignoring the structural dynamics keeping them down. In the same token, research by Graziella Bertocchi and Arcangelo Dimico confirmed that counties with higher concentrations of slave ownership in 1870 had higher levels of poverty and racial inequality in 2000. In the study by Matthew Blackwell it was confirmed that Southerners who lived in counties with higher levels of slave ownership in 1860 express more racial resentment and are more likely to oppose affirmative action. However, as Marx noted earlier, men make their own history, but they do not make it as they please. In actuality, they do not make it under self-selected circumstances, but under circumstances existing already, given and transmitted from the past to the future generations. When such a transmission is taken into account then the previously mentioned gene therapy becomes an interesting feature in healthcare development that encrypts mental disorders. The tradition of all dead generations weighs like a nightmare on the brains of the living when such a consideration is well taken. How we deal with that situation remains part of the question that can be asked about the current world order tribulations which could contribute to the possibility of the third world war or its prevention because charity begins at home as much as the healing of inter-racial tensions.

To learn and determine the answer to the above challenge or statement, it was in the last century before the age of ten years that I asked my mother the real origin of the current education system that we are being taught at school and beaten daily if we fail to speak English properly. My mother replied with confidence that education as I saw it in school was brought by foreigners and mainly the white people from England. Thus, as far she was concerned, I had to learn English language in order to look or become smart and find a good paying job. My next question to my mother was to assure me whether all our ancestors from whom we ascended were meant to be less smart in that perspective since they never saw a white man or learn their language from England. It was until the times of grade five that I began to ask who the person they called president was, how he was named and why as well as the importance of celebrating independence day in Kenya. My special interest was based on the importance of identity especially on the part of the president who was called Jomo Kenyatta without an English name like many other Africans in both our classrooms and outside. I was made to learn that the renaming of Jomo Kenyatta from his English names was the whole principle of the African dream of independence. Does that extend to other provisions in living operations under the same principle or they are still stuck and in need of an overhaul action?

The foremost African action or revolution that can work without requiring any conflicts, quarrels or weapons of mass destruction is an overhaul on the textbook development that has actually been discussed without attaining an implementable formula of mission accomplishment. The first grade could probably address the summary of this chapter in a simpler elementary or mother tongue language. For instance, the recent African union choice of Kiswahili as the official African language was demonstration that a revolution was on the way to be born. If languages can be invented by and for computers, then it implies that there shouldn't be the slightest of any problems in a reformulation of any other structural medium of communication on various instructions. That is even obviated by the fact that human beings are actually capable of learning many languages as witnessed in practical lives. However, it has been encountered within some African professionals with claims that by encouraging more usage of our own languages like Kiswahili for computer programs, it could be very costly and expensive to adopt. That it is better to keep forcing ourselves and our younger generations to keep buying computers filled with foreign languages that include Germany, Japanese, Chinese, Russian, French, and English other than developing the official African language to the same level of cultural competence. Well, as primitive as it sounds, it is better to remember that it is far easier to enhance one's self developed language other than spend all African lives struggling to become better speakers and orators of foreign languages. It is not only self-enslavement but an extension of primitive and self-destructive priorities.

The above discussion seems to pinpoint towards one important feature that is actually holding Africa and their dreams back as opposed to other nations. What some of the highly skilled computer professionals like the ones above seem to focus on is the monetary value that he could count on generating money regardless of how weak and what the long-term repercussions may tend to bring? Monetary technology is still being researched to determine how it can fairly serve all human beings without racial discrimination. Consequently, the definition of money of financial banking in general becomes a big issue. The definitive understanding of money is significant even though presumably complex that the world can never have unless fair redistribution of resources is extended to the larger population drowning in poverty. Most of the larger population in this reference is concentrated in Africa whose beneath the ground is a vast majority of almost all the raw material minerals that produce every precision instrument in the whole world. That was why I personally decided to approach a well-trained electrical engineer from an African institution that later specialized as a computer science professor and consultant in graduate studies. The idea was to talk about the consumer theory proposed earlier to determine whether his education could endure some supportive analysis on the issue of seating on a vast majority of raw material minerals and yet remain as poor as any other slaves in modern history. The challenge was to determine whether he could foresee the sense in such a question.

To answer the above challenging question, my proposal was that in order to be elevated in our standards of living with respect to the past and true discipline within our neighbors as the common foreigners, we should respect our natural resources in our environment. Respectively, we should start or equip ourselves with recycling techniques and in so doing end up initiating raw material smelting methods for tooling and extraction processes of various kinds. Thus, as an initial trial, I had proposed to begin such an institution by first implementing the scratch based small-scale recycling plants which could actually produce various tool parts that could include engine repair spares or electrical suppliers. The scholar, Doctor Matunda Nyanchama, who was considered a greater thinker from a scientific and political perspectives as well as a generous teacher, did not perceive it a feasible channel going through such a projection. The main reason was that it required a lot of funds and money from such places like the International Monetary Fund or the World Bank in the form of loans which less preferable by some like President Uhuru Kenyatta and others. However, finally he was convinced during the think tank chatting forums about the positivity of such an entity when I reiterated to the teacher that the previously mentioned dust theory of permittivity does not accept the general sole reliance on foreign aid as targets or consumers of both energy and skills. The only skepticism he maintained was that Africans needed that education first before recruiting them as full-time team members in good faith as most of them believed in consuming foreign products from education to clothing and sometimes foods.

While several Africans and their leaders are often very skeptical on the issue of incurring big national debts, many still lack the full understanding of the consequences that are to be realized for the generations that follow even with the simple part of interest servicing fees that keeps piling up on repayment schedules. The proposed hypothetical textbooks that need systematic overhauls should strongly reveal to both professional and laymen people that are still far from understanding the real source of money as opposed to the common belief that they come from foreigners. It actually originates from their own backyards if the right tools were in the right place at the right time to mine it. That is correct because something like a water fall as the one proposed by the name Nyakwana Falls of River Kuja, is a constant natural water energy power that has been flowing from the beginning of the world emptying into Lake Kisumu, but never tapped as source of money and other incomes. The failure to tap such God-given money is due to lack of deep thinking by the Africans themselves on how to develop a tool manufacturing plant or factory from where the knowledge of the smelting and the recycling methodologies could be cultivated to produce the necessary parts necessary for the Nyakwana Water Falls project implementation. That would not need any loans in the given perspective other than the local manpower. It is the best way to teach people to become fishers of themselves so called fishers of men and get completely self-reliant and economically independent as the case is with political independence even though not fully. Once someone learns how to fish then the teacher no longer needs to be there to fish for him and that is the most important feature of economic independence on money and other things in development. Thus, if one knows how to develop an economics pharmaceutical or medical textbook then they can make their own that fits their local problems. Failure to realize that will keep many poor people like the Africans from realizing their dream of getting out of inequality gaps and compete like everybody else. A good example looks like the former music champion, Michael Jackson on "We are the world" song. Thus, the big question then is whether the prevailing education is really teaching people on how to fish to become independent fishermen or in need of an urgent overhaul.

To answer the above question, one could need to utilize some good examples like the Titanium mining contract in Kwale district of Kenya that was awarded to a Canadian Company by the name Tiomin. During the final processes of the awarding of the contract, I had thought about making poor people the fishers of men. I initiated a talk about the serious problem of Africans not being able to take that contract even though most of the professionals have been through the formal schools and University systems to the level of doctorate standards and yet they haven't the slightest idea on how to become fishers of men in such contextual circumstances of economic terms. On the basis of such an example, an African parent usually plants a food or cash crop like corn maize in a small garden to raise money for his children's tuition that commonly takes a long time process and energy. The process is repeated once or twice every year for at least twenty to twenty five years which is regarded as the normal period that a student takes to realize returns from any educational investments on job placement or general employment. After working very hard for many years, the parents finally take a break expecting good returns from the children's employment if ever given any. It turns out to be a big disappointment when the children keep toiling from town to town looking for employment which they never find. Some could be professionals with doctorate degrees in Physics or engineering, but still as poor as ever and even homeless. While such examples are a high rise number in Africa, there are certain cases also found in the United States among African professional at the doctorate level of education and yet homeless as in the following case from two years ago at the writing of this book.

In 2011, the Homeless man with a Ph.D. Who Can't Find a job wrote this; what does this teach the world?

For Africans, times are always and ever tough. That perhaps can be best encapsulated by the tragic story of Dr. Maurice Johnson. Despite holding a doctorate in plasma physics from Dartmouth College and a masters in electrical engineering and acoustics from Purdue University, Johnson, 55, claims that he is homeless and without a job.

Though he has apparently declined part-time jobs in other cities due to financial and travel constraints, this overqualified man has allegedly been without employment since last November. Currently, he resides in a homeless shelter, describing his current situation as "just simply bad luck." In terms of his shelter experience, he says it is one he hopes to never have to repeat in his life.

Time's News Feed Maurice Johnson with a sign of not walking the popular talk on diversity in the workplaces:

According to the article Johnson spent all of his savings and sold all of his earthly belongings, including his car, to prevent foreclosure on his parents' house in Cleveland, Ohio so that his mother with Alzheimer's wouldn't have to move.

"They paid my way through school," Johnson said. "If it's going to take ten years, I'm going to make their final years safe and comfortable." He then moved to Boston expecting to take a job he had been offered, but found out when he got there that it had been given away.

However, Johnson wasn't giving up with life then and as of yet. He had been sending his resume out and he was hopeful that he could be able to get into either education or the sciences. When it came to the challenges he had faced, though, he seemed to have believed that his race had caused him difficulties. Additionally, he blamed the dry spell in employment on the fact that he was overqualified (after all, those degrees are pretty impressive). Below, see a screen shot from, which is also awe-inspiring: The important message is to digest the real meaning of the current education system and whether it is something which needs some kind of overhaul. To answer that question, it is important to revisit the previously proposed theory of Permitivity as well as the tribal-blind formula stated earlier.

However, despite it all, Johnson isn't giving up pursuing his dreams of succeeding like his counterparts. He's been sending his resume out and he is hopeful that he will be able to get into either education or the sciences. When it comes to the challenges he's faced, though, he seems to believe that his race has caused him difficulties. Additionally, he blames the dry spell in employment on the fact that he is overqualified and says that after all, those degrees are pretty impressive, but quite suppressive by human resources in terms of institutionalized segregated recruitments. He challenges the popular perception of homeless people by being an unemployed aerospace engineer with two Master's degrees which is a common case with African Americans without jobs due to employment discrimination solely based on race or skin color.

In view of the above and by taking the story of Doctor Maurice Johnson for what it is and especially if the details check out well, one can certainly surmise that we're living with some difficult economic realities and worsened by skin color for Africans. Consequently, it is worthwhile to conclude the times do warrant some immediate turning points some of which are responsible for a roaring Third World War that is basically nuclear in nature and one that can be prevented by simple related economic corrections on domestic and global inequality.

To offer a unifying example of the above case, it is important to describe a student in retrospect. Consequently, a student who has drained some parents on educational finances decides to go to a foreign country for further studies through an additional burden on the same guardians and probably with some governmental assistance or special sponsorship. The student who could definitely be able to become an adult by the time he or she earns a doctoral degree is capable of returning home from a popular university like Cambridge or Harvard. There is definitely a high expectation that time as opposed with a mere one undergraduate degree acquired before the accomplishments of the higher qualifications abroad. A new development begins to develop when a job placement fails to occur and the local colleges and universities while some faculties are over-filled with stronger credentials, but freezes on jobs. With extreme disappointment, the graduate professional in engineering could have nowhere to apply the acquired skills and either decides to live with friends as a partial homeless or perish. The professional could also find some means of hiding in the outside world as an immigrant to escape shame from home based on unwarranted failures in life. This is an example of cases that are broadly encountered among millions of people around the world which can only stand as a factor of a booming chaos or a contributing factor to the explosion of a possibility of a third world war.

On the issue of utilizing the titanium example for textbook revolutionary development, the raw material is so valuable a commodity that instead of using it to overhaul the educational curriculum in all levels, politicians considered it as an opportunity to make money and then decided to stick to it as consumers by hiring foreigners to start the mining. That sounds like a commensurate repercussion of the consumer theory mentioned earlier under the law of permittivity on investments. For some professionals like me and other pharmaceutical scientists, we have a broad spectrum of ideas which crop up into our minds when focusing on minerals such as titanium. There is common tendency by several scientists in Africa to wait until some foreigners come around and show up to define a mineral and describe or address its uses and the related future prospects. Such a definition could usually include the projected monetary value with the bargaining or purchasing power. That could usually be inclusive of the raw mineral as well as the finished product resulting from that material.

The above illustration on the titanium mineral is just but one example that can initiate a reformulation of the much needed educational overhaul. Another huge mineral deposit has been spotted in Western Kenya where the interviewing continued to dwell on while talking to the famous professional engineers. According to the interviews, much of the thinking was a closer match than expected because they both seemed to blame the whole problem that holds the African dream from being realized on the roots of corruption. However, they did not specify the exact point of focus that should be repaired in overhaul to expedite the much needed treatment for such a problem. The question to both professionals was to find out why Western Kenya that lied above the vast majority of Gold minerals should be one of the poorest among the poor developing nations of the world and yet Gold stood as the most expensive commodity for modern mankind worth trillions of monetary values. They both agreed that Africa is actually the richest continent if people were well organized to unite and put ideas together and understand the importance of knowing the difference between paper money and real money. Most Africans were too colonized to belief that paper money including coins was the real things that were needed to be counted wealth as a continent. Is that still valid or it was just a talk without substance? How could the previously mentioned BRICS organization look at such a problem?

Part of the answer to the above question resides on the recent events that were encountered in East Africa around the coastal areas that seemed to be a wake-up call to the rest of the world. It was either part of the solution to the problem of racial employment segregation, education, colonialism and slavery or part of the bigger problem to be realized later and for many generations to come. It was spotted according to a bigger picture as analyzed earlier. Consequently, it was noted that in an exemplary Kenyan slum, and according to Christian Science Monitor, Africa's first 'alternative currency' helps people fight poverty. Respectively, and near Mombasa, the year-old Bangla-Pesa has been used by about 181 businesses, schools, and churches as barter for goods and services that would otherwise be wasted without organization and format. In accordance with that, the first question is to find out how people can actually survive in this world without accessibility to a reliable medium of exchange that can be fairly distributable and acceptable by all groups and races of people in the world for better business purposes. How can people in the world's poorest slums increase their businesses even when they don't have any or enough money to buy food for use in daily nourishments? One solution found by residents in the slum on Kenyan coast is simply to print their own money. How and why that should be possible leaves a lot to be desired. However, for a year now, more than 180 local businesses in what is called the "slum near the coastal Kenyan city of Mombasa have used their own colorful currency alongside the Kenya shilling. That is a wake-up call and an indicator of something special about to happen in the world. In the making, it is called "Bangla-Pesa. It is slightly larger than a dollar and comes in 5s, 10s, and 20s, and is helping to stimulate trade in one of Kenya's most neglected places by its use in businesses, churches, and schools. That alone presents a big threat to the idea of inequality in all aspects of life and particularly in the United States of America.

The detailed explanation of the operations is that the slum is a home to 20,000 people who live with no paved roads, running water, or electricity, and is 100 percent native Kenyan. However, because of the ancestral backgrounds and connections, it is nicknamed "Bangladesh" and since locals say the place is as poor and congested as the South Asian nation where the name originates. The direct translation of the word Pesa is a Swahili name for money and Bangla-Pesa works by allowing trading operations between small business owners and even medium-sized companies. Since Bangla-Pesa is accepted only in "Bangladesh," the cash stays in the community without discrimination and allows people to save their Kenyan shillings for bigger bargains in various purchases.

The idea of Bangla-Pesa has attracted some attention to a few professionals including Americans like Will Ruddick and the Kenya government at the time it happened. According to Ruddick, the whole idea of alternative currencies was to help communities manage themselves with local economies and local leadership," says Will Ruddick, an American economist living in Kenya. It is Ruddick who introduced the Bangla-Pesa last May, sparking a large outcry from Kenya's central bank that he was undermining the shilling and something which he couldn't do in his homeland in America. That triggered his arrest and a lesson to the community. After government charges and a brief arrest, Mr. Ruddick went free as he explained that Bangla-Pesa allows people to tap into excess goods and services that already exist in their community, but that goes to waste because residents don't have enough capital to buy them when they rely on the shilling. There is a big and urgent need to look for alternative ways of survival if gaps between the rich and the poor continue to escalate the way they are currently doing and for real cities and local markets are the real unit of the economy as far as Ruddick is concerned. The question is how much excess do all these businesses have? How much more business could they do if they had more access to trade credit and contribute positively to the overall economy?

Whichever way the idea is viewed, it is true that the use of alternative currencies isn't actually a new thing. In reality they have become a trend of life because of the success of Bitcoin which has been a popular but expensive digital currency. Another example is traceable to the nation of Switzerland within the WIR Bank, which for a long time under the same example, has put out its own currency, the WIR-franc, for 80 years. That currency is currently used by more than 60,000 Swiss businesses in the country and beyond. Other examples of alternative currencies are found in various degrees of use in Brazil, on US Indian Reservations, and elsewhere without much of a problem. It is important to note that the only difference between theirs and the Bangla-Pesa is that it is Africa's first alternative currency and is designed to fight poverty. It is apparently having a good effect to serve as a new technological remedy to many economic problems which have stagnated over the centuries as in employment segregation mentioned earlier. Furthermore, it has proved that only after a year of use, there is both actual and anecdotal evidence that the new currency is real helping people's lives.

On the basis of Ruddick's studies and published data it was found that Bangla-Pesa users come out ahead by an average of 84 shillings a day, equivalent to 98 cents. While that looks small in a world market and sounds like a tiny increase, it is actually good for people living on a few dollars a day because it represents 16% percent more spending power within the larger currencies which is a source of feeding some of the peoples' kids in that perspective. Moreover, it has become acceptable even in big institutions which understand the depth of institutionalized racism like the churches and schools which accept Bangla-Pesa for donations and tuition, and in turn spend the Bangla-Pesa locally on lunches for worshipers and students' clubs or associations.

On a detailed and closer look of the alternative currency various establishments can be reviewed. Foremost, the establishments that uses the Bangla-Pesa actually places a large sticker on their metal shacks or wooden stalls after joining a formal network. In such a scheme, each one of the establishments gets 400 shillings worth of notes, though 200 is handed back to the network in a kind of tax to fund things like trash collections and health services. According to Ruddick and in a formal interpretation, one gets his or her own informal economy, their own currency, doing their own taxes for their own services. Whichever way we look at it, the creation is a huge burden off the government.

A lot of brainstorming has been taking place since the invention of the above alterative currencies in Africa. For instance, at a community meeting attended by more than 50 business people in Nairobi's estate at Kawangware slum in the year 2014, locals heard from Ruddick about alternative currencies. The response was quite good because in one case, Francis Wanjala, a resident who organized the meeting, concluded that working together will foster cohesion in a socially and ethnically diverse slum if such development can continue to be supported and take good course in networking. That is true because there is a lot of mistrust when people look at each other as competition. However, with a business community where you see your neighbor buying from you, and you also buying from him, it complements one another for the good of all people and even beyond the borderlines of any nation.

The above information on alternative currency seems to be adapting to a new type of inheritance in the financial world. However, a better comparative analysis leaning towards a new setup of a world order class scale level only took effect four months later when Russia made a tremendous counter money trade ratification by going for an alternative currency other than the popular dollar. Consequently, Russia is acting evenly so while it ratifies the Economic Union. It is also ready to trade in currencies other than dollar in the year of late 2014 onwards.

October 3, 2014 4:56 PM MST

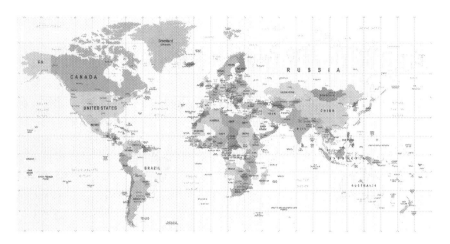

Courtesy of thediplomat.com

At the time of he above ratification, it was stated by President Vladimir Putin in a national announcement that he had signed a treaty ratifying the Eurasian Economic Union, and is set to begin a new era of commemoration on trade primarily outside the office, and in national currencies such as the Yuan and Euro. This Union already has the support of several of the BRICS nations, as well as associate countries, and will help facilitate trade to be done in a much smoother and easier way than what is currently used through SWIFT or other Western banking processes for past many years.

In the same sense Putin's signing of the trade agreement comes as a response to the weakening value of the Rouble, and the dumping of the currency onto the markets via U.S. intervention and other national agenda policies. And as an alternative to propping up the Rouble through a form of monetization, bond buying or additional currency strength on the U.S. and Europe, Russia is instead choosing the path of leaving the game entirely, and offering the world a competitive alternative to the current dollar based on global trade systems that are fair to all countries. Putin signed the law ratifying Eurasian Economic Union and sounded that optimism was very positive in that agenda if they hoped to prevent any outflows. Putin said earlier on that Russia wanted to shift to national currencies in trade deals with China and other countries, and contemplated the possibility of swaying away from the U.S. dollar as well as the euro itself. Surprisingly, the whole event seemed to be strengthened further that morning as Putin signed law ratifying a Eurasian economic union.

Much the same on principle as the Bangla-Pesa mentioned above in the Africa's Kenya country, the Eurasian Economic Zone, or Trade Zone as it is also known, is a joint venture with China, India, and several Central and Far Eastern countries that will tie into the ongoing construction of the new world order on the basis of monetary powers. Like the Bangla-pesa sorted help for the local community, the trade zone will allow nations to trade without tax or duties, and for the most part, in their own national currencies or with gold, oil, and other major commodities. Essentially, Russia and China have already begun non-dollar trade this year through a historic oil and natural gas deal that will bring in over $400 billion in Yuan equivalent to Russia for a 20-30 year contract. Additionally, Russia's primary oil company has paved the way for future energy sales to be done in either Roubles or Yuan, with both nations formulating a new alternative to SWIFT that will facilitate easier exchanges of one nation's currency for another. Thus, the Mombasa case on Bangla-Pesa is not alone or unique as some might suppose.

Economic sanctions by the U.S. are proving that they not only have backfired against the dollar and euro, but have accelerated plans by Eurasia to bring about a new global trade platform that leaves America completely out of any controlling interest or power to influence people as before. And with the dollar having strengthened against nearly all currencies in recent days, the potential of the Eurasian Economic Zone to equalize growing inflation and deflation around the world through the bypassing of the dollar, is quickly becoming a brighter alternative to another Great Recession of this decade.

On the basis of the above analysis and on the understanding of the real meaning of money, it is quite convincing that most of the world is finally learning much more on how to survive independently on their own without necessary relying on formal financial education in collaboration with colonialism and slavery at many instances. This kind of self-invention is somehow commensurate with the previously mentioned theory of permittivity in development where the future world order would depend on financial equality in opportunity. In so doing the majority poor who may have no other way out to survive in the current world and who are mainly concentrated in Africa can access more choices in such opportunities or actually copy the above 80 year old Switzerland strategy example and lead a new kind of inheritance that nobody else has ever produced. In the same respect, such or those inventions can either be original or simple generic innovations. Originality is definitely an interesting feature in this context because it so happens that Africa which is still counted out as a poor continent actually supplies the whole world with almost every raw material necessary for the modern precision instruments, but pays ten times the original price in order to purchase one of the final finished products like a camera. That poses an additional explanation to the previously quoted article question of whether there is really a living dream for Africans.

As far as the African dream is concerned, many conferences have been conducted from nation to nation with feasible resolutions being offered and sometimes passed for implementation purposes. However, when results are not produced accordingly as expected, the scapegoat is turned on to the African leaders on their full irresponsibility on corruptive systems at the high levels of governance that requires or qualifies for the much needed total overhauls. The question that needs a new world order impact from the foundations of the underlying context is whether diversity seeds of prosperity have already been planted for long term positive results.

Part of the answer to the seeds of diversity in question resides on the leadership examples of the groups that have been deeply affected on the American dream realization. Some of those great examples include former South African President Nelson Mandela, Jomo Kenyatta of Kenya, Julius Nyerere of Tanzania, Kwame Nkhrumah of Ghana, and Robert Mugabe of Zimbabwe. While the African American children still question the validity of a prevailing American dream if any, the above forefathers stood for the great African dream that was to be an independent Africa free of suppression, colonialism and slavery.

All the above mentioned former presidents were imprisoned by the European invaders and freed through bloodshed independence wars. Most of those presidents' dreams have rarely become fruitful because of too much involvement from foreign powers of the former colonial masters. However, some were quite notorious like Mandela, Nyerere, and Kenyatta for being really warriors of freedom by action in rejecting any offers in exchange for independence. Jomo Kenyatta resumed his cultural names by renaming himself as such to set the right example on the question of identity as a new seed in plantation under the previously proposed theory of permittivity. That example platform was defended by naming his son Uhuru Kenyatta who later became the Kenyan president at the writing of this book. That trend was continued by then vice-president to Jomo Kenyatta, Presiedent Daniel Arap Moi who took the torch and with speed got an approval of a new President Abraham Lincoln of Africa to save the Kenyan Union. It could be interesting to find out whether that was really true.

As far as former president Daniel Arap Moi was concerned, he had to continue on with the Jomo Kenyatta trend if not make it better. He even initiated a new dream of seeing the possibility of a future United States of Africa before or after he died. To introduce and implement that process, he initiated a possibility of a textbook development in revolution by challenging the local engineers to design a new make of our own car that they could name as UHURU. While that was the new focus of the new textbook development, it sounded almost impossible because there was not a single engine part that was being manufactured or produced in Kenya or East Africa for that matter. Consequently, president Moi seemed to have understood the weakness and thus simplified the challenge by requiring that the professional engineers and scientists perform just the assembly with some manipulation to produce the first Kenyan model car. While that was far from attaining the invention originally thought by the president for a new textbook development, it marked a first step initiative in that direction and an example to other important areas like Healthcare research and insurance in financial implications. Respectively, the engineers had not resolved the issue of materials science questions as previously illustrated above on the minerals of Gold and Titanium in terms of monetary values and from the scratch according to the recycling proposal to produce parts and tools.

The Kenyan example given above may not have been unique in context, but it stood as one of the foundations of the African dream that is yet to be realized or tapped into the current world order pillar in the making. However, some or many of those or such dreams have been hampered by the high level corruption projects where every little raw material production from the mines gets into the wrong misunderstanding or hands for further smelting and refinement to finished products elsewhere other than Africa. One of the best examples as to how corruption can be dealt with or even eliminated is Ghana under the governorship of General Rawlings. Ever since the death of former President Kwame Nkhrumah, Ghana operated and survived under a lot of corruptive activities. However, as of the year 2009 during the visit of the United States President Baraka Obama, Ghana was quoted as one of the most corruptive-free African countries in various surveys. Essentially, the Obama visit to Ghana and skipping of Kenya that was his father's homeland had a special message to Kenyans and the need for originality in textbook development overhauls and the proposed theory of permittivity and consumerism.

CHAPTER VII

WORLD ORDER – BY HEALTHCARE - THROUGH PHARMACEUTICAL HEALTH BASES

When Bernie Sanders compares the United States with Canada on Universal Healthcare, he finds that if every Canadian is truly covered by health insurance then all Americans deserve the same care. As much as he believes, it is a birthright thing for all Americans much the same as he does on education for all.

Healthcare is the foundation of a properly grounded and mature political powerhouse as well as military superiority and it is based on the strength of root-based medical or pharmaceutical drug developments. This Chapter is dedicated to Universal healthcare and particularly from the continents believed to be containing the world's most controversial health life issues, and where corruption, racism and tribalism have been used as instruments of containment to completely derail all types developments. The bottom line is that if third world nations and particularly Africans are not part of the manufacturing systems, they will not be part of the healthcare policy reform champions. It is designed to introduce a different kind of new inheritance to the world on African development that must be implemented before it begins seeing any progressive solutions including democracy and leadership. It is the author's commitment to deeply illustrate why Africa's past determines its future in terms of health and development and why a good textbook for African development needs to be very brief. At the same time I would like to point out why many frustrated Africans lack both the patience and trust in reading large detailed textbooks. I belief that for a nation to develop first and appropriately, it needs a summary of the important materials and methods so as to give a chance for self-digestion and creativity of the main idea. A healthful living remains one's happiness and greatest blessing and for which reason the author dedicates most of the chapters in health communication as well as grass root accessibility formulae. In the beginning, I start by explaining the theory of developmental permittivity, then dwell through educational setup schemes and conclude on the effects of general controlled systems on health, poverty and developmental planning.

The future of world healthcare would strictly depend on healthcare communication as well as the pharmaceutical developmental behaviors themselves across the manufacturing panels in research and development. Communication is best achieved by employing the easiest method of delivery with the simplest language terms possible (Tribal-Blind Formula). Jua Kali becomes an important entity.

In the proposed theory of revolutionary development it was stated that the smaller the size of a given purified formula or particle in a given development, the larger the magnitude of productive permittivity. It stresses that modern development has to be viewed just exactly as the human body developing pattern right from the scratch dust level particles. Just as such particles blend with each other to form larger ones through the formation of the human body, so does every development require for any progress to be realized as would be emphasized in the subsequent Jua Kali chapter. This theory was first proposed and formulated in the year 2001 at the time when the African country, Kenya, was preparing for the most popular election in the country's history since independence. It relates to the whole book in order to prove that Africa can only change by system other than by individual subject. That is why it speaks about a system in terms of its constituent subjects so that if only one is controlled then the whole system is affected. It was dedicated towards an acceptable resolution on ethnicity and diversity that threatened to dictate those elections regardless of what democratic method they selected and whether it was a proper or an improper one. It is a theory that fits most walks of life whether one looks at it from a scientific point of view or traditional human culture and it was entitled the tribal blind formula that will be elaborated better in the latter chapters and how the same principle can be used to develop all other areas of development including the Jua Kali proposal that I launched thereafter. It clearly states that every kind of development has to be viewed from the smallest particles or roots in order to attain the maximum yield of productivity. The theory refers to those particles as dust and that in every kind of development, there are many things that can be happen and a variety of changes ranging from mismatches, mis-readings or simply mistakes in terms of specific damages to the particles. Development will only be realized or made larger by recognizing the smallness in difference as well as the similarity among a given group of particles. Thence, it translates that the essence of this is to discover identity by restructuring the root differences required to realize real or any development.

As the author of this book, I have stated in various conferences and publications that development is nothing but communication from the grassroots. As a scientist by profession, I define grassroots as the smallest factors that are capable of communicating with one another towards the delivery of a given projected development. Some or most of those factors have been in existence for a long time but require new reformulation for better communication for better education and development since matter can neither be created nor be destroyed. When a new factor or idea is formulated it can only grow new factors of the same type and spread out if no barriers are encountered. Consequently, this chapter will focus on how well this definition fits into the above theory with other attachment factors. There are various examples that would be used to illustrate it and much the same as the subsequent chapters.

When the whole human life and the earth are broken down into distinct units called small particles, it is found to be actually of the same make up regardless of race or ethnic origin. That is why black and white communities are 99% similar in all aspects of life even though some professors have misused their chemical knowledge to say black paint cannot mix with white paint while we have seen fruitful and successful interracial marriages. Scientists have conducted a lot of research including the isolation of human flesh cells on DNA to identify every individual, but they do not have the slightest clue as to how these particles that make up those cells do recognize one another so as to communicate with each from the grass root scale to determine the physical ethnic or tribal languages that we see in the world. However, historically, we do read to see when the different languages that we see today came into being on the surface of the earth even though some still doubt it even when we can't explain beyond the atomic scale of events. The smallest level at which small particles communicate in order to develop into larger ones as visible by the human eye is not only amazing to scientists, but to the creationists too. Consequently, that particular problem has been left to the creation scientists since no scientist has proven that the origin of life was from a specific element or atom or how that atom came into existence.

After examining Africa for the past 500 years, our eyes tell us that in physical communication, it is the most underdeveloped continent even though it is known to be the father of civilization and holding vast deposits of minerals and resources that can lead to any invention ever. Based on the above theory, communication from the invisible scale is exactly the same whether one looks at it from the scientific point of view or the creation scientists. It is also a clear truth that physical communication is the most powerful tool that Africa needs in order to begin developing. It must be understood that the physical progressive and proper communication like the particulate communication, has to start from the grassroots. Modern scientists generally agree that the development of a human being during the first five years is as crucial as the life before birth. This agreement must therefore be true and applicable in all areas surrounding our lives of development.

The initial human physical communication is encountered after birth when the new human is newly born and gets detached from the mother's womb physically. This is what I refer to us the critical stage of proper human communication and development. The first communication is the choice of the name for the baby which it would begin hearing until further notice. At this state the particulate communication is over and depending on how well the organs like the ears developed, the baby will continue to develop based on touch, food, ears and eyesight. It is particularly important to note that development comes by hearing and hearing the words of development. Hence, the baby will develop according to what he basically hears as much as what he sees. However, hearing outperforms physical recognition in terms of the above theory of developmental permittivity. In most scientific philosophies, it is generally agreed that the essence of science is to discover identity in difference. Consequently, if the baby is identified by a particular name or label, he will grow up with that faith in the name. Like any other human race or tribe, Africans have their own clear languages to as far back as history goes including the biblical times when speech differed as the pyramids were raised in construction. It is therefore not only ignorant, but irrational to move from one's ethnic group to another in such of new self-identities or names at the early or later ages of life. However, the tribal formula states that an African tribe that has developed a national unified language can utilize that language to begin developing proper communication from the grassroots.

According to the earlier definition of communication, there is no stronger tool than the verbal communication which in this chapter is the tribal blind formula. However, it all breaks down to fit the theory of developmental permittivity because verbal is sound and the brain gets colonized based on the faith and consistency of the sounds it receives throughout life. The tribal blind formula stated that for a brain to learn national development as opposed to tribal development, the hearing receptors have to be colonized from the early grass root ages. In this formula, Kiswahili language was the model language which later on was voted and accepted as the official African language by the African Union. The Kiswahili language is a collection of language words from many African tribes in the range of 350 out of the estimated 500 hundred in the whole continent, but mainly the Bantus. Once the hearing receptors have been colonized into specific sounds, the same is transmitted to colonize the brain to that interest. The hearing receptors are subject to further manipulative colonization once they receive new sounds if different from the regular ones. However, if Kiswahili is consistently received from the grassroots age, it would be easily recognizable, absorbed and swiftly acceptable by the younger as well as the coming generations since the receptors would make more copies of themselves during the early stages of development and thence be transcribed and translated accordingly. Hence, quoting Mr. Kweisi Mfume as the example, it is quite conceivable that the model theory above is applicable in the most important joint in African development. Apart from the Africans, 99% of the rest of the world have consistently used their cultural names. The percentage of Africans using their cultural names is almost negligible. It is sometimes embarrassing to encounter Indians, Chinese and Russians in a workplace trying to find out why we use Arabic or English names while we are not from Arabia or England and not even born there. Some Africans have argued that it is a marketing tool to use such names while some say their denominations have the names listed and can only choose from that list, but many people have held a chain of degrees and yet find their Indian and Spanish counterparts winning in getting same jobs with less education as well as being less fluent in English and in none of those denominations. For those who have vast experience in these kinds of cases, it is quite conclusive that one of the reasons why we might not compete with such counterparts is ignorance on what really matters in development. It then becomes a bright idea to discuss the content of this ignorance in terms of its origin as well as the probable resolution.

For the past few years, a lot of Africans have talked about brain drain without proposing real solutions to that problem. Education as a whole has to be redefined so as to begin realizing some proper communication and development. Most Africans including leaders have been tuned to the belief that education is the achievement of a documentary tool that guarantees employment and jobs in general in a given public or private sector. This is the belief that any education minister in Africa would sell to his nation if not encourage graduates to look for employment elsewhere especially the developed countries. One wonders why the above belief was originally sold to the graduates to attain the credentials up to and including postgraduate level only to be encouraged to leave their own country. One might wonder whether Africa is on the right track as far as education is concerned. Since it was mentioned earlier that development is communication and while conceding that such a statement is quite imperative, it is relevant to quote the Kiswahili saying "Elimu ndio msingi wa maendeleo", which simply says that "education is the foundation of development". The question then becomes, why Africa hasn't realized any development over the centuries ever since education was implemented as we see it today in terms of large masses of skilled manpower leaving the continent. When did the rain start beating Africa and could fall under the African saying on wars "Vita Vya Pansi ni Neema ya Kunguru" that is currently beginning to take root in America with the internal civil wars?

Part of the answer to the above question resides on the kind and method of communication we use in our education and therefore development. By the fact that Africa has not attained much development since independence in the last 43 years, it is quite suspicious that the type of education and the applicable methods of delivery have not been appropriate. It is a clear fact that if one plants a tree and finds out later that the tree bears no fruits, then it necessitates the uprooting of that tree in order to plant a different brand as a probable trial. This theory has been binding in human existence since the ancient times in world history. However, human nature is always scared of change in addition to the fact that it takes a lot of time and patience to accept any changes regardless of how fruitful they may turn out to be in the long run. In the forthcoming chapters I will site most of the proposals that I have launched to aid in reaching out initiatives for major changes necessary for appropriate education. It would be appropriate to start with the number one problem with the number one resolution before Africa can begin developing.

I would like to start with the best method of communication and therefore education and development. As mentioned earlier, development being communication, it then implies that a controlled grass root method of delivery would change education. In a few decades back, a young Kenyan invented a simple broadcasting station and called on his own father to approve the invention by asking him to stay in another room to listen to his broadcasting station as he broadcasted. Even though the student did not understand the particles responsible for that kind of transmission of sound waves, he went ahead to invent the station. In that particular case a minister of education was supposed to recognize him as well as other African educators and encourage him to try to explain what he did in terms of materials and methods so as to produce more of the same young scientists.

In this introductory chapter, we have concentrated on the theorem of developmental permittivity and probably concluded that the number one resolution is that of verbal communication. In the next chapter we shall examine how the same theory can be utilized before we can achieve the implementation of the first developmental resolution.

CHAPTER VIII

NEW WORLD ORDER BY BLENDED EDUCATION RESEARCH AND LOCAL MANUFACTURING:

SELF-HELP SMALL SCALE GLOBAL MANUFACTURING

The big question about education in this world is based on who the learner should be as well as the educator in that context. The politics of establishment imply that certain groups of people are simply supposed to learn from others and not vice versa. That is if your genes belong to the Queen's family then you have to be important without question to educate the world as to which way or what the best thing is to do and whether you happen to be correct or wrong on justified events. Similarly if your blood contains the genes of Mandela or a De Klerk in South Africa then the world doesn't necessary need to learn much from you about any education or establishment freedom. Well, as much as most intellectuals know today, education is a very broad term that can be very costly if it is not well defined and deeply understood when considering prevailing cases as seen within most underdeveloped nations like the third world countries. In the Afro-third world the words "Jua Kali stands for Sun Hot" or more precisely Red Hot in the Sun to describe a particular class of people in manufacturing and is the basic principle or background of this book. Consequently, all the subsequent chapters will discuss developments with a particular emphasis or reference to Jua kali. As the above theory states, Jua Kali is practically a system that will sustain development by assembling other simpler systems as much as a body system works in the described perspective. That sector of the industry employs both skilled and unskilled manpower which many African governments have yet to recognize and support on a moral and material terms. It is a sector that is comprised of roofless open space houses that assemble few local instruments that are useful and affordable by all Africans. I first made the proposal to illustrate the developmental theory so as to recognize this particular sector after realizing that every precision instrument was either imported or manufactured locally by foreign investors and using foreign parts. It is a sector that like any other complete and workable body system really lacks many supportive parts to qualify it into a fully working machine or set of systems.

World history both from a theoretical and practical point of view clearly tells us that the famous industrial revolutions and communicable development has to start from the manufacture of small parts which once assembled can start the process of real healthcare and general development. Those small parts cannot exist without taking great account into the above theory so that many skilled citizens can put it into serious consideration. However, many people and particularly Africans have formed a habit of simply saying that once my Toyota engine car is dead, the only option is to abandon it to a total waste and wait for a new one from Japan if I can get another loan. This is a given habit in almost all Africans as they find it an easy pattern of leading lives for a few years as this can only be afforded by a few among many who survive under serious poverty. The purpose of campaigning for the Jua Kali proposal for almost five years before the World Bank approved the release of 1.7 billion towards the improvement of the related sector was to change that particular attitude. Most Africans whether at primary or University level of education are still brainwashed that we cannot process raw materials to produce finished precision products that could even include such trivial ones as needles for sewing clothes because of the implanted artificial impatience. That is with the fear that it takes a long process or many processes to arrive at even any finished good such as a simple wire product.

The Jua Kali proposal launched the first project that was carefully thought and researched to impact real change and we are still campaigning to achieve total implementation. The project was targeting the proper view of the energy industry as that is the number one industry to effect change if carefully planned. Africans students usually learn only the theoretical part of a given product such as the process by which an engine moves which is by the compression of a gasoline liquid till it explodes to begin initiating the movement of other parts in transportation. At the university level, that theoretical knowledge produces engineers who are only experts of maintenance servicing of such engines without the slightest practical knowledge on how the engines parts came into being from the grassroots. Consequently, it sounds and becomes a natural disaster when one mentions that a Jua Kali project can eliminate some of these misconceptions. The World Bank recognition of Jua Kali sector and its funding recently clearly means the government has to become very focused and totally involved as per the original proposal and according to the number one resolution for effective real change. Before elaborating on the number one resolution, it is appropriate to mention that Most Africans still suffer from the brainwash that a school or class can only be found in a colonial set up atmosphere with a syllabus published likewise. In the first proposed Jua Kali project, it was mentioned that once it is recognized by the government as outlined by the World Bank, it would be incorporated into the school curriculum as a special class and coursework. The intention of that is to reverse the brain drain by redefining education and school so as to know that proper development is one that is specifically based on the grass root foundations no matter what field we find ourselves in engagement. As we do know about Jua Kali today is that most of its manpower is either illiterate or high school dropout. However, the skills learned in the hot sun are special tools learned in such an institution or school.

Jua Kali as written or initially proposed is a wide range of industrial fields that have to be broke into various sub sectors before assembly of the whole product as may be desired. As mentioned earlier, the first project was aimed into looking at the number one resolution which I termed as "Recycling of plastics and metals. It is clearly true that if a given material is not recycled, then it becomes a total waste. I had two ideas in mind when I entitled the resolution this way. Cycling meaning burning to melt to learn more about different sources of energy. One idea I had in mind was to challenge and explore methods of melting and second was to produce spare parts for the number one resolution design technology. Essentially, the word recycling means towards making of circle. In that project it was mentioned that as the world spins around the globe and so shall cycling and recycling be the proper survival method of all creations. Africans must learn and agree that everything visible has been brought up from very simple minute substances assembled together to produce various shapes. Accordingly, then the theory of developmental permittivity fits into the cycling and recycling concept.

In the above project, various shapes of parts would be produced and used to design a tool manufacturing devise. This strongly implies therefore that the number one solution that Africa must confront to with reasonable aggression is the assembly of the tool design machine that would become capable of producing tool devises and instruments. There is a lot of misunderstanding on what it really translates into when large masses of people ask themselves why these are not left to the scientists. This is a big misconception because it continues to bar the names as the ignorance prospers. A tool design devise is the only instrument that can mark the beginning of development from where it is stuck. The big meaning behind it is that it would produce almost every little instrument beginning from the needle to the precision instruments. It would therefore create employment in terms of research, development and large scale total production.

The invention and therefore development of the above mentioned tool design machine can be defined and applied into almost all fields of economic prosperity. Hence, there is need to elaborate the related applications in various sectors.

The healthcare industry for the Jua Kali sector is one of the most controversial in modern Africa. It is most often criticized by the modern high precision industries, but when put together collectively, it shines a very strong green light that would give the world a future healthcare direction because of affordability. The relative methodology by which the Jua Kali products and their manufacturers would interact mutually with the modern foreign and world technology is a subject that has attracted a lot of attention to many African scientists. The truth of the matter is that there is no important Jua kali system in its sector than one related to healthcare as good health remains the greatest of all blessings. As much as the above theory suggests, a body remains impaired so long as part or parts of its system are not health or working properly. Consequently, the pharmaceutical systems which are specifically designed for rehabilitation or treatment of the human body diseases prove to be the most important in this theory. This is motivated by the historical factors often contained in many pharmaceutical textbooks as far back to the ancient times as possible in terms of drug origins of today's medicine. A careful survey of drug records indicates that modern pharmacy is actually based on Jua Kali origins and many of which go back to ancient Africa including Egypt as well as China and the Middle East. An example of a Jua Kali drug or pharmaceutical product that is still used in modern medicine is Physostigmine. Most of the drugs in the current diaspora have proven that while modern medicine is very focused within specific targets, some untreatable diseases and disorders end up being treated by traditional herbs better than modern medicine. With that in mind, then we are left with lots of ideas on where to search for resources in order to fit the Jua Kali roots.

Because of the current epidemic situation in Africa, Malaria and AIDS stand foremost to determine how well we can fit them in the Jua Kali sector directly from grass root resolutions. The roots of these diseases are well known by most scientists, but the Jua Kali needs such resources so as to fit some medicines in order that it is easily manufactured and revolved without limitation.

Malaria is the most infectious disease in most developing countries especially Africa because the anopheles mosquito survives happily in almost all ecosystems. This is quite a risk factor because the plasmodium parasite transmits the disease from one AIDS patient to another even though biological scientists still disqualify the fact that it may actually transmit the underlying virus. While many Pharmaceutical scientists and Medical researchers have argued that the AIDS virus is not transmittable by the anopheles mosquito, it is appropriate to leave the subject open for further research and scrutiny. The two diseases are the most deadly and with more awareness and education, the roots of these diseases with the transmitting vectors would be the most preferable target area for research in order to accomplish for total eradication of the spread of the tragedy in debilitating levels. In that respect, a particular plant grown in Tanzania so called Artemisinin is one idea that might be considered for future developments in the Pharmaceutical industry in the given perspective.

The Jua Kali Pharmaceutical institutions would have to adapt to a new kind of inheritance as they must learn more about tools and their assembly to sustain whatever plant that might be initiated by few modern technology equipment. The principle of selecting a Jua Kali plant like the one mentioned above and developing a method of isolation or extraction of the main ingredients is the same principle that should be applied to every prospective development among the partner institutions. Consequently, a new chemical ingredient might be obtained by isolation from plants, organic synthesis or simply molecular modification. While Jua Kali have generally not learned or used specific methods of analysis, they are still skilled in pure ethanol production methods and so much that they can employ the same ideas in other process developments and end up with very positive results. It is true and disappointing to note that alcohol, as much as it is used in the production of many pharmaceutical and medical products, there is barely any professionally employed institution that can scale up that ancient idea so that it can be utilized for production of various synthetic compounds. Most Africans only learn the method of production for use as food beverage without bothering on the potential to manipulate the process and scale up for industrial production technology. This is the case that applies to almost all other ancient methods that they might happen to be in possession.

Jua Kali is targeting a different kind of inheritance that can blend as many of both their local ideas and those from foreign countries to develop some of the best hybrid products of the modern times. Jua Kali would take into account the fact that medicine is an old art and that only few modifications including hybridization and recombination of substances need to be employed to accommodate any resistant epidemic evolutions. It has been agreed by many professionals both in village and in the urban sectors that the best opportunity is to set up the crucial structures on a one by one basis before assembly of those selected can be determined according to need. As a consequence, the word hybrid can be applied in many concepts including the molecular level business as well as in the formulation mechanics of each process necessary to produce a final product. In essence, if a project is to produce a remedy for malaria, both the molecular cause of the disease and the relative level of industrial productions of the regimen have to be deeply understood. Without such understanding, the problem will only be attacked for reduction and never eliminated. Hence, it proves that while production machines and skilled mechanics of those machines may be available, it is equally pertinent that some of the necessary tools be easily available from the Jua Kali sector. That is the definition of the different kind of inheritance that makes Jua Kali institutions as unique as they may appear in the future. Thus, in the Kua Kali pharmaceuticals, there must be an attached machine maintenance research department where different phase mechanisms are explored as possible.

There is a range of factors that need to be addressed to the sector in order to succeed in the Jua Kali pharmaceutical industry. The first strategy is to begin giving it a serious label as the most deadly weapon of mass destruction, the AIDS virus. It has been postulated that Africa as it stands, it is currently the home of human AIDS victims and without a cure as of yet. Starting a vaccine factory is one of the great ideas before the world gets closer to a cure. As soon as a perfect vaccine is formulated, the real cure will be just around the corner to be released. The idea of vaccination has been known for the last 100 years or so, but so far Malaria has been with us for the last 6000 years without any vaccine or appropriate preventive measures even though some mention of the first trials that are currently being tested on the first phase of voluntary patients. It is quite contradictory to find that the pharmaceutical world is well endowed with a lot of capabilities for a cure for malaria, but cannot develop or formulate a relative concrete vaccine. While that is part of the Jua Kali objectives, it will be second to AIDS in such a development if it willfully becomes successful.

The current and major objective is to concentrate on the pharmaceutical principles that will see us through in the eradication of AIDS as the number one and most deadly infectious disease. The number one structure is a collection of both local and international Jua Kali educators at a convention that would be well advertised and attended in a Jua Kali summit. The idea of such a convention is to implant the worthiness of Jua Kali and its objectives. The danger of AIDS would be presented as an incurable killer and labeled as a weapon of mass destruction for which anybody can be a launcher, but everybody remains a target.

While conceding that the above two statements are quite imperative, it is relevant to point out that human behavior as a factor in the epidemiological consequences of the above disease, is a subject that determines the basic principle in global healthcare. To understand the relationship of this principle and the AIDS virus, the Jua Kali scientists will have to utilize the opportunity of understanding the central pharmacogenetic background of cultural behavior. The molecular level at which that relationship can be recognized and treated is the most controversial, but the most pertinent if well taken and considered for research and education. In a recent communication from a pharmaceutical technology edition, the treatment of AIDS remains a big challenge to modern drug manufacturers while they focus on growing antimalarial ingredients at the same time. The report strictly stated that with the world holding many millions of people in hostage with diseases capable of being cured or mainly suffering from HIV or AIDS, tuberculosis, malaria, and other deadly contagious diseases, the pharmaceutical industry faces extreme and unforgivable demands for safe and effective life-saving treatments in mostly third world countries. The situation presents a challenge and an opportunity for pharmaceutical manufacturers to demonstrate their ability to provide affordable, effective treatments to fight these global plagues and contribute sensibly towards the healing of inter-racial tensions around the world.

To tackle the above challenge as indicated, all feasible options must be considered while inviting for more proposals without any discrimination so long as they offer some possible alternative. That is to say that even if it means herbal medicine in conjunction with vitamins, let there be freedom to contribute. The overall and most effective effort could probably involve an enormous scale-up of any feasible recipes in pharmaceutical manufacturing capacities without compromising product safety and efficacy. According to the current or most recent statistics it is very evident that the rising demand for antiretroviral medicines (ARVs) and Artemisinin-based Antimalarials is creating raw material shortages and stressing pharmaceutical research, development and distribution. These activities raise the threat of healthcare corruption and drug diversion from third-world markets to rich nations. As a consequence, many drug manufacturers are responding by re-assessing the licensing operations with generics firms to produce low-cost products while also encouraging small business distributions in drug delivery services. While that is happening, health agencies and regulators are innovating new strategies that can overcome any legal and political barriers so as to enable the development of the much needed medical products.

While the above developments are being tried with an intention of taking root it has also been detected that the lack of interest among innovator firms has led into the opening of more rooms for the Indian generic drug makers to formulate safe and effective drugs which should be encouraged and expanded without any disparities. On the basis of that understanding, the World Health Organization has demonstrated a lot of support in that effort by establishing a prequalification program in the last few years to confirm the safety and efficacy of medicines for infectious diseases like malaria, tuberculosis, and the immune-deficiency virus. According to the present situation it makes that the World Health Organization program is aiming at the assurance of health agencies in developing nations. Such nations are prone to a lot of healthcare politics because they are often limited on internal drug evaluation capabilities as well as the original necessary processes from the grass roots.

A major dilemma with the World Health Organization is the development of a universal gauge that can be unanimously be utilized as a standard of prequalification and final qualification purposes for proof of validation services. In that respect, the stated prequalification program above ran into trouble that year, putting pressure on antiretroviral (ARV) suppliers, when discrepancies in bio-equivalency reports forced WHO to remove a number of antiviral medications from its list. Controlling quality the bio-equivalency data problems raised questions about the reliability of WHO's prequalification approach, a skepticism shared by US health officials. Even though WHO officials claimed that its delisting action confirms its high standards, the US President's Emergency Plan for AIDS Relief (PEPFAR), which plans to spend $15 billion over five years to provide treatment to two million HIV-infected people says that drugs purchased with US dollars must be approved by the US Food and Drug Administration, generously to avoid charges that Americans are encountering lower quality treatments on poor nations whenever they travel for business and other matters. That was a big green light that many nations seemed to have supported for the development of approvable and valid standardization methods.

While the above is happening and in common politics, critics argue that the US position really aims to protect pharmaceutical manufacturers from increased competition from generic drugs across the health care systems from a worldwide perspective. A program that purchases only FDA-approved products, moreover, means paying more for brand-name drugs and, consequently, limiting the number of patients the program can treat. While the accompanying lobbyists are always keen to campaign for the respective large corporations, the US refusal to purchase World Health Organization (WHO)-approved drugs tends to pose challenges in many times and eventually create logistic problems because local clinics and hospitals must segregate those drugs purchased with US funds from others in order to survive especially with the prescription medications. The big question has not been answered as of yet because the dilemma is that in order to get around these problems, FDA promised to grant tentative approval to generic drugs that meet regulatory standards. In that respect, those products are consequently eligible for purchase by PEPFAR programs, but cannot come to market in the United States because of patent restraints as the main issue.

How the above operation translates into the healing of inter-racial tensions cannot be over-emphasized. Even though many observers still regard the FDA approach as a waste of money and resources, the prospect of qualifying for purchase by PEPFAR is attracting applicants, and the accelerated review policy has helped bring new AIDS therapies to market quickly. In the given perspective, it is revealed that speedy approvals could require quality applications and early inspections of bioequivalence data and manufacturing facilities to contribute positively and according to expectations.

Another dilemma is that even though FDA approval makes such generic products eligible for purchase by PEPFAR, manufacturers must register the drugs in each recipient country before they can be distributed to patients. A number of African governments also want FDA-approved drugs included on WHO's prequalification list so that they can use the same drugs for all programs. FDA and WHO officials recently signed an agreement to share confidential regulatory information, which will make it easier for WHO to access FDA data to quickly add any new drugs to its prequalification list. Manufacturers usually agree to any FDA requests to share trade secret data about drug formulation and manufacturing process with agencies such as WHO.

As challenging as the politics of world healthcare have implied, it is the most delicate industry because a health body is the greatest of God's blessings yet death may occur with a single error. For the past few years and mainly the last two decades, much has been talked about the relationship between healthcare and the economical or global financial crises. A nation with vision cannot and can never claim to be economically stable or more precisely an economic superpower if it lacks a satisfactory workable healthcare system. Only a few nations have achieved what is called a universal healthcare system for all its citizens. The systematic approach by which a universal healthcare revolution can be attained has become one of the most controversial of world issues. However, as I mentioned earlier, if the first unification factor of religion is resolved, then the others would follow gradually. How such a plan would be financed remains the subject of discussion in everyday business in many countries especially the developed nations around the world.

Part of the answer to the above subject resides on the power to change our determinative attitudes on healthcare administration in order to make the right judgments. It is the power to realize the much quoted talk by president Obama of the United States that, like the business owners' feelings, the workers on the factory floors have the same human health feelings as themselves without any slightest differences. We have witnessed healthcare disparities even in the most developed countries including America for many generations in the past and not only on the basis of income, but or race and national origin. I personally bear witness by working in many industries where healthcare discrimination has been practiced before my eyes. The most popular way has been achieved through unemployment. In the respective method, a healthcare institution begins to grow and develop right from the grassroots. As the process advances, one prime objective has to be fulfilled and consistently realized or the threat of taking the last resort or option of closure becomes an open possibility. The prime objective is to advance in revenue and have a consistent margin of profit improvements. That stands as an extended threat to a long lasting new world order.

World history reveals that mankind has traded with one another in different businesses for many generations. However, what remains unclear is the specific definition of who should be the obvious entitled breadwinner as to make guaranteed gains and profits and who should be the sole loser in all generations. That can be discussed more on the cases of insurance companies including Allegis which kept charging me one hundred dollars per week, but failed to pay for my child's drug prescribed for a distressful skin disease. Many books quite often quote healthcare as a risk term where a human being's good health is the greatest of God's blessings. Just like most of the world has realized the needs of an educational overhaul, and so is healthcare. Consequently, it would depend on the formulation of an ideological change of the educational systems to both merge and match a universal definition ranging from the guaranteed qualifying methods of implementations. The world has lived through many centuries relying on educational systems that some if not substantial, would describe as part of the weapon of class deception. The movements that have hinted in several parts of the world are quite indicative that the root cause is on track to be researched in more details. It is a beginner's belief that the design is focused and missioned to benefit only those few who can access the loopholes or the tricks that are sealed in secret destinations and boxes. In that respect, it is quite conceivable that any healthcare program that is simply focusing more on profits other than the status of the patient or customer should be rejected by both the government and the people of that government. That was the reason why the world recognized president Obama in 2008 campaigns on trying to take a completely different direction to reform healthcare as opposed to the past decades as a status quo where lobbyists from various pharmaceutical companies were required to stay aloof. When we see a big debate of the century that outbursts some senators like Joe Wilson to shout at the president Obama while addressing the nation on healthcare reform, then we foresee a big rift and fights ahead of millions of poor people around the world. Poor people are usually discriminated and live without insurance while they are the ones who produce the goods for the rich people to enjoy. A universal healthcare system is only possible if a compromise is enforced as much as the civil rights movements did for all Americans and other likewise nations. It is such an urgent state where policy makers have to agree to disagree with the majority who happen to be poor people and their representatives like president Obama. That would be a system that allows the right to happiness according to the universal constitution for all people regardless of how low the profit or revenue margins may be.

In the past many controversies have erupted to an incredible level that would actually cause complete mistrust if not checked on time. Such has been the case with research and development of medical products from pharmaceutical industries in collaboration with hospital practitioners. In that respect, some hospital professionals at certain instances have either performed dangerous placebo tests or research studies on various groups of patients without their slightest of any consent or understanding.

Again, this kind of behavior is only motivated by the thirst to generate profits and sprinting to the finish line with slim and thin minded desires of real help to the needy patients. Most of the outcomes have been positive, but with lots of side effects which sometimes can impact very negatively on the research professionals and diagnostic scientists. The greatest negativity or drawback lies on the honesty and trustworthiness of the healthcare system and the possibility of its validation as an independent secure institution. Thus, the healthcare professionals have to come to the point of no return and declare that enough is enough to revolutionize the respective modern educational structure right from the grassroots. How they can achieve such a revolution is a subject that has often called for thorough negotiation and compromise with the popularly renowned bipartisanship. However, it is still a tough question as far as a lasting union is concerned.

Part of the answer to the above subject in question lies on the idealistic innovation of the system of the health institution. The first thing would be the willingness to either share and spread the good living standards of the poor workers or use the revenues generated through the applied labor so as to guarantee the undersigned the healthcare benefits and insurance through retirement. When an American president ran for presidency in 1992 against incumbent George Bush, he scored huge political points by saying that if countries like Germany had advanced to achieve national universal healthcare, then a superpower like the United States of America should copy likewise or perform even better. That created some hot debate and tension as the incumbent; Mr George Bush dismissed the whole idea by wondering the source of the funds that would supply the money to finance the program and do all that was necessary to implement the program. Just like president Baraka Obama, former president Bill Clinton argued that if we could finance all the past wars including the Persian Gulf war while spending billions on military and national security, then how could we fail to achieve that goal. He insisted that the United States could oppose the wedging of some of the wars which were quite unnecessary like the one in Iraq and use that money for healthcare and educational improvements. On the basis of the famous financial crisis of the year 2008, it is reasonable to speculate that pride on military superiority is real costing America and Russia quite a lot of losses in education and healthcare. That is also true with those nations which are still counting and measuring development in terms of military superiority. In that respect, the war in Iraq alone for instance was a big failure and blunder as the suspected weapons of mass destruction were never found as claimed in order to certify the invasion. That is quite consistent with the rest of other wars which are pursued without clarity in substance to its cause. The end result is a creation of negative impacts and many repercussions lasting for generations without proper healing, settlements and reconstructions.

A real global healthcare innovation would have to look at a world of healthcare beyond our borders. In such an analytical focus, all humanity would be summoned to look at one another as feathers of the same flock that have been trapped in the same system that requires urgent remedies. That would be trivialized once the biggest obstacle in the first chapter has been dealt with appropriately. It has often been an old tradition to rely on competition as the greatest booster of business and economic prosperity. That is especially true when it is focused to transcend between partner states and greatly between continents. That tradition has created a big gap between the poor and the rich, and so much so that many world citizens have ended up losing hope not only in healthcare, but in general living standards. However, what just happened in the world earmarked by year 2008 global financial crisis, was not a lesson that can change, but in fact that the whole universal economy can collapse leaving anyone to stand as a victim while everybody remains a target. Consequently, the idea of looking at a world beyond one's own border grows high and gains a better consideration and understanding. That is why it can hardly if ever, make any sense for one to focus on politics alone in a neighboring country yet at the same time refuse or fail to use the same focal lens on a deteriorating healthcare system. The respective country might only be dwelling in verbal terms without actual existence. It would not matter how precious the operation is because once that goes to pass out of memory, there develops an angry and sick community where even the slightest illness cannot be handled with any rehabilitation element or clinical dispensation.

Healthcare has consistently remained the most challenging political hurdle in many lives, but the above dilemma can still be handled and get the attraction of every modern leader. That is true for the politicians of the current and the future generations of this world. As mentioned before, the real strategy is to try to inspire popular competition into cooperation so that the healthcare icon in campaigns spreads out to all nations. The universality has to walk the talk so as to be felt in many sectors like other industrial developments. That is the slogan that would simplify the universal trading in businesses as a two way traffic enterprises where benefits are neither doubted or monopolized in international relations. International relations are often viewed and substantiated by many as the import-export of products without limit to type and quality. In that respect, an international relationship becomes vulnerable to some kind of destruction once a particular nation outperforms another on a given enterprise development. That often leads to a forced trading regulation for which the buyer has no bargaining power in terms of whether to be or actually being covered by a healthcare institution of a universal status. Again, that can be due to either greed or competition without cooperation. In that order, it implies that quite a lot needs to be done in all related programming institutional systems for a stronger long lasting world union in healthcare.

For the past two hundred years, education and research have impacted and dictated how healthcare can become available for universal purposes. However, that kind of impact has not been felt in many developing nations because of lack of modern leadership and extreme political violence. While many of these nations have recognized democracy to be the best option, they have also cast doubts as to whether the loopholes can play a role for underdevelopments when the process finds 95% of the population in poverty and without employment or even food at their house. In a developing nation example one politician back in the 1970s, J. M Kariuki, like a sounding joke, made a good blasting statement by quoting how Kenya had turned into a country with ten millionaires and ten million beggars. Other news that confirm about urgent medical problems such as malaria being eradicated or ceasing to exist in some developed countries do indeed add more fuel into the issue of mistrust. Thus, for an initial start or spread of the belief that universal healthcare can actually ever be programmed, the basic doubts on the respective mistrusts have to be addressed and resolved urgently with immediate priority. How that can be achieved in a global financial crisis like the one of the year 2008 where banks were bailed by various governments and yet homelessness continued to rise. That resulted in the rising of the gap between the poor and the rich even more than any other time in human history. Just as recently as in the year 2008, the world witnessed how micro-soft owner and billionaire,

Mr. Bill Gates turned from the world's richest man into number three after a short stay as a number two. A new name took the first position as Warren Buffet and well worth over sixty billion dollars. That makes it a tough question about the money that was bailed out as to whether it was the money owners who really needed it or the homeless that had lost their houses due to foreclosures. A popular experience was witnessed by the whole world in the year 2008 when a bank executive could earn up to three million a month and still receive a bonus of an additional eight million at the end of the year. Nobody is or should be jealous about another person's money or wealth accumulation if it is honestly obtained. However, world governments should be ashamed of letting so much wealth accumulation take place within a few people or groups of people to take place when health is non-existent and homelessness is so abundant. The saying is "there is always a way out" which nobody seems not to have discovered as of yet, but it should be left to each one of us to ponder in analysis. It shouldn't really last longer than now nor should it have actually passed through the last century when most of the world nations fought and won to gain their freedoms. However, some still hold it to be true and do diagnose it as a necessary healing while many don't even consider it a necessary remedy.

Freedom as many of us understand it has been in existence in different forms for many generations, but few in number and with limited options. What many people do shy away from acknowledging is that no matter how much the phrase gets misused to certify or satisfy the misunderstanding, it actually boils down to a point of no return. That is where the truth resurfaces and explodes like fire and ends up burning any strands of lies with minimal struggle. Consequently, the loser is the individual who took the pain to understand, but failed to apply the correct universal formula of a long lasting investment of survival. This has been seen a lot in the past century with pre-independence struggles like in South Africa and many other nations who have gained such freedoms within the last fifty years. Many have misused the freedom phrase to accommodate corruption both in private and public institutions and none of the existing sectors has been affected more than healthcare. For the past few years the world has been introduced with the globalization song. That is the song which has actually seemed to have been one of the fundamental tools to streamline corruption under the umbrella of freedom. However, even though healthcare is a strong commodity in the whole world in marketing, it is actually non-affordable in the poor countries by more than 95% of the population. That is the hurdle to its universality for the necessary lasting world union.

While a lot of trading practices have been debated and workable agreements implemented, most poor countries have not seen the compromised and tangible prosperous results or benefits. It kind of gets worse when the same type of feeling is even felt in an highly industrial and developed nation like America and Japan. When further scrutiny is carried out, it is quite likely that other foreign ideas are going to be reviewed and considered regardless of whether it impacts negatively or positively on individual benefits from globalization. One African Kenyan professor of medicine and minister for health in the governments of both president Arap Moi and Mwai Kibaki, once said that while globalization is good, it has to be a two-way traffic channel. The interpretation was quite trivial because all he meant was that the medical institution has to walk the talk and accommodate innovation in all ways so long as the channels are safe for human living and consumer health. In so doing he tabled a proposal that would introduce the local pharmaceutical products to be shelved along with those produced in large scale international recipes. Such a proposal was in fact good if it had received enough understanding and support so as to design the set-up of the appropriate rules and regulations like it is with the common over the counter (OTC) products.

With world politics under different policies, part of any feasible healthcare strategies has to incur some or maximum opposition before implementation. However, the main point and background of such a suggestion as mentioned above is an attempt to tackle the negative impacts that may result from a healthcare disparity on the cause of modern globalization. Part of the most fought policy war in Washington was based on the healthcare disparity programs of the status quo. In that respect, healthcare has been making big titles with many underlying natures for many generations. A former United States presidential candidate, the Reverend Jesse Jackson, said during his popular speech in 1984, that "by the fact that one is born in a slum, it does not mean the slum is born in him or her. The whole speech was so inspiring to young America especially the African Americans. Since then, I have tried or tended to reverse the same saying by renaming it as "by the fact that one is not born in the slum, it does not mean that the slum is not born in him or her". That sounds quite awesome and kind of strong an expression and which I carefully interpreted for many people, and it can be very influential as to develop into a big weapon of mass inspiration for both parties as described. That is why in the same context, I did find Professor Sam Ongeri's proposal to be quite inspiring even though I do disagree with him on other issues. I do oppose some of his political attacks based on tribalism and lack of full cultural understanding on his own ethnic group in the Kenyan 2002 presidential sentiments where he terrorized his own tribe by disqualifying it on national and international leadership. That left a big drawback on him and his rival, honorable Simon Nyachae who was a presidential candidate at that time and which can be considered a negative factor for a long lasting world union in healthcare.

The philosophical background of Reverend Jesse Jackson expression about a slum is coincidentally based on my personal guide or wisdom book, the Bible scriptures which clearly states that love for the enemy means a lot including the teaching righteousness and correcting or treating evil whenever possible. There is no particular motive of rephrasing the phenomenon other than reverse inspiration to serve both the rich and the poor. In that attempt, it simply implies that an individual can be born in a rich family or environment, but misuse a lot of nice opportunities for the remote short term goals or reasons and eventually fall into the ditch if great care is not taken. That does not stand sticking far from the same guide which counts on wisdom or rather the power to make the right judgment. It is not by coincidence that the above philosophical saying clearly fits the United States of America where the popularity starts with development through the military superiority. However, it became more conspicuous in the recent 2008 presidential election that signified the miraculous powers which can come as a result of true democracy. The slum birth saying above fits in very well because it reminds the world that slavery does not endure forever. It is the truth which clearly does so and this time in plain daylight within a span of less than five hundred years that it stuck the majority of the world as a serious disorder. It actually comes as a perfect fit to the given world circumstances because after the collapse of communism which we counted as a slum side of the civilized political environments in modern lives, capitalism emerges with worrying news.

The emergence was earmarked by the threats of the collapsed financial institutions in Wall Street as well as Main Street. The big question is whether the western world has realized anything in relation to the long lasting world unity.

When we speculate about the bright part of our future lives, we usually base the argument on hope and faith. However, to be caught in a situation of financial threats of collapse of many institutions around the world, poses a significant wake-up call that no particular system or institution is simply perfect so to claim. It actually confirms that all have fallen short of the glory everlasting development and prosperity. In such a making, healthcare still stands as the central battleground in the unending war of economic prosperity. That definitely scares even the most wealth because they find themselves vulnerable to any depression on the basis of long global recessions destroying many billionaires. Thus, the future prosperity of healthcare would be governed by the amount of commitment that would be displayed from many governments and their opponents as well as private institutions or individuals. Profit is always good, but the wealth must be willing to invest more generously even when they don't achieve maximized profits. The good reason is that the poor people are the medium of exchange for many business foundations to survive. The olden days when billionaires used to enjoy the boastings are no longer valid unless the large masses living under poverty are uplifted somehow to some extent. Many of those found in poverty are those residing in poor countries where subsistence methods are the only option of survival. Many subsistence conditions are only aimed at seasonal farming for limited food without a foreseeable future prospect while many are struggling in the slums. While many hate to be idle, the conditions have forced many to find themselves in that gap. It is debatable whether third or poor nations' idleness is self-inflicted or foreign induced because my bible guide book tells me that idleness is described as a devilish workshop or more precisely "An idle mind is a devil's workshop". The bigger question is whether somebody can impose idleness on others so as to make them look evil as the case is with unemployment within the African community that stands highest even when so educated. That is a proven fact even when America claims to have eradicated racism or racial discrimination while I stand as one of the best examples. That has caused serious health issues related to unemployment stresses that resulted in homelessness due to the foreclosures on mortgage crises. The end result is huge healthcare costs that drains the economy while fighting for universal healthcare and deters long lasting world unity.

Many researchers including myself have been conducting serious work to determine the way as to how real universal healthcare can reduce crime and even terrorism as it stands today. As mentioned earlier, healthcare encompasses the greatest element of life which is translated into a state of being in good health. The most part of this book is dedicated towards investing on the whole future of the world which if achieved would simply rid it out of a lot of terrorism if not all of it. Accessibility and availability of most structures of healthcare institutions remains one of the greatest factors in that phenomenon. When a nation or a person is terminally ill, it does not matter where the rescue comes from so long as life can be saved. Consequently, in healthcare, it does not matter where the cure for AIDS or cancer comes from so long as it can treat the disease or even cure it. That is usually the time when cooperation becomes more important than competition. That was contrary to what I expected to see when I visited African in the country of Kenya way back in 1989-1990 on a healthcare mission and survey.

I arrived in the African country Kenya in January 1989 after my undergraduate commencement celebrating my achievement in pre-medicine concentration in the scientific trainings. I had not been enlightened as to how far Kenya as a country had advanced in development and particularly in healthcare ever since I had left four years earlier. Being a third world country where communication and accessibility were among the world's poorest, I could not expect them to have an advanced idea on how to approach or even handle a complex task that the whole world was facing like the AIDS virus. To think along that would be the same thing as thinking positive for somebody born in a slum only to rise above it and get to the top as a rocket science inventor. For a nation like Kenya which has become a magnet of many tourist attractions, the world politics and particularly the Obama election has added more fuel for the fact that Kenya is the ancestral homeland of the US first African American president. Otherwise one would only expect very little other than wildlife and the game parks with subsistence agricultural productions. President Obama visited the village slums of his father's ancestral homeland which marked part of the anointment of where he belonged. Consequently, his rise to the presidency was a clear tale to me that the 1989 healthcare claimed accomplishment might have just been a reality. Some or majority of other research competitors might question the validity of my claim, but the answer to such a query is a subject that can be supported in a number of ways.

First and foremost, it is a well-known fact that most of the world competitors are very difficult to genuinely unite or cooperate with one another. From a personal perspective and many colleagues, I have experienced such a drawback as a researcher in general science as well as professional pharmaceutical developmental. Likewise, I have witnessed a high profile politician claiming for instance that a league cannot allow many Kenyans to participate in a marathon race because it would end being just a Kenyan race with minimal outsiders getting closer to any winning tape. However, I did not hear such an argument when the Olympic swimming champion, Phelps, won eight consecutive gold medals in the year 2008 in Beijing, China. By comparing the above two statements, it is quite imperative to prove that cooperation among a competition can produce the best competitors. The results are displayed by the non-politicized race in the swimming participation. In that respect, the same can be expected in the healthcare and institutions and same should have happened in the 1989 Kenyan wonder discovery of Kemron, that may or may never have prospered depending on the weight of the underlying evidence.

The events that were taking place during the 1989 visit that I made to Africa, were actually a healthcare celebration on behalf of the achievements realized by the Kenya medical association. The respective medical association had compiled short-term based research results obtained from using an anti-virus recipe invented and formulated in their laboratory. The clinical treatment trials were conducted on local African women prostitutes who had been described as terminally ill due to an AIDS viral infection. On the basis of the results obtained and reported as posted at that time after treatment, the diagnostic tests revealed that the infectious virus had been either eliminated from their bodies or been exorcised to a controlled non-virulent status. Consequently, the celebration became so vibrant and overwhelming as it attracted a lot of healthcare researchers and scientists from more than a half of the worldwide countries. The main industrialized countries included developed nations like Germany, Japan, England, France, Italy, USA, and former USSR. That particular celebration was so popular that the then President Daniel Arap Moi called it a revolutionary breakthrough and approval of a poor country like Kenya. He highlighted the occasion so as to set up the basis for opening other avenues for which other inventions would be founded. For those who participated in the historic celebrations, some and mainly Americans seemed to have seen an uncommon green light that would unite the world. That would of course be on better terms than ever before with a new worldwide health organization order (WHOO). The name of the interferon as it was described or more precisely the antiretroviral formula was Kemron which many people have come across when researching through the internet. Theway Kemron popularity and prosperity failed to last or prosper for too long in years is a question that is still being politicized. It is still not fully answered from a scientific standpoint which is the only avenue of proper argument given all the necessary research tools. That leaves the possibility of universal healthcare in a long lasting union in dilemma that should not keep eroding.

Part of the answer to the above question rests on the vestiges of political competition as opposed to the politics of cooperation. Again, we encounter competition without cooperation which I have described previously as a destructive priority. The point is not whether Africa or Kenya was entitled to any wonder discovery, but rather focused on any possibility of attaining the ability to come out with some chemical entity that would shape up the deteriorating healthcare world. That would then impact and probably change the scientific and political hemisphere that is still taken for granted. Whichever way the events followed, the impact was felt throughout the world that change was actually on the way. That was much the same way that it felt when another version of similar winds spread throughout the world when United States president Baraka Obama engaged in a tight race in the 2008 historic presidential campaign. I tend to think that if the world had felt and suffered the same consequence of an economic crisis heading for a possible collapse then the Kemron idea would have been greeted with favor for guaranteed prosperity. However, after learning from the worldwide financial crisis, we are bound to believe that it can happen in any institution and embark on a special mission to prevent such a tragedy. Hence, we can reckon the importance of aiming at a worldwide healthcare unification system which can possibly be subdivided into various attachable strongholds of institutions.

As mentioned earlier, traditional healthcare institutions have suffered a great deal with lots of drawbacks because of less document scientific materials. Those are the ones needed to be available so as to fully support their trading or commercialization around the world. For that reason they have been isolated and kept at bay with little media recognition which has embargoed them to less profitable non-regulated environments which are mostly found in poor countries or locations. However, with the current winds of change, many of such dreams are about to be reclaimed and realized. There are many herbs that are now being harvested, packaged and shelved with the common over the counter medications for commercialization. However, some professionals have counter-criticized the popularity of natural herbs by saying that by being natural, it does not mean being safe. While that may be true, it is also true that many modern medicines do suffer from several worse of repercussions on the basis of the evidence from such companies as Merck research Pharmaceuticals on the suits related to the side effects of Vioxx. As a scientist, I do share the same vision with other healthcare professionals that every little thing in production actually adds up to make a difference. That can grow and become bigger into a major development much the same way as the birth of the industrial revolution into the world. Consequently, a common herb or medical beverage leave with its seeds and probably roots can serve different therapeutic needs simultaneously or at different times and destinations in a given normal body. That is an implication that on the basis of a given fair regulation on the less recognized medicines, healthcare barriers leading to exorbitant costs can be greatly reduced. That would soften the expenses and make it more affordable so as to discourage disparities so far experienced around the world. Thus, in terms of achieving a universal healthcare, complications would become history because there would be more choices work on and individual needs accommodated according to what suits a particular case. The fear of trading outcomes and partners would not become big factor. For one thing that might be a subsidiary to the success of the healthcare formula above, is the infrastructure that normally dictates the accessibility and communication in general which is highly magnified in the developing countries.

The above statement as pointed might seem to work best for the local villagers. However, without the proper tools of communication and particularly at the grass roots, the recipes would remain as unique as their mirror home images appear. Thus, some specific infrastructure and particularly the early mentioned Jua Kali rooted foundations; have to be injected into the systems. That would strengthen the maturity of any formula laid down in the foundation plans. As common as the daily lives go, people are always focusing on the development risks and which is normal in actuality because nothing ever grows easily from the grass roots without taking such chances. Even the first medical drug that was ever utilized or discovered for therapeutic reasons by any scientist could not have been perfect in the initial trials. It is usually a risk trial and so universal in strategic developments. At the current rate of mortality in developing countries and particularly those in the African continent on south of the Sahara desert, it is an extreme crisis which the world health organization (WHO) declared a worldwide state of emergency. In such an event where a state of emergency is declared without reservation, drugs like Kemron must not and should never have been politicized. It is more than twenty years since the discovery of Kemron that was not a perfect drug as most others, but the victims are still struggling in life without a cure.

As the understanding and complexity of the healthcare comes to be realized as a necessary highway where humanity has to ride many of the politicized arenas would begin to fade away. That would be contained in some form of saying about the consequences of an unhealthy world. The preliminary saying is that unhealthy processes are infectious and spread first and exponentially with very virulent factors like weapons of mass destruction where anybody can be a launcher, but everybody remains a target. Again, that sounds very threatening, but it is the reality of the matter. The scope of this book is focused on universal unity on the basis of healthcare. Other institutions can be classified under the same category without regard to who feels superior or inferior and whether Christian, Jew, Islam, Buddha or any other different believer outside that gap. A few leaders including President Baraka Obama have tried their best to separate faith from such issues as healthcare or other politically manipulated issues and ideologies. However, nobody has ever said for sure that if a scientific discovery is performed in an enemy country which may happen to be the only cure, then discrimination policies would be valid. That is why Iraq oil is useful and thus used by everybody. If both cases are true to some extent then it is prove that we all need one another in order to make and achieve any progress. In that respect the choice of healthcare as the first priority to the world unity secures a good case for encouragement. The priority would be looking more as to how universal healthcare can become a big product of a united world. The big question is whether the developed nations would be ready to buy such an ideology with freedom of expression without fear of labeling it world socialism for the purpose of winning political scores. The main point behind any cause to argument would be the mission to keep the old traditions of governance of the status quo where people simply talk for many generations without walking the respective talks in practice.

Based on a personal analysis, healthcare falls in the educational umbrella and stands as the number one issue in the world's strategic overhaul spectra. Education in the modern terms is centralized in cleanliness and that gets strengthened by the saying that "cleanliness is second to truthfulness". Many people particularly parents of the third world countries question a lot the fruitfulness of an education to a grade one child who seeks knowledge by commuting two to three miles and twice each day of school. As risk as the situation turns out to be, many parents advise their children to wait to at least eight to ten years in age before they can start attending elementary level school work. Even then it still remains a shoeless walk in most of their elementary level schooling years in addition to other unhealthy early life experiences where a healthcare program is non-existent. Thus acquiring a decent and health education is non-existent neither. That translates into the necessity of an education from the grassroots once again in order to open doors for any healthcare administration. That is a proven starting point for a real long waited ignition which needs closer examination and expansion once the new implementation takes place. The next question is how and where if the developed nations are trapped in the same similar struggle. Developed nations like America and Russia are still dependent on foreign loans from countries like China and consistently view universal healthcare as a distant dream. Such a dream is often blamed on the irrelevancy of the prevailing educational curricula as related to many hard-hit economies of the world. It would be interesting to focus on such a question in the sense it might affect the future lasting world union in healthcare.

Before answering the above question which would likely and definitely be very broad, it requires a frequent revision on taking a moment look at the freedom of healthcare on the basis of all human beings. Obviously, before the world even begins some exercising any dreams on the basis of a united universal healthcare, it must make it pretty understandable that human life is only measurable by one scale or yardstick. In his keynote speech in the democratic national convention in 2004, the then senator Baraka Obama, hit the nail on the head by saying that in quotes "there is no such thing as a conservative or liberal American, but there is the United States of America". In the same scenario and on behalf of freedom as human health, there is no such a thing as American health freedom or democratic and republican healthcare. There is one healthcare to adapt to and regardless of whether it is British, American, African, Arabic, and Chinese or Russian healthcare as all humans use basically the same type of drugs. There is the united world in which life must be measured with one yardstick much the same way as crime measurements. Consequently, healthcare cannot be united to achieve universality unless it is universally measured with one scale. That is in all phases and whether in stem cell research or in abortion and regardless of being in any wars as in either Rwanda or Iraq type of situation. Medicine and medical healthcare sciences in research has proven that life and death is the same in all human nature throughout the world. Hence a universal healthcare that could be long lasting would include a fair whole world participation.

What most people have tried to do in the past is to compete for a scoring game so called political scores. That happens even when it is quite obvious that some issues stand so critical and trivial without requiring much intelligence to prove a point. The fact is that in righteous definitions, crime is crime regardless of scale and is such a deep script in many cultural beliefs. On the basis of a personal experience, the seeking of superiority and particularly in militarism, has overshadowed a lot of intelligence that is often presented as pride in opposition to my guide book principles. At the same time, however, no particular woman would openly come out and declare that she likes abortion on account of the pain to be experienced for a long time if not already gone through the test. Many Americans have debated the scale of measurement by which killing should be analyzed. Some have pointed that the killings by abortion are more of a crime than those that take place in wars such as in the Iraq of 2002 on the basis of biological weapons suspicions or the Rwandan genocide of 1994. While that remains to be debated for any validation, it is also true that evil people cannot live or survive without terrorism or some form of war trafficking around the world even when many claim to be God's children in faith. Many who claim to be faithful and righteous on verbal terms do still survive by keeping strings attached to validate some rationality in the background of a war whose case has been presented and awaiting for a prove. Consequently, some conservatives argue that since evil is always evil regardless of scale, there isn't and should be no room to compromise with any enemies. However, that is immediately invalidated by the nature and principles of modern court proceedings around the world. In any case, such an intuition quickly invites a sacred failure which begins to get worse especially when we remember some past wars including the American civil war of 1863 through 1865. The American civil war alone was a great challenge that should serve as a permanent lesson as to what the real meaning of war must be. That is especially true when the underlying consequences are extrapolated so as to focus on the impacts of the future generations. It leaves a big imprint in question as to whether people really care and understand the clear basis of wedging a war of any kind. The magnitude of the above example of the American civil war was a loss of more than six hundred thousand lives just because former president Abraham Lincoln detected something wrong in the then prevailing system of slavery that was fully in operation. President Lincoln detected the future dangers of slavery because it could have brought the end of human existence if all men were not the same equality on humanity for a long lasting unity.

Most learning institutions around the world do teach a lot about human equality which is sometimes referred to as human rights. However, despite that fact that such freedom of learning remains the central world order, many people still believe that there should be no such a thing as totally free as freedom goes. Their argument is that for that to happen then even evil people should be given the freedom of movement. Those are the type of people who opposed former president Abraham Lincoln's ideology of equality on creation for all human beings. Some people later on turned around and claimed to have actually acted as such out of ignorance. What they might find difficult to certify is whether some vestigial structures of such ignorance are still having any strings attached and for how long in the current world. In the real world, such an argument can be injected into other freedoms that might be encountered in different cultures with various religious beliefs. It is quite doubtful that there is any religious institution that can openly advocate for the destruction of other human beings. When people argue that religious institutions should relinquish from political participations and yet those same politicians don't avail any mechanism for stopping unwanted teenage pregnancies, then it all boils down to hypocrisy. It is found sinful and yet those same people attend the same church and services which stands out as a contradiction. How can one fail to recognize the impact of teenage pregnancy as a serious sin to God, but only be able to detect the sin when the same observer commits the same crime? The misunderstanding of the meaning of true freedom has caused a lot of confusion in many world governments that even young boys and girls cannot be punished to any extent to discourage the unwanted teenage pregnancies that are the major causes of the wars on abortions. It should be started as a humble exercise around the worldwide learning institutions and particularly the universal healthcare as well as the Christian doctrines. Only then shall a universal healthcare plan come into being and grow into an implementable permanent entity in development. Those great civil rights activists like the reverend doctor Martin Luther King junior and president Abraham Lincoln, knew very well that nothing progressive would last long unless the attached ignorance of suppression had been rooted out first. That is why President Baraka Obama really celebrated Lincoln's birthday with great commemoration in high spirits.

The worldwide healthcare is likely to be given universal priority because the financial crises have proven that anybody can fall short of precious glories and become a victim of economic collapses. The world health organization should begin recruiting more people especially from poor countries where there could be superior sources of medical treatments. Superior medical recipes do exist in those environments, but there is lack of proper marketing regulations which makes them very unpopular and unknown for administrative purposes. Respectively, all those occur because of poor organization or inferior purification methods of instrumentation. Having grown up as a scientist in a poor country, I learned and trained myself as to how to survive healthfully by simple creativity principles which I later realized could become greater discoveries and inventions. Such training on scientific thoughts could inspire me to begin thinking on how to treat domestic animals out of imaginations based on life activities and illnesses. Later on in high school, I deepened the respective learning upon reading that famous scientist, Isaac Newton, discovered the force of gravity right in his garden or behind in the backyard of his house. It sounded so simple because while sitting down under an apple tree in his backyard, an apple fruit fell down and hit him by landing on the top of his head. Assuming there was no wind or any visible force blowing to have caused the fruit to cut off from the tree branch and fall on his head, Newton had to think what nobody else had probably ever taught. From that incident, Newton had accidentally discovered the force of gravity. That is how it is known today by many if not all scientists and without any opposing challenges even from the most brilliant of all scholars. In a similar fashion, I was seated in my garden during my elementary times at the age of eight watching in admiration my domestic farm poultry which I brooded. As I watched my hens keenly, I could see one or two of them grazing on grass most of the time, but rarely on a particular herb at the corner of the garden where such thorny vegetation was concentrated. One particular and probably special day I detected one of my hens biting on one of the thorny herbs and proceeding to a restful destination. I suspected something special because I considered such a herb to be wild and probably poisonous as no other hen or animal had ever touched it before by close examination. Then in the next few weeks there occurred an epidemic explosion of a sweeping disease that claimed many poultry lives including half of my own. Poultry healthcare became a big concern in my life at that particular time. That inspired into the career of healthcare at an early age which later translated into the current great interest in caring for others in many categories in daily living. I had to use all strategies to do whatever it took to save some or all of the infected hens reared in the same cages. I took the first initiative to prepare my first dosage formula like today's modern scientists, but without sterilization. That is similar to what most scientists do in what they describe as an in-vivo or live clinical studies. The good news were that the treated hens ended up to be among the only very few survivors out of the endemic disease in the whole village. Like Newton, I could only speculate without specific prove, but I had accidentally discovered a veterinary medical agent that would be scaled up to be formulated into various pharmaceutical products. There are may be many untold stories of that type, but to develop them into useful entities, the whole world must learn such few facts and begin developing the willingness to come together. That is the factor that would develop the required unity with the mission to focus on universal healthcare regardless of the source of resolution. In that respect, the ideology of teaching one's neighbor to feel inferior and insecure in most phases of healthcare must be eliminated if not outlawed. The same must apply in all other phases because it is now proven that nobody is immune to global crises as much as it is well known that none is perfect.

Many inventions and discoveries have been made during our healthcare lives, but a few have been documented. If the Newton's invention or discovery of the force of gravity had not been documented with good recordings, it could never have been known forever or until probably this age. The force has always been there since the foundations of this world through both evolution and creation mechanisms. Similarly, there are thousands of small discoveries and innovations or inventions for such matters which have taken place and still happening but simply become almost obsolete in terms of documentation for tracking purposes. For me to support the re-unification of modern and traditional healthcare, many factors are quite considerable including the central belief that primitive conservation principles are the main causes for the collapse of today's healthcare still dwelling in partisan politics. That is the place where help is discussed most, but only verbally without walking the talk. The impression can be likened to the much quoted saying in the Obama administrative strategies that calls for an overhaul not only in healthcare, but total political programs in Washington of which some are responsible for the current world crises. For those who benefited out of enslaving others and gaining out of free labor, change is not an option and would rather stay in fear or hatred than to see peace through uplifting of those victimized in those centuries around the world. The former civil rights leader, The Reverend Doctor Martin Luther King once quoted that "we'll still love thee even when you mistreat or even kill us". That was to say that a teacher cannot correct a foolish mistake by imitating the fool's behavior of hatred based on race or skin color. The only snag is that most fools don't actually know that hatred based on skin color or race is actually foolish and usually until it backfires. However, most dark skinned people would take all their time to display hospitality to all light skinned people even when they still hate them in all proportions. I keep asking myself as much as others do as to who the real fool is on the basis of the above scenario of doctor Martin Luther King because every time I try to do the best in everything, I receive a donkey's kirk in all levels of life with rare if any appreciation. My guidebook confirms to me that fools hate smart people and that would probably remain so until the end of the world because God was himself too smart to have used words only in order to deliver healthcare and for which reason he had to receive stones on his body. In that respect, any hatred or hateful investment has a long lasting sickening repercussions and or which reason doctor King advocated non-violence to achieve some ends meet as we know them today. I have studied for some time now and I am strongly convinced that healthcare disparities don't just start at the hospital clinics or in the capitol hill administrative governments around the world. They in fact start from elementary school grade levels and continues through the years depending on whether the instructing teacher is for love or simple primitive hatred regardless of whether liberal or conservative. Most people around the world are now actually learning that the criteria of judging by skin color is quite destructive a priority because unimaginable number of precious talents are dumped in such a strategy. I am one example whose talents have been suppressed over the years in addition to others that I detected because of the very fruitful proposal ideas that I presented in concept with negative reactions in the gap of competition without cooperation.

One of the best examples that I have always liked is based on the former scientist, Albert Einstein. The famous scientist had tried to conceive some special proposals, but some of them frequently landed him in trouble during his studies in graduate level educational researches. I strongly believe that most of his proposals must have been either too good to be truly acceptable by other competitive scientists or colleagues other than being too complicated or expensive without feasibility. That frustrated him a lot and caused him to transfer from one university to another at least more than once. It was through several temptations with patience that he finally succeeded and for which he laid the stony foundation basis leading to a major change in the nature of world wars. He was voted the man of the century in the times magazine of the new millennium because many scientists marked the beginning of a different new world outlook. Likewise, there are other scientists who made worldwide impacts like Vivian Thomas, who changed the vision of the cardiovascular technological surgeries. Vivian Thomas worked as technician in a medical healthcare laboratory caring for animals mainly dogs for experimental clinical trials and in surgery and frequently helped his boss who happened to be a professor in that institution. His work as a technician in performance led to the discovery of the by-pass surgery as it is known today. He was awarded a doctoral degree for that achievement even though he had never stepped in a modern medical classroom. There is currently a lot vacuum in the research and development of pharmaceuticals and it is certainly due to the same foolish talent suppressions as mentioned above as well as it was in the case during Vivian Thomas's generation.

Much of the above mentioned gap as described earlier has caused many healthcare crises around the world. Most of those gaps are self-founded and all on the basis of the same foolish competitions without proper progressive cooperation. For many companies that I happened to work for, it was very disappointing and quite primitive to encounter many treatments all based on skin color other than character content. For many who were African, it was our duty to such for ways of preventing blood pressure because of the daily signs that were only awaiting your last day of work. In Bayer Pharmaceuticals where I worked the hardest, a new boss came to my desk six times in my second to the last day to simply see me off through the door even without a social good bye with other colleagues. I kept asking myself the reasons as to why any Africans should even buy a Bayer manufactured medicine when I could experience the worst kind of racism in a professional class of people. How can the then world healthcare crises be resolved under such circumstances?

Like doctor King, I said I would still love them even when they crucified me so that I could have a chance to teach them the right ways by publishing this book. There are many ways medical institutions participate in killing universal healthcare and so much as to threaten any strategies towards a long lasting united world.

In another incident, I worked in a diagnostic company so called Quest diagnostics where I happened to be the only one with a master's degree in medical Microbiology in addition to the required New York license for that job. My education was second to the Africanism or my skin color and being one of the few in that department. My own nature led to a lot of mistreatment even when I stood as the hardest worker who could be the only one showing up for work on a snow storm. My hard work was so precious that I initiated some process development that ended up saving the company more than $250,000 per year. The department ended up awarding me with a fake certificate of achievement that even my immediate manager questioned the validity in pretense. The final result as before was a donkey's kirk. I called many relatives and other people in Africa to enlighten them about the issue, but told them to keep loving and welcoming foreigners as always and with more care. Then a time comes when I discover that an Arab co-worker had been working without authorization for many years in that company. That was while my work authorization had expired and the company restarted the process as a sponsor. I discovered it was a fake process, but my co-worker ended up with complete sponsorship. It was one of the worst tragedies that I ever experienced in the last millennium while many of the workers were not qualified to handle the assigned bench work while I was the only one with a graduate degree among all the technological scientists. What I actually experienced did not change my belief that America was still the land of opportunities, but it earmarked a highlighter in what discrimination is all about and its primitive or foolish consequences. That led me to return to graduate school for further studies in pharmacy on doctoral level education. While that was happening I thoroughly searched and was fortunate to have found a job as a temporary chemist in an analytical laboratory in drug developments. I had high expectations and probably different from my previous experience because I was a temporary scientist like my Asian counterparts. However, things turned out the same way because permanent positions kept being advertised on board every week until all Asians were completely absorbed while I floated all through to the deem end as a temporary scientist to eventual deletion. Tough challenges flew through my head every day in and day out with the main one being why Africans cannot be respected. I finally realized the answer which I sealed till the end of times or the last chapter of this book. Most if not all of the Asians who became permanent employees had foreign credentials, but were given more than ample time to have the United States equivalency evaluation. My total education in the United States did not make a difference and made a good point to ask whether it was sub-standard or some other reason was behind the behavior. This behavior had become a common factor because I experienced it in almost every company that I had a short or long contract with. On another last minute occasion at GlaxoSmithKline Pharmaceuticals, a plant manager stopped by my new office and yelled at me saying that they had hired a permanent employee from China for that desk and I had no right of moving to that assigned chair anyhow as I did. I quietly but angrily swallowed the bitter pill and I can imagine how bitter such a character could have been when he learned that Obama was the new and first African American president. The big question is whether that has changed if a healthcare professional like me could receive such a treatment and whether it ever changes if not now. I still question the defect of blackness in the above instances on many occasions because if someone cannot judge by intellectual performance in such environments as in healthcare drug developments, then a new and proper definition is urgently needed. Consequently, for a proper and long lasting universal healthcare to be reformed, all human beings deserve the same equality in healthful rights. For a long lasting healthcare system, many talks must be turned into real walks.

The search for cheap labor from foreign workers is nothing new in the Western world. Some people have actually defined it as the real basis of the definition of slavery across the Atlantic Ocean to America. Still some do exaggerate it to define it as the meaning of America. However, what has always and consistently remained a challenge is the explanation of how skin color is related to character that it is still useful to many people in their method of analysis on a person's resume. It is sometimes so thoughtful that one may see it as a curse as everybody needs love which can only be based on the content of character other than skin color. I clearly defined it as a form of ignorance that is treatable by an educational overhaul in the whole world. Thus, if the essence of proper healthcare is to discover identity in difference, then focusing on profits alone would lead pharmaceutical care into a big ditch that might never be rescued again forever. The current collapse of the world financial systems actually happened because of related ignorance where millionaires and billionaires only focused on profits alone without the other side of the coin. While the billionaires were advancing in wealth, the middle class and the poor were getting more and poorer as the number of homelessness from foreclosures were increasing exponentially. It is in on that basis that I tend to rely on my guide book principles which inspires me into this kind of publication. That happens while interpreting the exact problem and how it can be fixed in such places as in San Diego which has shown the signs of the great depression in terms of extreme droughts.

One of the best fixations of the above problem seems to have happened already when the election of Baraka Obama took place in the year 2008 and marked a big breakthrough in the world politics. There is a popular saying that many people can be called for a special mission and a good number may show up, but a few are usually chosen. Consequently, the Baraka election hit hard on the primitive stereotypes that still divide the world along racial lines. The stereotypes seem to be very frustrating to those who are still primitive in believing that all men are not created equal. Of course many Africans don't own more than 1% of the world wealth, but even when Obama is the president, the racial diseases cannot heal and the same old tactics are visible in most of the pharmaceutical companies that I had worked for before from the reliable resources. That is still a big snag in the development of universal healthcare that would be long lasting which is part of the barriers to the current passing of the 2009 healthcare reform in America. Most probably the charity organizations like Churches need to get more aggressive in delivering the truth about the message on to the governmental tables. Regardless of one's status, it is either all or none of the above and whether liberal or conservative for a long lasting united world in healthcare.

I was very much inspired by president Obama's speech of the year 2004 when reiterating for the push of a united world through a United States' liberal and conservative ideology. He reminded most Americans that there is no such a thing as a liberal or conservative America, but rather the United States of America. However, the educational institutions which reproduce the new seeds whether traditional or hybrid type, are still far from being liberated along the same spiritual lines. While I completely agree with Obama on the diluting education in both science and math, I do recognize that most corporate America are still stuck in the traditional goals where the interest is only based on the earnable quick profits through short term investments regardless of long term repercussions.

A personal philosophical belief strengthens me into the view of all the above materials with every generosity. It is through it that I view the popular scientists like Vivian Thomas in healthcare and Albert Einstein in physics. Due to the suppressive laws of publicity and African education in those days, Vivian Thomas remained an unknown figure until it was actually revealed very late that he was the father of modern by-pass surgery. When I watched the movie revealing the way Vivian Thomas led the process that finally became known as the by-pass surgery, I was rather excited than shocked. At the same time, however, it sounded like a frustration because there were and still some like him who could perform likewise, but skin color suppression in many phases of life denies that goal from being achieved. This is the same exact policy in many if not all pharmaceutical industries who could rather give credit to anything other than African, but simply harass and conceal. That is what has killed universal healthcare true reformation to prevent a long lasting world unity out and away from hatred.

The scenario presented above inspired me into the mentioning of the two Kenyan boys who had no formal engineering education, but one ended up and successfully invented a simple broadcasting station for his family while the one constructed an aero plane that actually flew the sky. How could Africans with all that disrespect as above be able to do that before going to any college or university? Well, those were boys who knew nothing about material science that most professors spend a lot of time teaching the undergraduates in colleges. That proved something that many of us are unaware of that many Africans don't need to go all the way to Harvard to acquire the best skills in education. The best healthcare doctors might actually not be residing in the modern hospitals and some of the worst incurable disorders may be treatable in unknown places through faith regardless of how poor. If the Jua kali (Hot Sun) kids could invent machines as indicated above, then anything is possible under God. Whether Albert Einstein would have done likewise is still subject to debate, but why not. It could be the reason of his quitting from one university to another and for which reason I usually place him in the same class as Nelson Mandela, Dr. Martin Luther King and Abraham Lincoln. Those are the characters that actually changed the world after lengthy struggles which were publicized as being rebellious before winning the Nobel peace prizes. Consequently, for the world to begin smelling the need for a long lasting universal healthcare and peaceful world union, the contents in this book have to be seen as rebellious, but they are the realities.

Sometimes, the above example that discusses a healthcare loophole that still keeps and maintains the retardation which fails the whole process is also detected in those who need it most. It is quite justifiable to use the same measuring yardstick because without the factory floor and manufacturing workers, pharmaceutical and other healthcare industries would be non-existent. In the same line of context in reasoning, we do find that without road constructors, there would be no possibility of commuting to those anticipated healthcare centers that may be constructed or initiated. However, due to the same ignorance as previously described, healthcare reform policies continue to be fought against by people like Sarah Palin after losing as a vice presidential candidate to John McCain in the year 2008 bid for the White House. For such people, it is rather to keep the status quo than to be vigilant about the future long lasting universal healthcare. Those who still doubt the power of ignorance should turn to read the following article that talk about the real killer of the poor without the existence of any healthcare:

The above article raises the question of whether the poor can use their voting power in numbers to change the world that seems to be ruled by money influence to corruption. Ignorance has often been used as the weapon of mass deception in both developed and the underdeveloped nations of the world. However, the impact is stuck strongly in the developing countries like a serious cancer.

As former and senior president George Bush once said during the funeral of Coretta King or Dr. Martin Luther King's wife, is that most people including himself commit many sins out of ignorance. Then about ten years when his son won the United States presidency, he reiterated that he did not believe there would be a time when the world could be operating without some form of evil. The two statements are somewhat inter-related because the source of ignorance is actually the same that is described as the father of all evil. For those who are not sure as to how to define the devil and the henchmen, it only falls in the loop of who stands in the lies. Lies are supposed to keep others ignorant in all developmental levels so as to remain poor from the smallest to the largest or of any international scales in healthcare and other sectors.

That is what is barring and killing the goal to achieve a long lasting universal healthcare.

Some of the books recently published that do hint on world healthcare include president Baraka Obama's book entitled "the dreams of my father". In that book he described his visit to the father's ancestral land at the village of Kogelo in Kenya. That is one province among many that has been hit hard in terms of the HIV and AIDS epidemic in addition to malaria and cholera. That still remains the biggest challenge in world healthcare in addition to the recently discovered swine flu virus. President Obama has been presented a war of the century in the universal healthcare reform fight, but also mentions a lot of cultural belief challenges in his book during Kogelo visit. At one point in the night during his visit, he mentions about a healthcare concern base on night time songs which he could hear from large crowds singing in total darkness. He described the experience as a nervous one, but when he asked his relatives what that was all about, he was advised not to worry as they revealed to him that it was just the normal night runners. President Obama could not imagine of people being in good health to be able to forgo sleep and go singing and running all night long and how they would fit into universal care. It was a mystery and still is because the mechanism of night visioning is beyond physiological or medical scientific explanation. Consequently, he could not foresee the plan of healthcare that could fit such conditions which were likely to fall under the pre-existing conditions which a few insurances subscribe to with certainty. That complicates the implementation of a long lasting universal healthcare for a stronger union.

After performing tremendous research on healthcare around the world, I ended up with the conclusion that president Obama's experience in Kenya/ Africa was not unique. It is actually a universal problem that only happens to be intensely extrapolated in poor countries because of various interests. It is a matter of what causes illnesses versus what the possible healthcare plans would be in a given place. There are some diseases or disorders which have proven to be completely incurable by modern medicine, by only to be treated by experts of local traditional herbs in the poor countries. In that respect, that alone is a prove that the exact definition of poverty has not been actually clearly given proper comprehension. The reason being that if a poor country can treat a disease like AIDS and realize some cure in recovery as it happened with the Kemron drug of Kenya in the 1980 and 1990s, then much can be expected. For one, such a discovery alone would have translated itself into a wealth creating instrument if it were well advertised with professional trading partnerships and commercialization. The cause for a failure towards proper trading channels was nothing but competition without cooperation which I have previously described as a destructive priority. The fear that if a poor nation like Kenya can outperform the rest of the world in medical research then who feel entitled to that rank would really get frustrated and degraded from the class of pharmaceutical healthcare stars. However, to some like the United States, that is quite contrary to the declaration of their independence that the whole world is likely seeming to follow. The declaration clearly states that all men are created equal and have the right to life, liberty, justice, and pursuit of happiness. That is what led to the emancipation proclamation which enforced the freedom of all the slaves in America. America was then made of the first few thirteen states in the union that stood as the basis of the American civil war costing former president Abraham Lincoln his life in the famous assassination. That in some language was the greatest reform in modern history that still serves as the basis of a long lasting world union including universal healthcare among other hot political issues.

The idea of leaders being assassinated on the basis of some special performance as mentioned above with former president Abraham Lincoln, seems to be still operational in many countries around the world. When Lincoln decided to defy the old traditions that seemed to let America down on the primitive beliefs of slavery, he had actually received a vision and arrived at the mountain top where he was viewed as a traitor. That was contrary to the beliefs of William Lynch who used the Bible to validate slavery before a large crowd at the River side in the name of God in 1742. However, for a long lasting American union, slavery had to be abolished and even those who were against him came to agree that he was really the most righteous president in the American history. His policy stands today and as the greatest weapon for the unification of the United States of America. It is only those who have realized the uniqueness of his presidency that would support universal healthcare which is an idea whose time is overdue and should now come out. Failure to realize Lincoln's uniqueness and apply it both at home and abroad on international terms that would be affordable is a very destructive priority. As president Baraka Obama often said on his campaign in the year 2008, it is only an easy process when it starts from the bottom heading to the top other than the the reverse process as many would suppose. In such a principle as many believe, it never works for the majority on long term investments.

To discuss the last and most important drawback against the success of any healthcare system or program implementation, one must mention the factors to be considered as the right representatives in all separate and independent powerful branches of government. Just like in the lynching brutality at the famous Riverside bank in the name of God some centuries back, politicians continue manipulating the electorate to award themselves with huge bonuses while healthcare continues to drown towards becoming non-existent. A good example is the most recent and probably the most popular fraud lynch in American history which was based on the Madoff financial institution. The Madoff institution ripped the world and mainly the United States of America more than 165 billion dollars' worth of assets. That was earmarked as one of the most deadly worldwide weapon of mass destruction because it resulted in a good number of suicide casualties. It ended up weakening the entire free enterprise system in its most stable and respected country and institution in the world that also threatened universal healthcare. When the world depends heavily on banks in all types of finances, such a voluminous corruption leaves a lot of suspicion as to how healthcare insurance institution can be trusted in taking care of universal treatments among all humanity. While the debates continue getting hotter around the world on the future of healthcare, the majority seem to be thinking about alternatives ways of surviving when poverty is encountered in large numbers. The collapse of the world financial system that ended up requiring government bailouts to resume survival, strongly suggested that there is every possibility of an existence of similar frauds that are yet to be discovered if ever. They might be in small scales, but it is a green light that mindful people need to keep track on to avoid future imitations of such disasters. Consequently, if respective representatives are subjected to frequent heavy strict screenings before being given the job of that caliber then a lot remains to be desired. It is very conceivable that if the United States achieves universal healthcare then it would really be through national and international levels for a long lasting world union.

While research continues on finding out the best of any resolutions of discrimination, the world has to be aware as well as realize that it is the basis of all sources of weapons of wars and mass destructions. Without some form of discrimination, the weapons of wars would cease to exist. The greatest of worldwide researches that can ever be honored with endless accomplishments are those related to resolutions of ethnicity and discrimination. It is stands as the most magnetic cause of almost every conflict that eventually leads to wars or some kind of terrorism. That is true whether the argument is based on the terrorism of the world trade center in the year 2001 claiming more than 5000 lives or the programmed apartheid in former South Africa's minority ruling regime. On the basis of the proposed law of revolutionary development under the consumer theory, discrimination is actually a consequence of textbook education consisting of a scheme of underdevelopment loopholes that must be addressed for proper resolutions. Some believers and scientists still argue that it is all more to do with genetics other than a learning phenomenon. However, such a theory is more dependent on assumption than approvable facts. My argument is based on the fact that it has been witnessed completely in a situation where white children have been born out of two complete black or African parents. Such many cases have been witnessed in Tanzania which have ended up being victimized for some cultural or witchcraft beliefs. Consequently, then if the genetics argument were correct, it would have been impossible to produce such children who are commonly referred to as "Kiibari" with completely white skins out of black skinned parents where the reverse has never been recorded. Thus, discrimination is a learned ideology usually according to the consumer theory of ignorance, greed and selfishness. It happened to be quite interesting when I interacted with the Kiibari gentleman while he played the rare accordion in that community because I greeted him in English of which he understood nothing. Then he revealed to me that he was not from England or such places where I would expect him to have come from. He simply told me he was a complete Kenyan Kisii. While research is an endless exercise and continuing to answer some of those difficult questions, it has not yet recorded the above case in reverse order or more precisely two white skinned parents producing a black skinned child. And even if it happens in the future, it might not fully explain the above argument to obtain a concise resolution even though some scientists have used that to certify as to who came first in the theory of evolution.

As a believer of creationism and science, the Kibari case mentioned above drove me to a partial belief of evolution, but within such small circumstances. However, the main proof was that there were not the slightest detectable superior structures both mentally and physically that could support and certify the discriminative tendencies or policies that are still leading to worldwide terrorism. It actually proves that all people are created equal as it would actually be supported by many biological scientists as opposed to many politicians. Seeing is believing and some of the most populous villages with the Kibari type of people are only sixty miles from United States president Baraka Obama's ancestral homeland. The big question is that if the genetic mistake that produced Kiibari did not cause any issue to alarm discrimination in superiority development, then the defect is neither genetic nor an inborn error of metabolism. In that respect, ethnicity and discrimination as we see it today, are simply more of an environmentally influenced disorder under the consumer theory of ignorance, greed and selfishness which would also be a preventable disease under its own merit. Consequently, that can serve as a prove that the world dream of a long lasting unity would clearly have a chance of realization as an achievement. The only dilemma is whether both the victim and the victimizer would ever have the chance to read this message and comprehend it to the best of their benefits and the world at large.

Part of the answer to the above question resides on the idea of text book development. Such an idea has to be able to focus on the grass root level of humanity which is nothing but healthcare. Healthcare and pharmaceutical development would always dictate the healthcare industry as a whole whether from an educational or therapeutic point of view. There is no revolution that can be long lasting on a textbook development if it falls short of a healthcare reform that can target the term caring for all and from a universal point or perspective. It would be tantamount to the real structural goal of health. The proof of the matter would then be that the Rosa Parks strategy would be weakened by such a loophole because pharmaceutical sectors deal and through handling, encounter far too many materials than any other profession. When closely examined, the pharmaceutical sector stands as the backbone of all healthcare because it researches, discovers, processes to purity through formulation of the finished health product for human consumption. Likewise, it does performance of all clinical consequences likely to be experienced from their production as well as any interaction towards nature itself. Most remote parts of the world particularly in Africa, have large deposits of the basic materials both in the soil as minerals as well as above the earth as natural herbs or edible plants. One of the great blessings of the tropical climates is that plants are ever growing and supplies are abundant throughout the year. That is one of the good reasons as to why many Africans rarely put serious thoughts into large scale healthcare in pharmaceutical production or factorial industries. For one, if they really need a pain killer out of an emergency situation, they can walk down the garden or along the river and get some herbal plant medicine out of the natural shrubs or sometimes in their backyards. Consequently, with all these counts of researches for universal healthcare resolutions in overhaul, it would seem quite conceivable that a Rosa Park strategy is very stigmatically inclined for a real good fight against discriminatory policies in any of such developments.

The idea of dismantling healthcare disparity and discrimination is and has always been set to start from the early stages of development right from elementary level schooling through university education. The elections of the United States presidency in the year 2008 dwelt on health reform possibilities more than any other policy. It was interesting to encounter the fight continuous in 2009 while experiencing a few protests in some states while addressing town-hall meetings and some commencement activity during a graduation. It seemed quite clear as to what the cause of such protests could be and as such nothing more than the intention to keep the status quo as intact as before. When pharmaceutical companies support the status quo, then it becomes conceivably clear that they still disregard the fight to consider pre-existing conditions in the healthcare reform. That is not what the world healthcare calls for in order to achieve a universal caring of all people. Consequently, the future of healthcare must not keep relying on the bureaucracies of the big pharmaceutical companies' lobbyists because they target more on stomach politics than the desperate patients. For one, it is well known that if everybody affords health insurance or maintain a standard healthful life, then the life expectancy would be improved so much as to reduce hospital visits because prevention would become the weapon of survival. Second is that a healthful living would be generative of superior healthful brains and think tanks who would in turn develop further preventive inventions against serious diseases like Malaria and AIDS. A careful view of such a development would seem to be perfect fit into the revolutionary overhaul focused on the textbook developmental strategy.

For many years, many groups of people from large world populations have been held captive in healthcare dilemmas because it goes hand in hand with financial status that is deep rooted on unemployment disparities among black and white among different races. Extreme cases like pre-existing conditions of cancerous disorders would surpass heart disease or hypertension which is motivated by inter-related economic conditions of unemployment. The main victim if not a target has been the poor and ignorant which some say depends on their own fault even when they are created to be so when the argument goes back to the founding fathers' historical analyses. It is not beyond imagination for a person or group of people to fall under that category to be able to survive in the current world if they fall sick and have no money, food or healthcare insurance. Yet that happens to be the group that is useful for the consumer business. As before, ignorance does not only encompass the uneducated, but can actually include a group of university graduates ranging from sociology through pharmaceutical and medically related institutions. These are the same type who can never devise a strategy focused on universal healthcare. Some of them are mere victims of the disparity policies in pharmaceutical manufacturers. However, the really target are those without employment that stands more than anything else as the basis of survival in self-feeding of themselves and their children or families. That is also true when dreams keep occurring in questions as to how to survive in case of a tragedy such as sudden illness. Can such dreams be cared for if profits are the major driving forces in the machineries of the pharmaceutical industries? Most likely never and for which reason the future of pharmaceutical business would definitely be defined by a total overhaul with a new type of inheritance. That was one of the lectures I had presented in the popular pharmaceutical ingredient industry that was based in Chicago, Illinois in the United States of America so called Roquette. It was a half of an hour lectures which only a few would foresee the seriousness of my focus of the future of the shrinking pharmaceutical businesses.

The strength of the world and a long lasting union depends on the ability to focus on the future of universal healthcare. The question is what if more and more people get better and less vulnerable to diseases and disorders as it is likely to happen on the basis of the current worldwide analysis. An even bigger question is whether those research scientists who are likely to become idle and jobless would prefer such health world or in fact an unhealthy one for their employment security. That would be a fair question only if employment was free of discrimination especially in that particular sector. However, because it is not, it is proper to focus on a different type of strategy and particularly for those who are to be victimized as such. That is the strategic principle on which this publication is based and basically similar to the lecture I had delivered in the above chemical company in Chicago as mentioned earlier.

In view of the above, many research institutions around the world have encouraged drug development in various classes with government sponsorships, but the same diseases keep killing the same group of people over and over again as the pharmaceutical formulations keep producing weak recipes that yield minimal cures. An appropriate example is Malaria which one time existed in certain countries, but ended up being eliminated without usage of any necessary vaccine developments. Many politicians and scientists can debate on the reasons as to why it was possible to conquer malaria at that time when the world was still on its root foundations with limited modern resources. If there were limited research tools and scientists then why wouldn't it be possible now in the developing countries. It is highly unlikely that the current modern pharmaceutical institutions are focused on eliminating the malarial parasites because if that were the case then discrimination on research employments wouldn't occur as described earlier. Most victimized communities suffering from the parasitic infections have come to believe an hidden agenda behind the big failure. It cannot be more than the politics of health economics. Such a motive is not a late stage development of pharmaceutical institutions. It is actually a textbook development which needs an urgent overhaul according to the proposed vision of revolutionary development under the consumer theory. That is why pharmaceutical companies would hardly support or sponsor any research that may target the elimination of malaria at any university institutions or high academic learning. Consequently, an advising professor would suggest to a prospective research fellow student that in order to complete a dissertation thesis in the shortest possible time then the candidate must simply look for something simple and straight forward. The moment any mention of malaria comes as it did happen in my case, then it portrays the beginning of hatred towards destruction starting with the candidate's character assassination. On the other hand, the problem is worsened when the issue is delivered to the real people and victims because of politics of competition without cooperation. That is the kind of problem that Keith Olberman of the MSNBC television station often describes as the party of "No" when discussing the Obama healthcare reform bill. It is actually the feathers of the same animal that only differs in scale when we talk about the party of "No" and the consumer theory that affects if not afflicts most Africans. All this happens because the required remedy of a textbook development has not been implemented or initiated.

The issue of using the malaria example in the proposed pharmaceutical healthcare textbook is an idea whose time has come. I arrived at this conclusion after several years of analysis with the objective of searching for the best tools to handle underlying discrimination. It has frequently shown up on my list of ideas proposed in the working places which could be both an income earner and problem solver to save the one hundred million lives in Africa alone. Most business developers preferred an idea that could target vaccine development. However, my personal preference has been an actual proposal towards the eradication of the disease carrying parasite in whichever way possible. Deep down in my heart, I knew the proposal was going to be received as a bite in the neck in terms of prospective future profits within a range of projects. For instance, I did that for the GlaxoSmithKline and Bayer Pharmaceutical giants and it became a big bite in their business developmental structures because my manager, who was friendly and respectful, suddenly lost his common smile as he reminded me to revise their real vision and mission. However, we always interacted and he discussed various plans that the company was focusing on in terms of helping Africa on AIDS, tuberculosis and malaria. While I didn't rule out any pretense, I could still sense some form of discrimination. In both of the above cases, it was conceivable that such proposals were quite feasible because there were similar actions taken in filing the copies under their desks until an opportune time. That was most likely because they did not originate from the right scientist for such candidacy. However, I did my best interpretation by describing it as simple competition without cooperation which I often describe as a destructive priority under the consumer theory of greed, selfishness and ignorance. That is the kind of snag that affects developing countries more than anything else towards a long lasting union. Consequently, the problem is more pronounced in Africa and for which reason malaria cannot be eradicated as was one time done in most developed countries in several centuries ago.

In view of the above, it is quite convincing that discrimination in whichever way it goes, the respective resolution is heavily owned by Africans themselves. That would be valid once they decide to learn the side-defects of competition without cooperation and initiate a new overhaul of textbook development. The text has to take priority in addressing that to a more degree or percentage, discrimination is a learned other than an in-born error of metabolism. That while trying to be the best academician in any field of competition, one has to do the best in cooperating with the surrounding colleagues on honest resolutions to win as a team. A single success without cooperation is only short-term or short-sited that ends up as a useless ideology where false pride is initiated, but a bridge is built to nowhere in terms of the future generations. In such a development, the individual still suffers as a slave of himself or some employer regardless of title. Based on that analysis the main important development is to focus on building a bridge that can eradicate a common problem such as malaria and poverty. That was the reason as to why the late Rev. Dr. Martin L. King Jr., once said that "we are either all free or not free at all". That translates into the current idea that if the future healthcare is to succeed, it cannot only be to the benefit of a few or certain group of people. That would be like building a bridge to nowhere in terms of the future generations. That parable was repeated several times by United States vice president Joe Biden when comparing Sarah Palin's choice of words in her Republican Party 2008 campaign speeches of quoting her vision of Russia from the roof of her house in Alaska. Joe Biden said such a vision was fine, but translating it into the future American vision was like building a bridge to nowhere. Consequently, the idea of embarking or relying on treatments as designed by pharmaceutical companies is not only irrelevant on the strength of the United Nations dream, but a basis of discrimination from the early stages of the proposed textbook development. However, it may sound complex to understand such a basis, but there are a few ways through which the complexity may be explained to uplift a brighter union.

When looking for a better understanding of the above case, many people end up focusing on the victims of healthcare discrimination other than the common trend. Such victims are the ones who remain sick and may remain so for years and generations to come. Money becomes a big factor and for which reason we keep seeing the large pharmaceutical companies either merging or buying out the smaller ones before downsizing discriminatively. It is doubtful as to whether the law of pharmaceutical economics can compromise profits for the sake of caring towards real cure under a universal healthcare focus. Some diseases like malaria should not be compared to recurrent painful disorders like diabetes, cancer and hypertension. While profits are fine to make, they should not be the sole driving force in pharmaceutical business developments. However, because the whole world is becoming more and more elite, pharmaceutical growth is likely to shrink as self-care is likely to expand in the future when botanicals take the front line in many backyards. Some historical records such as my guide book, describes money as to say that too much love for money is the root cause of all evil. Consequently, the future of healthcare would be more reliant on those companies who would focus more on caring other than money profits without bias on employment on the basis of race, creed or national origin. In that regard, then if people like Bill Gates and other worldwide billionaires like former Zairean president Mobutu Sessesseko, and Oprah Winfrey, were interested in using the power of money influence to reduce healthcare disparities that originates from pharmaceutical discrimination, then they could mainly focus on prevention and cure other than mere recurrent treatments only meant for business expansions and profits. Oprah Winfrey has already taken the first few steps on education as seen in the foundation girls' school in South Africa as well as the participation in the 2008 presidential campaigns for changes that we could believe in. However, Bill Gates who is 30 times richer than Oprah Winfrey, frequently donates hundreds of millions of dollars to the same pharmaceutical companies which practice business in the same old style of focusing more on profits than real healthcare. In that respect, he could afford to donate millions to GlaxoSmithKline pharmaceuticals when I worked for the same company which had rejected a real caring research proposal for malaria and other diseases in the developing nations like East Africa and Africa as a whole. However, in those same years GlaxoSmithKline could afford to demonstrate bias in their employment policies as I could be laid off and someone right from China get hired and only to produce nothing two years later after complete sponsorship. And I could experience some open prejudice when a facility manager could sound so arrogant by saying, hey my friend, I don't care who your boss is, but you can't keep on transferring from office to office and whoever instructed you to do that was out of his mind. And I am the facility manager, he said. I was perturbed by such a statement because these are the same people Bill Gates trusts so much that he sponsors research for their developments in terms of hundreds of millions in dollars. It may not be appropriate to blast Bill Gates because his prime target is his business development and money other than the healthcare resolutions in pharmaceutical development. I didn't blame him for not donating even a single dollar to the organization I had founded for the same exact purpose, but more focused and specifically to AIDS initiatives because it may have not been one of his interest locations or a more unified long lasting world unity in business.

The determination as to how discrimination can be dealt with in healthcare in the pharmaceutical roots rests more with Africans themselves and using more examples as Bill Gates in the above analysis. In that respect, Africans like Oprah Winfrey, the late Michael Jackson and former Zairean president, Mobutu Sessesseko could have marked the main initiators if they had to discover and understand the real nature of discriminating roots. For somebody like Oprah Winfrey, the establishment of a girls boarding school was a tremendous move. However, on the basis of the above analysis, the textbooks to be used in such an institution, are still those designed to brainwash and maintain the status quo that eventually strengthens the same behavior of pharmaceutical discrimination among other things. As a consequence, it is more about the context of a new establishment as opposed to a photocopy of the same old ideals of teachings that are based on the same textbooks which focus on recurrent treatments other than total cure or prevention. Such a principle can enhance the discriminative policies in other related sectors as in pharmaceutical healthcare industries.

The construction of a bridge to nowhere is to embark on copying other than inventing from the grass root point of view and whether it is a medicinal pharmaceutical or a simple broadcasting station. On the question of inventions, I have always confronted the matter in different levels. At one time around the beginning of the 2002 Kenyan general and presidential election races, the Kenyan Americans under the Kenya Umoja Association for which I was one of the representatives, we invited one of the candidates into the New Jersey City University. On the issue of copying, I confronted the candidate seated next to me at the stage and asked him about the whereabouts of the student who had invented the simple broadcasting station by a mere construction of home wires. I asked him about the boy because the Kenyans and Africans are generally less sensitive in terms of tapping such special talents for industrial development. The Kenyans had only seen him on one newspaper where he was seen calling his father to go to the next room and asking him to listen as he broadcasted. The father was amazed, but the presidential candidate, honorable Simeon Nyachae seemed to be unaware of that development. Later on, I read another article portraying a student who had developed an helicopter out of simple scrap of the Jua Kali materials that were of his own making as opposed to the factory made parts as normal. The above two cases were a complete demonstration and prove that copying is not quite necessary if the Africans actually need to develop as they wish. That would really mark the beginning of the end of discrimination and complete gain of the respect we deserve and as a necessary tool for a long lasting world union. There was no single textbook from which the two students could obtain any information to guide them in their respective inventions. Not one engineer around that community or even in the whole nation could figure that out including the university professors who are in constant work in teachings that use the same old syllabuses of textbooks. However, Many Kenyan and African leaders can always afford to purchase private helicopters from foreign countries through corruptive processes.

The instance of encountering geniuses such as those students mentioned above who have never stepped in a college or university classroom is not only amazing, but inspiring. Developing countries such as those in Africa can keep on producing geniuses of very level in various fields of research including the law makers' institutions, but still be made fruitless because of the infiltrated defects that originate from the consumer theory of not recognizing them appropriately. In that respect, universal healthcare opponents in pharmaceutical discrimination was greatly enhanced when the discovery of the AIDS drug was introduced after positive clinical trials from the development of Kemron. The advancement or improvement of the related clinical trials was derailed by both national and international politics. Political war was successful because of the lacking will power towards institutional building developments which could have guided the founding roots to strengthen further research on Kemron. The development of Kemron could not prosper if the original sponsors had included money focused individuals and of which Bill Gates is no exception for the reasons explained above. For one, Bill Gates had refused to encourage or support any sponsorship that would aid the establishment of rural electrification in such areas in Africa. When I submitted my first proposal on the establishment of a simple local electrification for demonstrative purposes by the name Jua Kali Shinning Organization that I founded, he turned it down as much as he had vigorously done to other similar objectives. That was a clearly published attitude on various newspapers in local and international presses. The question then becomes the validity of his support on AIDS on healthcare. If he had supported the discovery of a possible cure for malaria, AIDS, and tuberculosis, how did he expect such an accomplishment to mature to fruition without electricity and particularly the one encompassing the direct victims? Our proposal was designed to be a win-win situation because we figured that the electrical technology through the establishment of electrification was the root basis of Microsoft and general computer information or internet communication for which Bill Gates has become a billionaire through tremendous product manufacturing and sales. Even the current computer researches and developments are focused and dependently more reliant on computers in various programs especially those involving chemical analysis. Again, it is a focus on money other than caring in healthcare resolutions as presented in those donor awards to pharmaceutical companies regardless of results or level of discrimination.

The idea of institution building must be root based and in accordance to the true utilization of the two student inventors mentioned above under the theory of revolutionary development. An effective establishment of a textbook overhaul must include that particular case or argument because most institutions are usually focused more on money other than performance towards a specific resolution.

For the proposed revolutionary textbook to become a valid entity, innovation with creativity welcoming inventions must stand as the core program of adaptation. That means the establishment of revolutionary textbooks right from the foundation roots through the ages of the above student cases and beyond while giving credit where due without corruption or ethnic warfare. Discrimination would prosper for generations so long as Africans continue to capitalize more on copying other than originality from core grass roots. That has to be an endless war because education has to be decolonized from the politics of establishment where Universities like Capella cannot approve research on African studies in any perspective. The two students, who invented the broadcasting station as well as the helicopter, serve as the best examples. Copying especially in the current systems of textbooks is almost unaffordable by many poor people and mostly Africans. That is of course in the majority of the institutions where a poor African may desire to initiate such an aspiration, but discrimination delays the process for superiority complexes until made unemployed as the first victim. It happens after copying all the years until post graduate level through a terribly expensive textbook syllabus that is designed to shape one into what he finds himself when it is too late. The small scales inventions demonstrated by the two students mentioned above are the real institutions which by simple scaling up, would become the roots of the revolutionary textbook development like any other advanced nation operation. The two students had no money and were as poor as anybody else, but the inventions came into place as a lesson to those who still find it hard to believe in themselves. An even important lesson to learn from such an experience is that money is not actually exclusively necessary for the process of institution building including that of the proposed textbook revolutionary development and other needs. It can be very much established the same easy way a political overhaul is initiated with minimal financial requirements. Thus, many can greatly appreciate an outsider's help like Oprah Winfrey or Bill Gates if there are no strings attached that limit the long lasting establishment of a future stronger world union.

When United States President Baraka Obama frequently mentioned during his 2008 year campaigns about a descent education, I often remembered about the above two students educational achievements. Those are the types that can be included in the early childhood development programs in a similar umbrella as quoted above. It was particularly interesting when I tried to relate the above two cases to Oprah Winfrey's foundation of the girls' school in South Africa. A personal concern and probably a few others with the same vision is that Oprah would be definitely doing such a thing from the bottom of her heart when in fact the real problem of discrimination is only half way accomplished. The same girls she will end up helping with educational credentials could still stand the same conditions as I stood when discriminated by such healthcare pharmaceuticals as Bayer and GlaxoSmithKline as before or Capella University Online on my universal healthcare proposals. That would be long after having been educated in the high class system of schooling in her institution through the same textbook of syllabuses for many expensive years. At the time of rapture, Oprah Winfrey could look many years back only to witness the same policies of poverty in more or less the same scales which she hoped to eradicate through education. The question that Oprah would remain asking is whether she had actually approached the real problem and from the right angle at the right time in history. It might not be an actual total embarrassment because it is always better to try than never to try at all. However, if she reads this book, then she could wish she had approached it differently so as to resolve most problems from the roots. That could and is the only way of building long lasting institutions in such places as the one she built the girl school as well as some of the poor American communities wherever possible. To do that, she must read this book and avail more time to such authors on her popular shows because that would make her more of a problem solver than a talk show entertainer. She must encourage more inventors from the poor communities with various awards in her shows. At the same time, the Africans in the African continent must get it very clear that for an overhaul to take place, mostly small things need to be invented and particularly in healthcare through pharmaceuticals in the same manner as in political developments. That is in complete consistency with the above students' invention cases as well as with the proposed theory of revolutionary development in the consumer belief. With competition becoming more and more cooperated, the necessary faith on spread and establishment would definitely change the strength of the awaited long lasting world order.

While pursuing the deliverance of a more cooperated world in competition, some organizations including the Kenya international Community abroad that particularly resides in the United States of America, I have taken various initiatives on such a case because it is simply caused by discrimination in education and employment. The message has been consistent and embarked more on the reduction or eradication of poverty. That is why we have always invited many African leaders to our podiums so we could enlighten many on the same subject whenever they are willing as communication to the poor victims might as well be best delivered through those who represent their constituencies.

One of the worst drawbacks in the African politics is qualification by association, but one of the writers of the world's oldest constitution, former United States president, Thomas Jefferson, said that there should be no taxation without adequate representation and compensation. How can the African politicians utilize such a theory or likewise to effective change on those who need it most. Could president Obama's ancestral homeland, Kenya, stand as an example or Africa for the future of universal healthcare towards a worldwide point of order?

To answer the above question, the ignorant must be enlightened on such basic protective laws as the constitution of a state in all walks of life. An Appropriate strategy is in a textbook communication such as in this book and particularly in this chapter. The reason is that book communication is the least expensive with no dictatorship attached strings that can monopolize without any barrier standing along its way. From many statistical resources, it is quit embarrassing to find that many children around the world go to school and proceed on through university without knowing the basic content of their country's constitution. As a consequence, the greed politicians having mastered the art of hiding the self-interests would come around during the election times and simply keep repeating the same tricks towards unfairly rooted underdevelopment. They would definitely avoid talking about the importance of ratifying a fair and valid long lasting constitution in reform that can protect their citizens for the current and the future generations. In that respect, a honest and truthful future presidential candidate for true change must address the issue of a textbook level type of developmental law from the grass roots. Such a development must be clear, short and concise for all groups of voters and even children to read and understand as a daily song. Many citizens would wonder how that can become possible in a place where money has corrupted a large percentage of the politicians who ride in helicopters, Hummers, Range Rovers, Land Cruisers and Mercedes vehicles at a time when the common poor people are sleeping in sacks without food in some days. Conversely, and even though seemingly difficult, president Baraka Obama defeated the corruptions of elections and cleared the barriers of many impossibilities that can bring the world closer to a long lasting unity.

The issue of delivering a long lasting constitution that must address freedom, liberty and pursuit of happiness is as easy as the delivery of this book and to the right population of people at the right time. The current African Kenyan example is composed of 70% new members and only 30% old group veterans. This was accomplished after post-election violence, but a real indication that people can get change when they desperately need it even if it means a major constitutional reform. However, to the electoral disappointment, the new members ended up being absorbed into the old system where nothing works to completion without involving a bribe or some form of corruption. A 70% change is almost equivalent to an overhaul, but something is lacking in Africa that seems to keep recycling systematically. The most important prove for a possibility of an overhaul was witnessed during independence struggles in the middle of the twentieth century in almost all countries of Africa except a few like Egypt and Ethiopia. There was a complete overhaul of government representatives when celebrations were being conducted with new rising flags, but an exact copy of the system that was revolutionized by the respective movements. Just like those particular overhaul acts in their performance processes, and so would the process of expedition of the development of the new revolutionary textbook take place. The failure of the new majority 70% team of parliamentarians in the Kenyan example was due to the lack of grass root changes in the proposed textbook development of a new system. It is not by error that most of them would either be unaware of the flaws of a system or the needed constitutional reform for the long term investments. They find under the same system that shaped them up since the education they received was directed to the similar fruits as witnessed. The constitution having been led by Martha Karua as the minister without any slight reform act, it would be naïve to expect her to make an about turn to try to kill her colleague liars before specializing on killing the lie itself. It would be irrelevant and it won't work and that is the content in the basic structure of this chapter or the revolutionary textbook development for a long lasting world union.

The first initiative in the new textbook revolutionary development is to target the lie other than the liar. The biggest lie and kind of strong conspiracy is that directly related to money and education. An important note is that money should not be a big dictatorial factor on constitutional education. Consequently, if somebody of some political stature tries to factor money into the constitutional education law in development, it should be rejected as a lie in the making. In that respect, the reading of a message in a book targeting such ignorance must be shared and proven to be relevant to the grass root developments of the most important code section of the constitutional chapter. It is not easy to reach out and hope for change overnight by simple grasping of a point in this chapter. The intensity and frequency of the song has to keep scaring the lie as the liars keep listening as well as read between the lines of this chapter.

The current and most constitutions around the world limit other people from achieving their dreams indirectly while creating immunity against many corruptive acts or money laundering. In that respect, the real credible and legible honest reformers of any constitutional amendments must be from independent groups of associations voluntarily representing mostly the poor people in both urban and rural areas. That would be in conjunction with the students of the early childhood development as discussed in the proposed theory of revolutionary development and the consumer belief. For every popular achievement that the world has benefited in full harvest, a grass root movement has often served as the main engineering processor or else it proves to be short lived investment. The exact title of the message is that a real change in this context does not only require mere change of guard, but both the characters as well as their methods of serving the people. A mere change of guard similar to the 70% of the new parliamentarians simply produces more or less the same old type of recycled products and services in same skins in different colors. That is why Africa has been independent for over 50 years, but grown worse and worse in warfare because of the recycling of the same old groups of leadership with almost no new ones with originality in grass root development initiatives. It does not mean to say that a son of a former leader like Raila Odinga or Uhuru Kenyatta both from the first president and his vice president, are unlikely to become great governors, but Africans have to change guard at times when real change is their highest motive as witnessed in corruption. This African ideology of being led by the same recyclables all the time is what creates dictatorships in as much extremes as in former Congo that was led by Mobutu Sessesseko as president for 32 years. Consequently, the full support of the proposal to change the recyclables and resort to a complete parliamentary overhaul is strongly endorsed and recommended by many patriotic specialists. That would be the basis of the constitution that abides by the revolutionary textbook in development and utilizing Kenya as the initial first example. If that becomes successful, the information would be spread first throughout the continent and beyond for the betterment of a long lasting world unity and particularly in healthcare.

Just like any other movements that has been utilized in the world and seen in history, there was none that ever succeeded with a smooth ride. Even the Obama presidency in the United States of America was a movement achieved through a lot of trials with resistance through several years. However, unlike the former movements in Africa or the so called colonial independence struggles of wars, a textbook knowledge such as the authoring of this book and chapter, should encounter the least of any rebellion. Any slight detection of such would disappear in shyness within a short time. The only limitation would be the publication of enough copies of the message as authored, but those victims and to whom the majority would be the voting population, the result might be broadly instrumental. It would be very instrumental in interpreting the urgency of constitutional spread out knowledge that would be part of the textbook of grass root changes in overhaul. Some of the visiting MPs have on occasion tried to mention about various political operations on dirty money as recently did by one prospective of presidential runners. At one of such moments, I have sometimes been concerned about the source of such dirty money because time and again I have described it as the root cause of all the failures of African unity and developments. Part of the above understanding as well as in the previous chapters is that the textbook in development takes the initiative of clarifying money as the root cause of all evil when it is loved too much. The only dilemma is the pretense by many people including professionals to set up limits that can clearly define when too much is real too much. Consequently, there would be no valid movement and hence trustable change for a long lasting unity if money is our greatest lover in our lives. That particular teaching is taught in most cultures without significant stressing. From the past history, it is often indicated that greed and selfishness for money ends up suppressing even the most fruitful movements of which the constitutional law in amendments is the most frequently mentioned as above.

Upon the full understanding of the definition of money, then liquid capital would no longer be a factor on the revolutionary textbook in development and particularly the constitutional replenishment. For one, declaration of wealth would become an important code of regulations under that title. Second, is that donations would be monitored and controlled through a federal reserve other than through the neighboring borders. For many generations, several movements have been derailed by money traffickers during campaigns who have instituted the belief that political democracy depends on how much a contestant has managed to accumulate regardless of the sources. Those kinds of cases have come to be described as campaign funding scandals. After several of such examples were exposed in the United States funds originating in China and other places, the response was to impose legislation that would target the control of such scandals. That became very successful because America's basic textbook knowledge emphasizes performance other than the amount of dirty money dispersed and circulated during electoral campaigns. Likewise, Africans have the obligation to learn that money distributed during campaigns cannot satisfy their short or long term needs. They tend to look like the flow of the wind. In that regard, the contestant who may become or remain a member of Parliament has to be well known and open to background checks through several televised interviews and scrutiny. That should be an adopted constitutional law in the textbook development. Hence every student should grow and develop along with it and through the educational life cycle of the related special curricula. In this chapter of the textbook, there are several areas that need to be discussed with precautions in order for the movement in question to sail smoothly. Consequently, the scramble for Africa as written in the famous novel would continue to guide the alienation of the African from his cultural past to keep it controversial and attractive to many scientists in competition.

Part of the answer to the above challenges resides on the hidden laws of corporate investment. That is particularly connected to the land ownership programs with respect to the defects seen in money trafficking in continental Africa. The channels of the constitutional law that lays down the accessibility and admissibility of foreigners to a general control of African investments on both corporate and land settlements is not only amazing, but scaring to the brim on most reformers and native localities. However, it is so attractive to non-reformists or the so called duplicate copiers and often described as puppet politicians who only focus on selfish ends meets. Such politicians have been carefully addressed in the revolutionary textbook of development.

The most profound framework that stands as the most precautious element of revolutionary movements is the banking corporate investments. The banking technology which has only been operated partially by Africans and only for a few decades is still partly understood because of several factors. Foremost factor is that of ownership because almost all major banking investments are non-African owned. Africans only work as part-time employees with a slim understanding of the roots of the respective popular industry. Thus, the great question is the process by which Africans can be acquainted in determining whether a particular bill like a constitutional amendment can have a smooth ratification without a proper control and good understanding of the special interest groups like banks. That is particularly true when a respective bill is encountered by such institutions that doesn't protect their interests and kept in operation from one generation to another in their favor. In that regard, some African countries can be oil-rich like Nigeria, Libya and Sudan, but still stay poor because of complete reliance and dependence on foreign banks for their capital basics in development. Some particular prominent references are Nigeria and Sudan which are oil-rich, but far from development. It is about twenty five years ago by the writing of this book that Nigerian currency was stronger than the dollar, but the Naira has drastically deteriorated and mainly because of oily wars and ethnic conflicts that are based on corruption. However, a major fuel to the issue must have been money laundering based on the lack of full access to understand and control the banking system in relationship to the rich oil deposits. It is interesting to note that the banking investments has strengthened through the generations and even when its business is down, there are always possibilities to recovery such as the recently witnessed bailouts from the roots bases. The root bases are usually the mother countries or headquarter destinations.

When a rich country like Nigeria cannot build a foundation institute like a continental bank to compete with old ones such as Barclays or Citibank, then there is misery in that environment. That is because Nigeria resides the richest man in Africa so called Dangote that is worth about $30 billion dollars. For one, oil alone is a potential bank that only needs to be translated into liquid capital. Second, it can lend oil directly like investment capital and earn the same interest the banks earn with other exchanges without the necessity of liquid capital. That would actually stand out as a small scale of an IMF or World Bank. If such a challenge is only instituted at the level of this textbook development, then the next generation would grow seeking an advancement of the same type of inheritance. Consequently, the issue of banking and its basic influence in Africa remains a potential threat in the success of the above movement as well as other similar textbooks in development. However, once this chapter in publication is delivered and spread out to the right target, a lot could be achieved with respect to that potential to influence a common lasting progressive world unity.

While many people still believe that the bank is the source of all types of boosters and barriers of movements across the world, the issue of land ownership has never been put off sight. The most recent influences came as revolutionary movements in both Zimbabwe and Israel. The two countries have a lot in common other than race with respect to their movements as represented by the two famous presidents, Robert Mugabe and Benjamin Netanyahu. President Robert Mugabe was one time the favorite of its former British colony or Britain as well as other Western nations like the United States of America. He therefore as one of the freedom fighters against colonial Britain, came along with the late Joshua Nkomo, as the prominent co-workers to see Zimbabwe gain its independence. However, the doctor and currently the president Mugabe, played a better music for colonial Britain and matched their preferable choice as opposed to Joshua Nkomo. Definitely for Mugabe to win that great respect that influenced the support for the first election whether rigged or not, he must have negotiated with price and interest agreements. That was the reason behind the calmness that prevailed for many years with the pretense that everything was good after independence. That was after an almost total change of guard of honor and ownership in the land that had been torn for many generations through independence wars with the Britain. According to many sources, President Mugabe was disappointed for the failure of Britain to honor the signed agreements even after decades of the signatures or treaties. Consequently, he claimed to have decided to dishonor the respective agreements in retaliation. He moved on to initiate the drastic measures which led to the redistribution of land ownership owned by the British in favor of the landless African or native Zimbabwean citizens.

As much as the nature of democracy goes, the basic control is money and numbers regardless of its sources. In that respect, Mugabe almost paid a big price when the 2008 elections came by and he almost lost to his main opponent resulting in a short temporary curfew or state of emergency. While it was true that money from Britain must have been influential in the election trafficking in favor of Mugabe's opponent, land issues counter-offered the election result in favor of the incumbent, Robert Mugabe much the same it just did for Israel new and former Prime Minister, Benjamin Netanyahu. Whether rigged or not, the two cases are quite similar, but not exactly identical. It was even more interesting for Netanyahu to declare that their land dates back to three thousand years and it is their right to continue expanding construction in new settlements. The United States was kind of fair as much as they could for both countries because if they don't then the end result would be for everybody to return to their ancestral homes dating to three thousand years even though Mugabe's case is as recent as three to five hundred years. The question is whether the world would favor the two above mentioned presidents movements and equally exclusive. And is democracy a big factor in that scenario towards a long lasting world unity.

The attention given in the above subject was greatly diluted when the prime minister for Kenya, Raila Odinga, recently as in 2009 and quoted in prime time live DVD, that elections in Africa are never won. He reiterated with a full smile on his face that elections are actually rigged regardless of the results. After watching the broadcast, many would end up asking whether he had also exercised the same process in order to get to the top seat that he now holds. While that was taking place, he had also attacked Robert Mugabe's overstay in power through the subsequent rigging of the 2008 Zimbabwean general and presidential elections. The attacks might be genuine since he happens to be in the similar system. However, on the basis of the events we have witnessed in the world of democratic elections, there is a lot to be desired that dictates the urgency of replenishment of the prevailing conditions. In such a development, it becomes worth of mentioning the Iran elections that were also conducted in the year 2009 and settled after a long and bloody protest similar to the Kenya's 2007 that led to the creation of the second prime minister's spot in the country's history. Conversely, it was in the year 2000 when the world's oldest and strongest democracy smelt the wrath by experiencing one of the greatest failures that threatened the world. In that famous dispute, Albert Gore won the popular vote, but seemingly, the opponent, George Bush won the Electoral College vote. That created a long dispute that eventually had the be settled by the supreme court after several protests. Rigging was thought to have taken a different format by the claim that certain counties and districts with majority African Americans had been disqualified from the valid tallies to final results. It was a deadly political deadlock where every trick and strategy had to be utilized for a winning result. However, there were hardly any big blood conflicts or casualties that would be compared to match the Kenyan, Zimbabwean or the Iranian election for that classification. Nevertheless, the descriptive nature is all in the name of rigging as the weakening agent of democracy no matter how popular it may claim to be. Such a description is a big threat to the democratic institution development that requires urgent cleansing for a united and long lasting future world union.

Just because of the belief that democracy could be the only option left for a freedom towards a people's choice, cooperation is hindered by the confrontations presented by stiff competitions among given contestants. At one time or another democracy would either be threatened by ethnicity or racism as the only major weapons of discrimination? Consequently, democracy in Africa has struggled with a lot of direct and sometimes indirect failures. The main failure is the ethnic belief that the race or tribe is more important than character content. That has resulted in a lot of corruption in all elections and hence the daily operations that follow the respective elections. The parable that states "a house divided does not stand" is best described in Africa by given examples ranging from Rwanda in 1994 through Kenya in 2008 among many of her nations. America escaped from becoming a perfect example in such a description when the former president Abraham Lincoln worked so hard to safe the United States of America union in 1865 after the civil war. However, in many other countries around the world, it might take many generations to realize anything closer to a clean democratic election. It is important to realize that the main item that Africa lacks is the saying that "united each achieves more" which is often translated into the philosophy of team of workers or TEAM (Together each achieves more). I have often formulated the new version of the first and opposite parable quoted above on the house divided does not stand as DEAD (Divided each achieves death). Africa must resolve that terrible disorder before anything closer to development can even begin as it stands as the number one disease in the whole continent. Instead of being described as a democratic development, it actually turns out to be a dictatorial format of governance. In such cases, an incumbent leader always gets threats from various sources around the world most of which are trade related that end up shaping the next conflicts. Consequently, an incumbent would utilize every kind of resource including the police to influence the outcome of every election. In that respect an incumbent would stay in power for 30 years such as former Congolese president Mobutu Sesseseko, Uganda's Yoweri Museveni, Zimbabwe's Robert Mugabe, and even Kenya's former president Daniel Arap Moi. That does not exclude leaders like Libya's Muammar Gadhafi and Hosni Mubarak of Egypt before extending to the middle East and China where democracy doesn't seem to take roots. However, it is the number one ideology that would be necessary to shape Africa into the status of a war free zone on the basis of the above sayings or parables and for a stronger lasting world union.

According to the forgoing information, it is quite important to determine the relationship between democracy and discrimination. An important establishment in the new millennium is that relating the product of a former slave and their slave master or rather the master and the African American formerly the negro by description that became the first in the American presidency. That was marked by the election of Baraka Obama as the first of his kind in American five hundred year history since its discovery. Not even the native American has ever had that chance. No other nation has ever come even closer into conquering racial discrimination as the Americans demonstrated in terms of judging by character content or merit other than skin color. Some or many tend to think that it could never have happened if it weren't because of the great depression. At that time it required merit more than mere skin color as still many would end up turning to after the expected fixation by Obama. Such a behavior is very common as I witnessed in many pharmaceutical companies especially Bayer healthcare. The election of Baraka Obama was indirectly a set up for America to the rest of the world that discrimination is actually a long term digging of a self-graveyard. It became a lesson for those longing for a long lasting world union in political development which Africa lacks more than anybody else. It is reasonable to understand that achievement has a deep rooted endowment because the first United States president, George Washington, owned more than three hundred African slaves. As the father of the nation, he must have known more than well that it was extremely wrong before man and before God to enslave other human beings. However, he still continued to harvest on the basis of slavery and cheap free African labor without the necessity of a great intellectual around him. Then it took more than ninety years for a better intellectual to fully detect the wrongness of such evil acts when president Abraham Lincoln took over the leadership of the country and for which he was assassinated in 1865. That did not end, but it marked the turning point because it took another one hundred years for another overhaul to be initiated with the civil rights movements for which president John Kennedy and reverend Martin L. King Jr. were both assassinated. Many other strategies have taken course, but not more than what the world has come to learn about the new and current one that is based on the Obama election. The Obama strategy tends to tackle the relationship between democracy and discrimination especially when Africa is a reference for that purpose.

While believing that Africa's biggest challenge is corruption, it has also been closely determined that ethnicity has remained one of the greatest drawback influences in democratic elections. How discrimination coordinates corruption practices to ethnicity to produce a complex bond of an institution is no longer far from being understood. The method by which a special interest person or group from either within or outside many victimized countries would approach and coordinate the issue, is not only irrational, but dangerous in a strategic developing democracy that must be guarded for a long lasting world union. On that basis, China was accused during the United States presidential campaign funding of the 1990s. Similarly and as much later as the year 2007, we encounter a lot of campaign funding donations in Kenya leading to no clear winner in the tally results that turned out to be the country's bloodiest election in its history. Democracy tends to fail when there is no clear winner as much as the world witnessed in the United States presidential election of the year 2000 between Albert Gore and George W. Bush. Just like the United States elections of the year 2000, the Kenyan incumbent, president Mwai Kibaki barely won the popular vote, but seemingly lost the electoral college vote to Raila Odinga. Not too many Africans could understand the difference and thus the determining factor became scandalized as to cause a bloody post-election ethnic war. Lack of clear victory on either side made it extremely difficult to concede defeat resulting in casualties in the range of a half a million people who died in the post war conflicts while destroying billions of properties in money value with displacements and human burnings. Kenya became a spotlight in the whole world and particularly in the continent of Africa because it had retained a superior status as the best or number one example of a stable country with the highest democratic objective goals accomplished. While many were stranded and left wondering around the world as to what had gone wrong or transpired within a short span of time between 2002 and 2007, it was a big lesson to the world in addition to the United States democratic flaw of 2000 between Albert Gore and George Bush. The two separate but similar turbulences have to be corrected evenly so as to prevent the same happening in the future generations for a long lasting world union. It is so tempting yet so possible if the cause can be elaborated.

Part of the answer to the above question resides on both avenues of corruption and ethnicity as well as the special interest groups or persons lobbying and participating in the coordination of the business developments. For the third world countries, high level corruption involving an election that is based on democracy is actually enhanced by money laundering from special interest groups. Consequently, for a high level corruptive scheme or scandal that targets money profiteering to be successful, funds are usually given as donations towards a prospective good will for best returns. Depending on the size of the funds that are usually donated in large volumes, it would eventually be distributed as hard cash to the rest of the loyal contestants for a specific interest. Such interests can involve new or old incumbents for the purpose of stomach politics. However, that is not usually described as dirty money because it was donated by the same agents who cannot admire an African unless there is some money business in profit going to be generated in any focused exercise without a win-win strategy in hand. However, if that same person happened to receive likewise donations from China or the like as in the Clinton years, then it is labeled a big scandal as the name "White Water" often quoted in those years in the 1990s. As before and by using the Kenyan example in conjunction with the Baraka Obama election in the United States, the Kenyan election of the year 2007 was marked by a lot of chaos. In that development, a lot of individuals and corporations from around the world had donated so many contributions in funds that were designed to support the opposition party. At some point it appeared as though the opposition was actually receiving the main sponsorship from those nations with some special lobbying interests that they could pursue after the conclusion of the elections. As much as the talk concentrated, it duplicated the Obama language of words as to how the special interests had messed up things in Washington for decades and going as far back as the great depression of the 1930s. The same song was prevailing in Kenya even though it almost knocked out the incumbent administration.

The special interest people and groups have been in serious operation for quite many decades in Africa and they have managed to influence several elections. Even when Kenya is used as an example and we have President Mwai Kibaki winning an election in 2002 in the popular Tosha slogan and landslide, the special interest groups wanted a share of the result popularity. However, because President Mwai cooled it off by not receiving any donation from any of them, whatever the choice for the country was, could become his favorite and his opponent ministers could continue the fight regardless. During his bid for the second term, the opposition became so strong because of the enormous support from the opponents that originated from the special interest groups. The strength that developed from the special interest groups grew to a level that was so troublesome as to bring business to a standstill while human burning was accelerated at the countryside. It was particularly interesting to witness some special interest groups that were openly and outward in campaigning against president Baraka Obama's bid to become the first African American for that office in terms of acting very peculiarly in format. The political behavior was quite contradictory because of the same group of people with special interests who had done the best in supporting the opposition parties in Kenya, but were painfully campaigning against Obama for being an African and to lead America. In that respect, a special interest person or group could afford to donate fifty million dollars or shillings to an opposition candidate and still continue denouncing president Obama's bid to the White House. For most patriotic people from either Kenya or America, the analysis for such a donation becomes a big question mark under special interests. At one point the special interest appears as an angel of light in supporting the opposition in the name of democratic development whereas the same angel turns out to be a racist when appearing against Obama who won by majority sixty five percent of the votes in a landslide for worldwide vision change.

The above understanding points out that a democratic process can never be clean on transparency if a special interest group happens to be the driving force in judge with an upper hand in that process. In that respect, it wasn't very clear as to whether the statement from the Kenyan Prime Minister in the year 2009 was a change of tune when he said that "we are not here to listen to American or foreign lectures". That was a strategic timing because at the very time, the United States secretary of state, Rodham Hillary Clinton, was touring Kenya on a special visit. The statement seemed to be a reaction towards Hillary's call to reduce corruption and as drastically and as possible. To some extent, it could just be a talk which none of the two would actually walk in practice when things happen to mature to fruition of reality. For one, the special interests prime objective is expansion of business with increases in revenues. Secondly, the reaction might only be a lip service as experience often indicates that such emotions only last just a few days. However, very few Africans can decline campaign donations which are not controlled or even monitored as the 2016 Presidential candidate, Bernie Sanders keeps attacking on such a trend in American politics. Even when the assumption is made that the reaction is intact and valid, the special interest groups would quickly shop for a possible alternative which might rarely be patriotic, but ready to make new promises and agreements. As usual, the easiest alternative is to identify a candidate who might fit the system by ethnic arithmetic since that would presumably guarantee an early psychological win by tribe other than by merit. The special interest person or groups would continue pumping money as the campaign strategies are laid down while visiting those countries frequently to offer moral support for their interest candidates. Thereafter, anything is possible as a future repercussion.

On the basis of the above statements, monitoring becomes very crucial in any business development. As in the case of Kenya and other surrounding countries, the lack of monitoring for campaign funding creates an environment that is full of dirty money. The amount of dirty grows to a level that it can buy rigging through the policemen themselves even though they are supposed to be the law enforcement units. As a consequence, the next thing is nothing but the development of wars which many African hate to see on their quiet environments through the ages. Sometimes, people learn from historical experiences and redirect themselves through past mistakes leading to new changes while some keep on repeating sane errors. That was why the Obama campaigning strategies concentrated on the younger generations as opposed to the special interest groups of the status quo. The new make is for the discrimination victims around the world to have a clear understanding and determine whether a special interest group can real bring credible change anywhere in the world when they utilize money to buy an election other than win it on merit and honesty. Is it possible for Africans to base their argument on merit, and Obama of the year 2008, can they clearly sing the song "yes we can", and from their hearts as opposed to the common lips? Thereafter, try to do the same by singing the same reverse song "Not this time".

To answer the above question, the previously described hypothetical proposal for a related textbook development would be highly recommended. The main point is to change the attitude that still holds in many psychological minds of Africans and the rest of the world. The attitude that Africa is a dark continent and the poorest in the world has to be totally cleansed from the many in the Diaspora. That has been the foreigner's greatest sale for many centuries and still on for many special interest groups around the world in the common struggle often descried as the scramble for Africa. One realization is that most if not all rich people have kept the old tendency of not associating freely with poor people since the times of poor Christ and beyond for fear of losing some tiny wealth in donations. That has been the causative agent in the world that has seen it in endless discriminative policies that keeps tearing the world and preventing a long last union. Such a rare association is usually observed in people like Bill Gates who went back to number one as the world's richest man. He has mostly presented himself as generous, but the true special interest colors have not been too hard to detect as can be read in the other chapters. In that respect, it is kind of reasonable to conclude that Africa is not as poor as it is frequently postulated or else Bill Gates would not want or be as free as he usually is in terms of associating with that continent. It doesn't matter how many billionaires keep developing around the world. Nevertheless, Africa would always be an interest to the rich man which he can't do without directly or indirectly as it would be explained in most of this book' chapters.

The discrimination that is being displayed and presented above is actually twofold in nature. For a special interest person or group, the major driving force happens to be money first. The second type may be perceived as an ethnic or racial instinct, but the bottom line comes down to money as the backbone of all the disgruntled conflicts as indicated. In that regard, true democracy and especially in the discriminated African black continent, money remains the greatest temptation as the weapon of mass deception. As mentioned earlier, any misunderstanding on the word money would keep on being used as the likewise weapon of enslavement in the modern times as well as the continuous colonization of the mind. As a consequence, the low money income prejudiced communities often present a big burden into the imposed family systems in Africa leaving a lot to be desired. Africa as the main discrimination victim over the past several centuries have the obligation to take this text in the publication and clarify that there is no way an interest can develop leading to the scramble for Africa if there weren't vast deposits of goldmines attached to it or underground. There is no way a claiming rich man or a foreign special interest group and whether political or medical pharmaceuticals, can so intensely decide to scramble for Africa according to history over the centuries, if in fact there were no riches to tap and expand their revenues. Again, it turns out that the greatest supplier of some of the most precious materials on planet earth such as copper and uranium, are actually mined in Zambia and South Africa respectively in addition to vast deposits of oil and gold. From the collection made in the famous Sarafina movie that focused on Whoopi Goldberg or nicknamed as MS Masambuka and Hugh Masekela, it was reiterated that Africans come all the way from Zimbabwe in parked trains to work in the South African mines for the longest hours for almost no pay. Masekela then says that deep and very deep down in the mines, those people work all days without lunch while the families left behind keep only hoping as they are never sure whether they will ever come back home. At that same time, special interest groups continue to be busy in media deception by reporting on very egocentric based statistics to show that South Africa is the richest country among all African countries. It becomes very difficult to verify or disqualify such deceiving reports even when the African Union is challenged with such a responsibility because most of them have been elected through some assistance from the special interest groups. Such a problem is created by the vestigial defects of William Lynch often mentioned by Louis Farrakhan and of which the best product is the endemic disease of AIDS that one time produce two conflicting groups in South Africa when Thabo Mbeki rebelled against the theories of some new academic concepts in particular medical institutions.

When Hugh Masekela stresses that the work is extreme for almost no pay, sounds like an extended form of slavery. The question is actually why there should be willingness to self-enslavement by people who clearly understand where and how far the alienation of the Africans has come from. By the writing of this book in terms of timing, it is quite conceivable that the few who seem to understand are actually suppressed every time they rise to inspire the pretreatments and maintain the inspiration spirit. It is extremely significant to inspire the truth of the whole matter by declaring clearly that every good and shining man made structure is directly linked to its origins which are nothing but the dirty and risky mining environments either wholly or partially. When most Africans come across a shining office, they tend to hate the mining jobs out of ignorance because the really origin of every shining material is a dirty environment whether it is oil or minerals. The only correct attitude change and textbook education is that the same people working deep down in the mines are actually the best engineers because they know it from the roots. All others are mere academic scholars who have been brainwashed and colonized to believe that they can only act as intermediates as either instructors or assessment officers. Africa is busy stressing her children and senior citizens to rely on academic textbooks which are meant to alienate the real education based on the roots of development from its production that is the basis of jobs and justice. That is why a lot of African engineers are jobless after having been tuned to live on paycheck to paycheck from generation to generation and become the first victims of any economic crises whether in a first, second or third world country. This is the most important element lacking in Africans wherever they may be. In that regard, the best and only solution is that the miners should become the process engineers and self-made through team trainings as any other country that has developed on its own like China and India have just done in the twentieth century. There is no such a thing as going to another country like Germany, India, China or Britain to acquire the necessary tools of development because I and many others have lived in a foreign country for twenty six or more years and experienced discrimination all through even after graduating with a chain of advanced university degrees that I consider next to worthless as explained earlier by the Bayer consumer healthcare pharmaceutical example. Consequently, self-made processing engineers could be made by mineral root inspiration in textbook development as outlined under the proposed theory of grass root dirty of revolutionary development. A mere travel for hundreds of miles to look for jobs in South Africa by other Africans including the Zimbabweans mentioned above who would never return home to see their families was, and would be always be normal exploitation without value or simply another modern form of slavery under the consumer theory. In that respect, it becomes virtually important to determine why Africans with all those popular vast deposits of wealth as in the case of mines in addition to fertile agricultural soils as in Zimbabwe, cannot be able to create jobs and employment for all its citizens. That is the exact factor that keeps being utilized to undermine the rich continent as a mere dark place of habitation where happiness is far from realization. That theory has been standing as a drawback offering a license to many foreigners coming in as self-seeking investors in the name of job creators and still treating Africans as second class citizens in their own beliefs of a God-given large land mass. My experience would still remain a special type of remark because I had to follow the colonial textbooks and attain a total of four degrees including three post graduate ones, but never really get considered for a commensurately good matching occupation on a reasonable or respectful job for all the twenty-five years in America. Most or all that I received was barbarism and humiliation as one Bayer healthcare asked me why I had not left to start my own factory in Africa or Kenya as a way of humiliation and chasing after offering future feasible proposals for their pharmaceutical business. I kept thinking of any other place to migrate to that would be as good as my original home where I grew up that eventually was torn by the William Lynch theory, but kept options open because Kenya was still in political turmoil and ethnic war fare originating from the consumer theory mentioned above. It is amazing that just a mere processing of the huge money earning resources that could create employment while exposing the goldmines of vast minerals that is of an abundant wealth that could change the world image, is still standing as the only single element holding Africans at bay that keeps them solid victims of discrimination and a threat to a long lasting world unit.

By traditional cultural standards, processing in engineering has been tackled in small scale productions. A good and simple example is the production of alcohol where most mothers can perform and as much as they have been extracting same syrup from corn with yeast fermentation. The small scale industries are able to perform process engineering that produces a very strong beverage called Chang'aa. However, the liquor has been discouraged because of impurities in the purification systems and the consumer theory of underdevelopment rooted in ignorance, greed and selfishness. The discouragement has been worsened by some illegal additions of intoxicative chemicals that have claimed lives while projecting to better organoleptic properties in that equation. The perspective here is that there are still many subsistence processing skills which can form a base of presenting a big challenge for scale-up services, but which are rarely recognized. One thing that Africans must come to learn is that real development is strictly dependent on a transformation from a small research-like scale of production towards a large one. That is what led to the development of factories of everything that exists today that has made a difference in job creation and justice along with employment. That is why some type of alcohol like ethanol or Chang'aa as the Africans call it, has come to be found useful in the driving engine machines like automobile and particularly when blended with the normal petroleum gasoline. In a similar respect, other processing of various productions can be imitated under the same principles in order to develop a stronger textbook of revolutionary development. Consequently, the world would avoid the oil wars or any other energy driven ethnic conflicts for a long lasting world unity.

As I have mentioned before, very little is likely to be achieved in the world crises unless the core broker is offered justice and the core of the urgent matter in discriminative policies is fully addressed in the proposed revolutionary textbook on development. In that respect, at that great development, an elementary child would have an assignment of both the thinking and practically researching about different fires as well as their respective burning temperatures or extent of heat on a possible melt out of various substances. That is not only a parable, but a reality because other than producing light to the whole world, fire is the actual background of modern industrial developments and hence one of the greatest of God's gifts only second to health. As much as the child knows the dangers of burning, the glowing of a wire burning out of electric current generates light to suppress darkness just like the sun does for the earth and other planets or bodies in the outer space galaxies. That was my ideological background on my first proposal in the Jua Kali Shining organization founded in the year 2001 and projected towards a recycling industrialization from scrap materials to spare part productions. There is no single textbook in the whole of the African continent that addresses even the slightest knowledge at any level of educational information as to how such related developments can be initiated towards light production whether from the conventional hydro-electrical dams or simple solar panels. African engineers are brainwashed to believe that such help can mainly be obtained from foreign countries like Germany or Britain and the like, which has never been so and will never happen until discrimination has come to an end. While such an end still remains a pipe dream, the engineers would either stand jobless with endless outlook searching for employment or simply walk proudly in the streets of Johannesburg, Nairobi and others. Those are the times when they get pasted with big titles as associate directors or chief engineers of such things as the Kenya pipeline or Ranbaxy pharmaceuticals at the mercy of the foreign owner of the company. That is the target of the proposed theory of revolutionary development because the whole problem is social and psychological torture deep rooted in the slave mentality of colonization that requires serious treatment or stick to the status quo under the current textbooks. Consequently, if that happens to be the case, then the above Jua Kali Shining proposal would never be fully successful to produce the necessary fire that would be required to generate light required to wipe out the bitter darkness from many phases of the African lives. A partial darkness in the world such as the one encountered in Africa is a big threat to the future of a long lasting world union under the United Nations agenda.

It so happened that during the beginning of the course of the new millennium, I decided to become part of the foundation of the newly formed church in New Jersey in the United States of America and as a new member. The then my pastor, Peter Gusuta, who later died due to a fire accident had developed some strong bond in Christian love as I used to counsel him on his general health as well as on his prescription medications from his doctor. During that very course, the pastor requested me to become his assistant in all pastoral activities in the church and particularly in preaching the gospel. I have since that time assisted in the preaching of the gospel holding the assistant pastor title while working in my main job as a pharmaceutical research scientist. My employer was never affected because that was only a weekend part-time job, but I figured how much hatred existed in pharmaceutical companies in regard to Christian people who are likely to pray for sick patients with a possibility of being healed in the process. The hatred is based on the idea that Jesus would be invited in the healing and that would result in the reduction of revenues generated from the selling of drugs that trigger the similar healing results. Anyhow, my love for preaching inspired me to discuss a lot with the late pastor in whom I had first searched opinion on the above mentioned Jua Kali Shining proposal. He received it with a lot of excitement which made me to extend the submission to a presidential candidate, Simon Nyachae. The then honorable Nyachae discussed it with me and fully endorsed it to include it in his Kenyan vision if he won leaving a few of my opponents of that proposal grumbling in despair. The proposal became a real major campaign tool for his run, but got derailed after his final loss to Mwai Kibaki who won the presidency. Out of this proposal a lot was developing because it was an electrical ideology that was electrifying many walks of life that had been dormant in ages past. When Nyachae visited the United States to promote his vision for Kenya, a stranger for African who happened to have attended to his focal address, rose up during the time of questioning and introduced the name of his country Lado which most of the crowd had never had ever before. As a consequence, we demanded some kind of explanation as to what the real meaning was behind that name and its lack of exposure to the modern maps with evidence. In the process of offering that respective explanation, the gentleman displayed an 1893 map that showed the map of Lado in between the former colonial boundaries of East African community so named British and Germany East Africa. The next page of that magazine handout print that he distributed in the conference of about three hundred people contained a special article talking about the importance of decolonization of the African mind. Some people would digest right away while some could not understand anything at all even after many weeks and probably months. The lack of understanding was most likely due to the limited knowledge offered only on the basis of the textbook designs and still being used as the only syllabuses of school instructions in all levels of the academic curriculum. Then during his explanation, he reiterated that the kingdom of Lado used to be in the textbooks of the 19th century syllabuses because it was never colonized by those who did the same thing in all other African kingdoms excluding Ethiopia and Egypt. He continued to say that when the partial decolonization was initiated, the colonies became independent republics such as Kenya, Uganda, and Tanzania, but Lado was not given the same recognition because it was never colonized. In that respect, it has continued to be in the conflicting situation for more than seven hundred years. The validity of that explanation depends on the United Nations charter and resolutions development for the independent African States for a longer lasting world unity.

The foregoing discussion mentions and points to some kind of misunderstanding within the United Nations organization in terms of being somehow blind in some significant resolutions as to lack a direct answer deep rooted in freedom, liberty, justice, and pursuit of happiness apart from the African Union. As a volunteer counselor and Assistant pastor in my newly formed church, I found the issue of decolonization to be quite interesting. The issue of seeing and witnessing the presence of Lado in the 1893 African map was kindly an apparent prove that the kingdom was in existence and recognized as much as it is now by those same colonialists along the same generation of inheritance. After researching many historical books, it can be found out how Israel parallels that particular Lado kingdom because after the colonization and total destruction of Israel in 587 B.C it decolonized itself 2000 years later and came back to the world map in 1947 which it is still resisting with the help of its allies. According to my guidebook and most popular historical records, Israel was one time a kingdom in the Middle East as one of the nations in the region. However, somewhere between two to three thousand years back or around 587 B.C, it was completely colonized and destroyed from the map and scattered around the world that only recently reformed and reappeared to be recognized by the same colonialists along that chain of inheritance that is still fighting. As ignorant as in the above case, many leaders and people around the world including Amadenajad and Netanyahu could not figure out how people who had been scattered all over the world and particularly in Germany for so many generations were able to simply return home as they did in 1947. The whole world had been colonized to the belief that Israel ceased to exist after their escape from the invading Babylonians almost two thousand years back. However, through slow developments mainly by decolonization of the affected people, many around the world have come to recognize the original map and hence the right to co-exist as independent states for both the Jewish and the Arabic Palestinians in the two troubled and struggling Middle East nations. Such an understanding has come to take root through a new development of textbook revolutions in educational overhauls that is still far from being understood while it only dates back to the reconstruction of the Middle East map in the 1940 as opposed to the Lado of 1893 or 1960s. It usually comes as a hard nut to crack and sometimes by events such as the Germany holocaust of 1940s that left people like Dr. Henry Kissinger to narrate more about Hitler's genocide over the Jews. Like a few other political boundary wars, the Israel case is exactly similar to that of Lado because by being unrecognized, the Lado people are the same as the previously scattered Jews, but different in proportion and scenario. However, they are both presenting serious tests to the world of United Nations that can prove the ability to govern itself for a long lasting world order or perish like fools.

As broadly mentioned and discussed, the world is still being kept in captivity in various perspectives. The issue of discrimination is enhanced by deep rooted corruption in various developments around the world and remains the greatest barrier towards a long lasting world union under the United Nations agenda. The struggle to achieve that agenda must be based on equality by all human beings that inhabit the earth and open to free participation as freedom goes. The agenda to achieve that struggle is currently being hindered by irrational competitions without adequate cooperation that is based on the consumer theory of ignorance, greed, and selfishness as discussed in the previous chapters. The urgency of a new textbook development that would serve as part of the basis of such a resolution for a long lasting world union cannot be over-emphasized. However, the publication of this book delivers part of that resolution. The emphasis would rely on the lay down of a concrete textbook for educational overhaul right from the grassroots. Such an achievement would focus on the right to life, freedom, justice, liberty, and pursuit of happiness through fair employment according to taxation. That must never exclude the kingdoms mentioned above in terms of their right to exist and whether Israel, Palestine or Lado if a long lasting world union is to be expected. Consequently, Africa standing as the oldest victim of colonization and still living under the William Lynch theory of slave development must digest all the information presented in this piece of a book or publication to carefully shape its future with every possible justice that endures forever. It must then be distributed and serve as the new guide towards the development of the proposed revolutionary textbook in the expected educational overhaul. Likewise, the rest of the world has the obligation of supporting the respective ideology so as to make it a more liberal and just home for all mankind. If we all take that responsibility, there is no doubt in peacemaker or anybody that the world would become very close to a long last union without any fears of nuclear proliferations and economic depressions. That is the kind of world that our dreams can foresee as the happiness to be realized for the current and the future generations.

CHAPTER IX

WORLD ORDER BY COLLABORATIVE TECHNOLOGY

Before starting and getting into the real current crisis in the new millennium as of the time of writing of this book, America learned a lesson recently which I think should be used as a great future analytical tool for a long lasting technical world order. Currently, when we begin a discussion about the plight of American industrialization in manufacturing we realize that something had gone radically wrong with the American economy. A once-robust system of "traditional engineering" the invention, design, and manufacture of products has been replaced by financial engineering which is nonsensical if it is not shielded by a strong base in raw materials engineering. Raw materials lead to a vibrant manufacturing sector for which without it we witnessed Wall Street creating money it did not have and Americans spent money they did not have. That led to the crisis that is still greatly being felt and one which was worse than the great depression of the 1930s. In that perspective, Americans stopped making the products which they continued to buy including: clothing, computers, consumer electronics, flat-screen TVs, household items, and millions of automobiles and many other things.

America's economic elite has long argued that the country does not need an industrial base. The economies in states such as California and Michigan that have lost their industrial base, however, belief in that claim because they cannot compete anymore with the Japanese automobile developments. As mentioned earlier about the Jua Kali industrial bases that Africa needs in order to begin developing and competing, it is true that without an industrial base, an increase in consumer spending, which pulled the country out of past recessions, will not put Americans back to work now or anytime sooner. Similarly, by lacking the tools of basic industrial initiatives, the nation's trade deficit will continue to grow. By lacking an industrial base in our economic developments, there will be no economic ladder for a generation of immigrants, stranded in low-paying service-sector jobs. By lacking basic industrialization tools, the United States will be increasingly dependent on foreign manufacturers even for its key military technology for which we shall keep on begging for jobs in order to succeed.

As far as the current United States economy is concerned and for the American manufacturers, the real worst years didn't begin with the banking crisis of 2008. In real operations and in numbers, the U.S. manufacturing sector never emerged from the 2001 recession because of too much predatory lending that was practiced. That was a circumstance that coincided with China's entry into the World Trade Organization. From that time in the year 2001, the country has lost 42,400 factories, including 36 percent of factories that employ more than 1,000 people. An additional 90,000 manufacturing companies are now at risk of going out of business and become homeless, or lead to a terrible drawback in a developed country like the United States.

The question is to determine the real cause and to what extent all of the above trends have occurred and the status of the foreseeable consequences. Respectively, long before the banking collapse of 2008, such important U.S. industries as machine tools, consumer electronics, auto parts, appliances, furniture, telecommunications equipment, and many others that had once dominated the global marketplace suffered their own economic collapse. Something too worrying took place in the manufacturing sector because manufacturing employment dropped to 11.7 million in October 2009, a loss of 5.5 million or 32 percent of all manufacturing jobs since October 2000. Consequently, we did recognize that the last time those records showed fewer than 12 million people working in the manufacturing sector was in 1941. Thus, in October 2009, more people were officially unemployed (15.7 million) than were working in manufacturing industries.

Factories are the bases of industrial development. Thus, when a factory closes, it creates a complete breakdown that has far-reaching consequences for the current and the future generations. According to a past study, the Milken Institute estimated that every computer-manufacturing job in California ended up creating 15 jobs outside the factory. That scenario applies to almost all situations in factorial development. Consequently, if one closes a manufacturing plant in a given sector, a supply chain of producers will disappear along with it. In sequence, dozens of companies end up getting hurt such as those supplying computer-aided design and business software; automation and robotics equipment, packaging, office equipment and supplies; telecommunications services; energy and water utilities; research and development, marketing and sales support; and building and equipment maintenance and janitorial services. In the same limelight, the burden spreads to local restaurants, cultural establishments, shopping outlets, and then to the tax base that supports police, firemen, schoolteachers, and libraries and much more in recreational facilities.

People have talked such sayings as "No Empire lives forever" when they see a deteriorating United States economy as above, but is it true that the U.S. manufacturing has declined because its companies are not competitive or is it according to that saying considering what the Roman and the British went through before they all failed? It may be so, but hard to contemplate. That is because American companies are among the most efficient in the world on the basis of some analytical characteristics. Respectively, the nation's steel industry, for instance, produces a ton of steel using two man-hours whereas a comparable ton of steel in China is produced with a dozens of man-hours. Furthermore, the Chinese companies actually produce three times the amount of carbon monoxide emissions per given ton of steel under similar conditions. Those facts are similar for the same kinds of comparisons in other industries.

Another defect resides on the financial currency devaluations. That is because American companies do encounter some obstacles in competing against foreign countries that undervalue their currencies with cheap labor, Health insurance or actually paying health care for their workers, supply or offer provision of subsidies for firm estates, energy, land, buildings, and factorial or engineering equipment. They also grant tax holidays and rebates as well as provide zero-interest financing in almost all financial institutions; they pay their workers poverty wages that would be illegal in the United States, and without rules they never enforce safety or environmental regulations in their industries.

Many experts are still searching to find out what went wrong that is making the one-time vibrant economy of the world or what is actually bringing it down to its knees even when it counts itself the most powerful in the world. Before or even during the recent declaration of China's superiority as the number one in the world on the basis of many analyses, proponents of free trade and outsourcing operations argue that the United States remains the largest manufacturing economy in the world. Many conservatives are not even bothered about the decline of the American economy because wealth accumulation has been on their side from the time of slavery and still on. While such a status has not yet begun to diminish based on the decline of American manufacturing, many people could most likely be interested in reading the article entitled 'Winwood Reade's 1872 volume *The Martyrdom of Man*', in which he chronicled the economy of ancient Rome with specific terms. At that time dung was their return cargo after instrumental and coordinated operations focusing on economic development.

According to the dung theory then mentioned above, the facts are that the largest U.S. exporter via ocean container in 2007 was not even an American company, but actually Chinese. The name was described as the American Chung Nam, which exported 211,300 containers of waste paper to its Chinese sister company, Nine Dragons Paper. Respectively or by comparison, Wal-Mart imported 720,000 containers of sophisticated manufactured products from overseas factories into the United States, followed by Target, Home Depot and Sears which recently acquired and now owns K-Mart superstores.

In many perspectives and given the various world competitions and conditions on free trade agreements, the United States is losing the industries of the future right from the West to the East in an alarming rate. That is well exemplified by the solar industry where there was only one American company or the First Solar among the top 10 worldwide in photovoltaic-cell production in 2008. But the European Commission does not even classify First Solar as being an "American" company, instead labeling it "international" because it does most of its production in Asia. That is a clear prove that the United States has been outsmarted and actually thrown out of the shell of the uniformed competition for which even billionaire and 2016 presidential candidate Donald Trump wouldn't attempt or dare to debate on.

Further evidence in support of the above analysis is revealed on the information that states that in 2007, only a tiny percentage of all new semiconductor fabrication plants under construction in the world were located in the United States. Twelve percent of new fabrics were being built in China, 40 percent in Taiwan, and 6 percent in South Korea, according to Semiconductor Equipment Materials International. China has now surpassed the United States in motor-vehicle production by a big margin of more than 2 million cars. The U.S. steel industry is still lagging behind in total productivity competition, despite the far greater efficiency of U.S. steel production in terms of quality that is often based on safety and efficacy.

Many scientists have maintained an advocacy of a tool manufacturing expansion in the United States to keep up with the prevailing superiority in industrial development. As it is well noted, machine tools have long been considered essential to maintaining the country's national security. In 1948, Congress passed the National Industrial Reserve Act based on the idea that the "defense of the U.S. requires a national reserve of machine tools for the production of critical items of defense material." In 1986, President Ronald Reagan, a staunch free-trade advocate, supported a five-year Voluntary Restraint Agreement with Japan and Taiwan on imports of machine tools based on national-security grounds. The experts and advisers of that administration succeeded in helping make Reagan's determination who later reiterated that the industry was a "vital component of the U.S. defense base and which should not be politicized for that matter.

At the same when the above events were occurring dozens of other industries were nearly disappearing from United States of America. However, one major American manufacturer which remained was Summitville Tiles of Summitville that was based in Ohio. The company's president and CEO, David Johnson, on his analytical speech on competition, concluded that the industry had been virtually wiped out by international competitors where it seemed that his industry was gone or just about to be finished. That was a very discoursing report by an owner of a company in an industrialized country like the United States of America.

While the above report leaves a lot to be desired, another consequence epidemic condition was witnessed in the rapid relocation of the world's manufacturing belt from the U.S. to China which has also meant a shift in these nations' technological capacities. Thus, as foreign manufacturers flock to China to take advantage of its cheap labor, devalued currency, and manufacturing subsidies, they have also shifted their research and development endeavors to China. That is the kind of competition that needs scrutiny as it is the basis of the healing that is heavily needed to counter the inter-racial tensions in America that originate in economic instability to inequality.

Universal education is yet to be standardized for everyone's benefit in the competitive business world. The continuing shift of manufacturing to lower-cost regions and especially to China is beginning to pull high-end design and research and development capabilities out of the United States because of cheap labor and overall costs in production abroad. In the same perspective, healthcare is not excluded at all because without surprise, the Bush White House did not publicize any or all the trickle-down economics in the above shifting in research and development that could include the pharmaceutical companies. However, the above report recommended that the U.S. should make its research and development tax credit permanent and irreversible. However, it has not been done as such at the writing of this book. Once the world's most generous, the U.S. research and development tax credit is now lower than those of 17 other nations and that is something that is discouraging and detrimental to healthcare development and the economy at large.

An obvious reason for the above consequence is actually originated in the way taxation works n the United States. As with the old establishment from domestic manufacturing as it has been, the tax credit no longer pays for itself as it once did in many business sectors. In such a perspective for instance, if our innovation system discourages an invention from being manufactured in the United States because of primitive competition, then the American industry will not be able generate the taxes that will in turn fund the federal investment in research and development.

In the current political arena, there are two major candidates that are actually addressing the issue of economics and the future we can believe in that include Bernie Sanders and Hillary Clinton. All that is necessary and actually what domestic manufacturers want is for the United States government to shift its economic policies away from consumption to incentives that favor investment in new factories, equipment, and jobs in the United States. They want the United States to abandon policies that favor geopolitical world police or global interests that have no regard for the economic health of the United States and its millions of taxpayers and retirees.

To the disappointment of the domestic manufacturing community, the Obama administration has yet to devise a strategy aimed at creating the industrial jobs needed in America to generate trillions of dollars of tax revenue. Without a surge in U.S. production and exports, how will the United States pay off its mounting debts and cover the retirement and medical costs of the largest generation of Americans in history? Creating more jobs for dental hygienists, health-care workers, retail clerks, and bartenders will not do it unfortunately.

There are convincing signs that the administration is awaking to the need for new economic policies aimed at private-sector industrial investment and the creation of good jobs. President Barack Obama had appointed Ron Bloom, a financial healer, to be his "senior counselor for manufacturing policy." Interestingly, Bloom, a graduate of Harvard Business School, worked for years in the investment-banking industry before taking a job with the United Steelworkers, using his experience to help restructure companies to assure their survival and their ability to employ American workers. He also worked on the Obama administration's Task Force on the Automotive Industry, which at least for now saved General Motors and Chrysler from extinction. Bloom is piecing together a strategy that will build upon investments being made in the $787 billion economic stimulus package aimed at helping the U.S. clean-energy sector that is really catching fire in policy development.

In addition to the information presented above, it is quite true that the idea of industrialization has become very challenging considering Chinese and Russian superiority on Super-computers and nuclear technology build-up. That is because most of it is based on the industrial revolution of the eighteenth century that all people have ended up learning to leave no consumers as before to boost businesses. Much of today's developments especially those that involve mechanical movements resulting from some assembly of designative metal parts has become too common or likely to remain magnetic attractions of modern businesses. At no other time in world history has there been such a tremendous revolution which spread out so fast so as to cause the initiation of the establishment of schools and colonization simultaneously. The revolution of industrial development resulted in the evolution of stiff competitions in all sectors around the world. However, there evolved some competitions without real productions or anything new combined with old developmental theories. That was the kind of experience that led the world into another global financial crisis that most of America refers to as the second great depression so similar to the one of 1930s. America had maintained the number one position as the king of industrial development. However, the question as to how the king of industrial revolution and therefore development comes to a level of a second world nation is probably answerable by this book in the rest of the chapters. An extended answer would be the deep relationship between evolution and revolution lines in development. It is a challenge that has attracted a lot of attention to many leaders as much as the scientific researchers and law makers.

Part of the answer to the above question resides on the colonial revolutions that took place in most parts of the planet earth including the first thirteen colonies that made up the American Union now called the United States of America. Colonial rule was intentionally made by the law makers of those days to deny some people or races out of their natural freedom. Their goal was to enforce slavery among the African race so as to achieve free labor and maximum profits and revenues out of it for wealth accumulation. While the historical records reveal that former president Abraham Lincoln, did sign the "emancipation proclamation" as part of the new revolutionary development of that time, it is also true that a different format of slavery was initiated indirectly for at least another one hundred years after he outlawed it. It continued through the times of the civil rights movements during which president John Kennedy and Reverend Dr. Martin Luther King were both assassinated because of their support based on the Lincoln struggle. A careful examination of those three great leaders confirms that a big breakthrough on intellectual evolutionary development was very apparent. It is commonly true that human beings resist foreseeable changes in their communities even when the respective changes are meant for the good of everybody. But it was a great evolution of the brains that most likely supported the various movements including those of industrial technology itself. All of the above mentioned leaders were assassinated because of the changes they initiated that actually ended up making it a freer world and safe environment to live in. The big question is whether any vestigial structures of resistance to such a revolution are still fighting those initiatives that are only meant to destroy the progressing world after achieving so much in that perspective.

In view of the above, there is still that worry that some vestigial structures are innate and could be fighting forever. However, the real threat could be the super greed and the ignorant. It is quite true that real change doesn't come easily and quickly as expected by many people and even scientists do have the same general agreements while they accept that evolution is a continuous process. Ignorance like any other infectious disease process or disorder can be treated and cured, but there is still that possibility of mutating itself to afford re-infection to attack many people and probably most of mankind with the common respective consequences. That is why history had witnessed the four hundred years of Jewish slavery in Egypt as well as the similar case in more numbers during the two hundred years of the African slavery in America till 1863 and bearing defects that might last a thousand years according to William Lynch theory of 1712 at River side bank. Whether there is any relationship between the above two types of enslavement, it remains a question for further scrutiny. However, the industrial revolution was quite influential in the partial eradication of slavery in the latter case. From that perspective, it is quite conceivable that as many brains of mankind continue to evolve and so would be the industrial and democratic revolutions. Consequently, the remaining vestiges of slavery would eventually be eradicated if well planned, but nobody knows how long that might take. It may become determinable by some new theories as illustrated in this publication or special mathematical calculus. That is true because there may be prospective methods, but different forms may recycle several times before meaningful evolutions become real visible according to many scientific researches in various literatures.

One of the evolutionary scientists who contributed a lot towards more freedom to the world in the last or twentieth century was Albert Einstein with the quantum theory on mechanics. The proper interpretation of his theory with the addition of further scientific inputs, quite honestly initiated the real end of major colonialism towards a new beginning with modern acceleration of the civil rights movements. The revolutionary episode of that particular industrialization prompted the rest of the world with the special alertness that the world would be filled with a lot of bombs that might make some to backfire. After the bombing of Pearl Harbor and then the atomic bomb that burned the Hiroshima township in Japan in 1942, a major arms race emerged around the world and led by the former Soviet Union and the United States of America. Later on, China joined the race and other smaller countries around the world except Africa. As more and more evolutions continue to erupt around the world, we shall keep seeing the race get tougher and tougher. That was particularly true upon the time when the world witnessed the launching of nuclear missiles in North Korea. The world can also foresee other countries gaining more and more expertise on the same race by observing the Iran and Afghanistan type of revolutions. The question is not the fear of dropping a bomb on someone or some town like the New York World Trade Center in the year 2001. It is actually about dropping a bomb on everybody. Most intellectuals think along those lines because many crimes have taken place in humanity so much so that some have decided to keep their grudges indefinitely without any prospect signs of forgiveness. For a peaceful and long lasting united world, forgiveness must be one of the options or face the consequences of Dr. Martin Luther King quote "perish like fools" which could remain applicable anytime indefinitely. It is often described as a Christian cultural norm, but it is encountered in most world cultural customs and traditions. However, the approach and method as to how that can be achieved is a big question to the world even when the military or nuclear intelligence continues to spread exponentially.

Some of the answers to the above challenges reside on the definition of enmity in broad and detailed terms. Firstly, it is important to bear in mind that human beings are more of dramatists than realists. It is often difficult for many people to accept openly that a specific country or continent is either being friendly or has been a friend to another so as to remain in that status regardless of new errors. World history has noted that no nation is a permanent friend or enemy of one another. Leaders can sign treaties from time to time and again, but still fail to walk the talk to abide by the respective rules. It seems close to some bill signing such as those that took place during the civil rights movements around the world. However, to be a friend of a certain country, a lot of consultation is conducted and the respective constitutions examined to find the matching factors. When constitution in type of government aligns with another, it is often expected to be the defining factor of friendship. That is true when we examine the similarities between two republican types of governments. But one can still find a communist type of government exercising friendship to a democratic or republican administration based on business matters and certain trade agreements. The best example is China which is a big friend of the United States especially in the year 2008 at the time of a big recession in America. We heard so much during those depression times with the presidential elections taking place in the United States that China was being so generous in lending a lot of money to America to help in the financial meltdown crises. That was one lesson for those of us who love democracy because then communist China seems or proved that at times it could do better than democratic nations as it has never been thought of before. That is the same time when China got accused of leading its people through a system that is dictatorial and frequently violates human rights. It could be true or may be a simple confusion, but that creates the necessity of re-defining those systems regarded to be dictatorial in nature more closely so as to determine the real way of attaining a long lasting world Unity. That means real in friendship as opposed to a simple race in war fare nuclear arms. An arms race is like any racing competition, but quite risky and dangerous in nature because in such a contest anybody can be a launcher, but everybody remains a target. Precisely, it sounds like an infectious disease that is airborne and from where everybody breathes oxygen for survival. As a one-time philosopher said "If you need peace then prepare for war", it is also true that if you prepare for war then prepare to die if peace does not cultivate. I tend to trust that philosopher because it looks like evil has been lingering around us ever and as far back since the earth was formed. However, my philosophy is that "one cannot eliminate truth by killing the rightist", as in the case of civil rights activists who have previously died in that context because truth always prevails and wins forever. Likewise, "one cannot kill evil by killing the devil". That leaves a big dilemma as to how or what method should be used to resolve evil issues as we know them today as opposed to just death penalties or random killings. It seems then that wars are not going to resolve any terrorist activities because at one time we had Timothy Mcveigh in America and yet at another time we had a Hitler in Germany or an Osama in Afghanistan. It is common to all human beings that humanity is a feeling of loveliness or a mere sense of love is a powerful weapon of modern development. Consequently, for a long lasting inter-racial healing for world unity, we must clearly be honest to ourselves and define real evil as much as we do for real love. Regardless of whether we perform good or badly, we are always interested more on being credited than corrected on our past mistakes so far committed. The idea and nature of human behaviors to reject the acceptance of their own mistakes is the basis of the common greed or the emergence of the arms race. That is of course whether it is in accumulation of wealth through mass deception or in dictatorial regimes. The main reason why we see various protests around the world is because many are suppressed with deception that there is no single government that can satisfy everyone even with what many consider to be the best defined laws and policies in a given place.

One of the most difficult laws to enforce on all mankind is the one of love followed by jobs and justice. Even when industrial revolution has played a big role to change the world, we still experience some form of serious discrimination as in the case of the Bayer Pharmaceuticals mentioned earlier. That is while slavery is still being experienced and real in Sudan and other less publicized communities. Also, that is in addition to the fact that there are various protests witnessed around the world and particularly in the civil rights movements. Again, it becomes a rather challenging task to walk the peace talk because of the failure to implement the much preached justice as presented. That reminds some of us about the popular parable by a onetime philosopher who said that there is no easy walk to freedom. That was said by the first president of democratic South Africa, Nelson Mandela after publishing a book in the 1990s upon serving a prison term that was forcefully terminated after 27 years. Most scientists where I happen to be one, do believe that general development of which the basics are industrialization, can play a big role in peace investment. A good explanation is the recurrence of ethnic wars in less developed countries. That is due to lack of industries and particularly small manufacturing factories that can improve infrastructure to reduce poverty and unemployment. While that is true, it is also truthful that the more the knowledge spreads out around the world, the more the naturally evil minded people misuse the skills to manipulate projected destruction. That has been clearly seen in the Oklahoma bombing by McVeigh as well as the world Trade Center both of whom were United States citizens. That makes it very difficult to determine who the real enemy is and whether within or outside of any country and how such presiding intelligence should be distributed.

Part of the answer to the above dilemma resides on the worldwide educational overhaul guidelines and principles. As mentioned earlier, it is the industrial revolution that has changed the world up to the level where we have internet communication as a perfect mobile information tool. The spread of any information is currently unstoppable because more and more people are gaining knowledge on the basic needs required to develop satellites which would continue to enable wireless transmissions. That is great pride to the world as it brings everybody closer to one another with the easiness in communications. However, that same pride can become great danger if the world does not try to unite under those principles and get the control measures in place because competition without cooperative justice can lead to total destruction of human species. The question is how that can be accomplished before the situation gets out of control because internet has contributed a lot in many business advancements around the world.

One of the answers to the above question is based on the willingness to unite under the principles of equality, respect, peace, and justice much the same way it is portrayed in the United States American constitution under the bill of rights. On that bill of rights under the first 10 amendments, it is clearly stated while not necessarily practiced that everyone has the right to life, liberty, and pursuit of happiness. It only turns out to be the greatest human right that everyone seeks to achieve. For the past two hundred years ever since that bill was drafted and written by Thomas Jefferson, it has been the most popular in terms of world democratization processes and movements. However, much has been on the contrary because of failure to walk the talk they inspire the masses with because dictators hate to hear it. Even after losing about six hundred thousand people in the American civil war, the same people who had escaped dictatorship and religious persecutions around the world, could not accept it. They could not accept former President Abraham Lincoln's call to all America for an emancipation of proclamation that was designed to end slavery imposed on the African Americans. President Lincoln was finally assassinated with an intention of suppressing his call by his opponents, but it all came to an end after another one hundred years of continuous enslavement through the civil rights movement actions. That was at the climax when the civil rights leader, the reverend Dr. Martin L. King was assassinated along with President John F. Kennedy only within a span of a few years. When a collective analysis is well performed to assess the above assassinations and others alike around the world, it becomes very obvious that there is no easy walk to freedom which all human beings are always longing for. Likewise, there is no easy walking of any talk even when it is meant for the good of all because a few good numbers are only born and circumscribed to believe in greed, selfishness and hateful. That is the definition of what may be called evil because why not do to others what you want others to do to you? That is an element that has been resolved before and can still be resolved because there is more than enough food for all human beings and for which they can all enjoy in pursuit of happiness for a long lasting world union. That should be the daily song to be sung to the whole world.

The target of the central message is the consolidation of the worldwide regimes into a fit close to a real United Nations with a more elaborate universal world order. However, the stumbling block is a question of whether, most people including those preaching the gospel could ever reach a state where they see that all human beings are real created equal before their eyes and before God. With the previous warning about information technology and how it is strongly spreading the improvement of communication, many nations are bound to the fact that most human beings are now capable of accessing extra ordinary skills at the touch of the button fingers. That is what would mostly account for the strongest spread for the winds that are urgently needed for real change to every corner of the universe. That is why many were not surprised when the world witnessed a small country like North Korea, launching the nuclear missile in the year 2009. While many of developed nations did condemn the act, it was a prove that many of us are now capable of utilizing every piece of research information including the internet resources which can basically lead to such risky constructions.

Many generations have passed without changing much on various outdated machines around the world. Man does not solidly know to his awareness as to whether there is any easier way of simplifying work other through the use of machines. Many people have to become the medium of change as soon as they identify a dying regime in a particular nation. Despite the differences among leaders in small organizations, it is certainly true that differences must be talked over and resolved with respective achievements. However, if the industrial revolution with all the scientists and the missionaries manage to come and reason together, then they could be able to get to their early and light a candle that can give more light to all people who are still locked under that loop of darkness. Only then can anything planned on either underground or the upper side could be expedited for the betterment of a long lasting world union with minimal fears of self-destruction in an industrialized community. That is definitely a factor in inter-racial healing.

For many generations, the world has encountered several types and classes of researchers and scientists. While it is appropriate to quote other scientists as I did in the early part of this book, I sometimes utilize myself as one of my best examples. I have often been inspired by researchers like Albert Einstein and Rosa Parks on the basis of their ideas that really transformed the world. Consequently, it is with that inspiration accompanied by special interest that I do expand more on a lasting world of United Nations on inter-racial healing criteria. Such an expansion has to dwell through all the educational aspects of industrialization. That prompted me to the inspiration of co-founding the organization I had named Jua Kali Shining. An important thing to realize is that such a foundation was only part of the initiative to expand and spread knowledge while confronting the obvious barriers over the past generations. There is still that fear among some groups of people as to what could happen if everybody just had enough food as much as the basic needs require. Some falsely think that they could lose their wild pride in that process. That seems to be the triggering factor in the race for nuclear superiority and suppression. It is not hard to formulate some thesis that can defend such a proposition.

To answer the above question with a view to enhancing an implementation of long lasting peaceful future, we need to realize that with or without evolution, the world has always revolved. That is of course without any special impact of the underlying scientific theories. As discussed in the other chapters, religious freedom has experienced some peculiar operations that man could have utilized for the better and may never understand even as it has been dating back to the times of Christ and beyond. Many historical researchers have even indicated that when Columbus arrived in America, he actually encountered different types of people or tribes of people which included both Black Africans as well the so called Red Indians as they were named. That posed some feeling and is still posing a threat to non-African pride which has thrived for many generations since the fifteenth century slavery. That was because of the implication that Africans must have arrived in America before the Europeans and thus a prove of being the pioneers of civilization and hence industrial revolution. While that is open to debate, the basic belief should not be over-emphasized because there must have been some special means of transportation that led Africans all the way to America before Columbus whether by steam engines or some kind of inventions. That should be noted in the proposed new textbook of revolutionary development for better understanding as needed for a long lasting world union and inter-racial healing of hope.

The above statement is an indication that nobody can real stop somebody else's revolution once the ignition key has been set in place or while it is still in operation. That applies in and to all areas of freedom-oriented lives and so long as different interests are collaborated with scientists aggressively. Consequently, the world would probably have to accept unconditionally that as much as truth and freedom keeps spreading throughout the universe and so will the speedy spread of industrial revolution with new and renewable sources of technological advancement. When that takes place and with a particular reference to the past one hundred years, many changes do occur in world treaties and orders so as to balance the abiding equation in evolutionary schemes of development. A major change that was kept in suppression for some time was the emergency of religious freedom which included the Bible and the Christian doctrine that has really expanded. Most of the people in the world's largest continent, Asia don't believe much in Christianity since most of them are Muslims. However, Louis Farrakhan, the Muslim leader has often indicated that he believes in Christ as well as in Muhammad. However, Indians believe that their God is actually the Cow from which most milk is obtained. The most surprising thing with plain statistical truth is that most Americans trust Asians for almost everything in the workplace and one hundred times more than the African Christian counterparts. That poses a big question as to whether there are real Christians in such regions to fully trust. It is true that Africans can fellowship with all other races and attend the predominantly other peoples' churches, but when it comes to issues like jobs and justice, they have to be discriminated and get judged by their skin color in order to eliminate first hand on any over-qualified African who are dark skinned. But love endures forever because Africans have never stopped loving the non-Africans upon recognizing that when they particularly visit the African continent, a lot of people do sacrifice their day's work or weeks to welcome and serve their needs as well as entertain them even when they receive a donkey's kick in return in terms of equal employment opportunities.

A specific consideration is the extent of all human understanding based on the Godly historical books and what they say about human rights. That is quite important because many interpretations have been presented to define the same doctrines in several religions. In some the confusion is indicated as intentional till some time according to superpower schedule that is far from human comprehension. That is why some things appear like miracles and at different times yet at times they are considered to be just nature which nobody's theory can explain satisfactorily.

The consequences of the above translation can become epidemic when a big rift or bridge is built to cause division. Different interests from various groups can lead into that and in most divisions there usually develops some sort of conflict many contradicting rebellions. However, for united industrialization to take root with a new seed, there must be peace makers whose tireless work is to unite the whole world as one. Those are the ones who usually built the bridges of negotiations. When we hear especially that the Unite United States President Baraka Obama is talking about bringing the democrats and republicans together, he is in actuality in the process of resolving a big issue dating back to the time of Abraham Lincoln that keeps the two look like real rivals with two different types of ideologies yet it is democracy. The world then wonders whether something like such an ideology is possibly attractive as to copy by other countries towards a universal long lasting interpretation and as a unit of inter-racial hope.

Before answering the above questions, there seems to be a specific need to understand what the most basic human right ideology should be. The most popular example is whether all people are really equal as created. Many of those people who know the answer right by their fingertips would be the first ones to violate that popular right. That is why the world is still encountering slavery in certain parts of the African continent and particularly in Darfur in the country of Sudan, which is actually the largest in Africa. It is quite amazing that a country like Sudan which is free of the deadly weapons of mass destruction or a defense machinery missile system in their disposal can continue violating that basic human right while the whole world is watching and talking other than walk the talk. Sudan has rich deposits of oil and other minerals, but shouldn't there be an interest in every suffering country to receive aid from other African states or the more developed nations. It is probably true because Rwanda could have received the necessary aid during the 1994 ethnic genocide if there were real interests like oil and other minerals for profit making businesses. That was never the same case when we encountered the invasion of Kuwait by Iraq in the 1990s that led to the Persian Gulf War between Iraq and the United States. The question of how each country should respond to the disasters of others has not been deeply examined to compromise for a universal devise that can be workable and applicable without other reservations. It is astonishing that many Americans have not really seen any profits out of those wars and as dirty as the term sounds when there are no weapons of mass destruction found after a decade of a blind war in Iraq.

Except in the written records of history, man has always known that the really excuse or prime objective of war is for self-defense. That is proof that the devil exists that is out to attack the physical or spiritual nature of humans or animal life. Even the scriptures do mention about self-defense in the course of attack by an enemy. However, such an important passage has been misinterpreted by many people and their elected leaders so as to conclude that an attack or invasion of a neighboring nation is an act of defense. However, it is usually found that such invasions are actually out of greed and selfishness or colonialism itself. The biggest invasion in history is actually the colonization of America by many foreigners even though some would say it was Africa. While America was totally colonized, Africa retaliated and left some room to breathe without respective extinction of language and culture and still fighting for sovereignty. That should be a reminder to the invaders that it is incorrect to underestimate the potential power of any nation whether big or small even without the presence of deadly nuclear weapons of mass destruction. Biological weapons are even worse because they are easy to formulate and launch and for which any country can acquire at any time and rate. They include deadly viral germs that are capable of spreading easily and fast. They are more threatening because they are not easily detectable as they spread and constantly mutating to resist any available drugs in the medical or pharmaceutical developments. Again, this kind of threat to humanity is resolvable by a united industrialization in collaboration with proposed text book of revolutionary development on inter-racial healing of hope.

The so called monopoly of world things is and has remained a big issue since the beginning of the world or as far back as history can take us with the written and reliable records. In one explanation, it can be described as colonialism which is still responsible for many of the worldwide invasions of some countries by others including the first and second world wars. In another explanation, it simply talks about patents and their protections. The business strategies of patents have been so colonized and monopolized by some countries so that it can seem to be correct that others are actually not producing anything other than plants in this world. Consequently, patents have been very popular in protecting the misuse of others talents and skills without permission which actually depends on both the location and accessibility of the prevailing system on filing or registration for permanent recordings. That is what happens in the healthcare industry of which is one of the best politicized for example with the Kemron drug that was discovered by the Kenyan scientists in the 1990s. It could have been one of the greatest patents in the Kenyan history if politics wasn't the major stumbling block. After its clinical trials, it was determined that a complete elimination of the AIDS virus had taken place in those patients that were treated in the Nairobi city studies led by doctor Koech. The AIDS virus has since been only slightly controlled, but it is still regarded as biological weapon of mass destruction by many Africans like Nobel prize winner professor Wangari Maathai of Kenya in 2005 and doctor Jack Felder of the former US Army.

The above example spreads out a lot to many organization and particularly the pharmaceuticals industries including the Bayer incident that I described earlier where one can give many ideas, but still become the first victim of discrimination on the basis of skin color or simply an African. Nevertheless, for a long lasting progressive world union, a united industrialization is eminently needed for safety purposes for everybody. That is about to be achieved with the given information and expansion on grass root ideas and the development of the text book of revolutionary development without necessarily injecting the Rosa Parks strategic overhauls on the re-definition of education that is in support of 2016 presidential Bernie Sanders call to be free or debt-free for all Americans.

CHAPTER X

WORLD ORDER ON CONTROLLED TRIBALISM AND PREJUDIZED CORRUPTION:

A world order attached with tribalism and racism is invalid and unworkable. It is either a tribal-blind or color-blind strategy for all people or remain in full-time disorders of conflict wars from generation to generation. That means no peace as there would be constant fears within and among all human species. That is why a few people like Bernie Sanders of the 2016 United States presidential race and others do talk about ridding America out of institutionalized racism and tribalism based on skin color, religion, and national origin. For a given system to work, it has to be controlled from some root source just like the human body system works under the pumping of the heart or the car moving dependent on the engine drive. Consequently, tribalism and its repercussions of which corruption is the most ruthless cannot thrive without an engine drive at some point whether we look at it from a social or scientific point of view or not. The root of such a drive shares the same basic origin as the Jua Kali roots described earlier. As much as Jua Kali cannot thrive without principled foundations as indicated earlier and so is tribalism. Tribalism used to be the order of the day during the ancient times and especially before the Christian age, but Christianity and other religions added a lot of impact towards its reduction until and through the beginning of industrial revolution. The beginning of industrial revolution was the major factor if not the only cause that took us back to the ancient times of official tribalism as slavery had to repeat itself once again based on race and ethnicity. While we do know that each tribe or ethnic group on the planet deserves the right to self-determination, Africa has been one of the most popular in terms of adverse effects of ethnicity. Africa has been hit so hard by ethnicity and to such an extent that a one-time tribal war in Rwanda caused close to one million deaths in a couple of weeks. That was quite instrumental towards a resolution for most Africans in terms of reviewing the prevailing methods of treatment and development without considering clan, tribe or ethnic identification.

For the past few years many leaders and scientists have been so concerned about the world peace which has been and will remain at risk so long as race and tribalism remain the basis of judgment. While religious organizations are performing great progress in preaching peace in daily communications, scientists are less concerned about ever inventing any devise or formula that can tackle the problem from the roots. However, it is the concern of the author of this book to test different types of any probable and available formulas with an intention of achieving a workable formula in the long run. The tribal proposed blind-formula mentioned earlier became so magnificent after launching in the beginning of the 21st century and was solely based on scientific principles. It has occurred into several people as the most workable in all progressive growth and development. It is therefore to the best interest of this book to elaborate fully on the formula and hence offer an attachment that is historically proven as to how it could eventually reduce if not cure the problem of ethnicity that stands as the main source of corruption in the world.

As far as the tribal blind formula is concerned, every kind of development in the world begins from simple substances that by collaborative partnerships of inter relations become more and more advanced to become reproducible elements and multiples of one another. The simple substances are described as seeds that are basically made of specific chemical or dust particles. The formula takes into account the fact that like in most life developments, an error can always occur to reduce the uniformity in any growth process. Tribalism in a diverse environment where all people are supposed to co-exist is one of such errors which dignify some psychological consequence that one ethnic group can take advantage on identity to molest another without any foreseeable cause or long lasting benefit. In such a context, long lasting means coming to this world and leaving without anything shortly.

Failure to understand this is one of the worst errors that has terrorized Africa and other developing countries either within itself as a continental body or by outsiders who often take advantage of the ignorance to offer empty unworkable formulas. In the circumstance that ignorance takes the center stage as often as it has happened in the last five hundred years, there is often big space created for the outsider to penetrate into the community leaders with an intention of awarding according to particular interests. Once an error is awarded according to interest other than reality, it has greater chances of increasing into multiple proportions where corruption is the main product making tribalism even worse. From this perspective, it is probably easy to recognize that corruption as we see it today has a root cause that is treatable if thoroughly considered and understood.

For any formula to be fruitful and reproducible, a proof is often very necessary to guide in the future feasibility in many related predictions. For the healing of inter-racial conflicts, the proposed tribal-blind formula that calls for closer examination of identity reclamation can be proven both scientifically and in historical theories with circumstantial evidence that is often physical in nature. While some people cannot understand the origin of the current ethnic groups, as we know them today from the historical point of view, it is generally accepted that the original parents spoke one tribal language and were actually one race that most people currently believe as black or African in nature based on evolutionary lines. However, sometime in history and according to written resources, the people were transformed by spiritual powers into the confusion of speaking the many languages as we see them today for which science cannot disapprove with an alternative explanation. This division in collaboration with the racial differences is the basic cause of worldwide crises and wars over the centuries and as much we see them today. From the scientific point of view, all human beings are 99% alike and have not the slightest idea as to the cause or evolution of different languages. It is the goal of this book to convince the concerned readers that the proposed tribal blind formula is partially based on the Pavlov's experiment in collaboration with the spiritual historical knowledge outlined above that reflects our ancestral lines of development where hearing a word can result in a physical or chemical change.

For the purpose of sharpening the healing patterns of the inter-racial healing, The following extract is an explanation from the Nigerian

Nobel prize winner in 1989 that was based on his invention for Super-computing that happens to be closely compatible to this publication.

According to the Nobel prize winner, Globalization or the ability of many people, ideas and technology to move from country to country is more of an old fact than a new one as many may tend to believe. In his narrative language he stated that in Africa, it was initiated by the slave trade and given impetus by colonialism and Christian missionaries. During that time the early missionaries saw African culture and religion as a deadly adversary and as an evil that had to be eliminated within the shortest time possible and by all available means. Thus, in 1876, a 27-year-old missionary named Mary Slessor decided to immigrate from Scotland to spend the rest of her life in Nigeria. That was the beginning of the elimination process that is still being expanded or opposed as of today. In that respect and for her efforts in trying to convert the people of Nigeria, Mary Slessor's photograph appeared on Scotland's ten pound note, and her name can be found on schools, hospitals and roads in Nigeria which most Africans still don't understand the mission behind it.

In the collective excerpt, the introduction to Mary Slessor's biography titled: "White Queen of the Cannibals" is quite revealing because it has a lot of impact on the Nigerian or more precisely the African culture while there may be some dilemma. Consequently, she states that on the west coast of Africa is the country of Nigeria which contains a lot of ethnic backgrounds that she felt were not real human enough to qualify into the class of light skinned people. She continued to state that the chief city of Nigeria is Calabar and that the country seemed to be very dark and backward because the light of the Gospel was not shining and had never shone brightly in that part of the world. While African or Black people live there many of them are cannibals who eat other people or at times their own children. Such an allegation seemed to have been extracted from local native citizens within the same ancestral lines without practically any physical evidence. Those around at that time were actually more familiar with some Africans often described as bad people according to the lady. She insisted and stressed that for truly they are bad because no one has told them about Jesus, the Lord and Savior of all people from all the sins of the world. Moreover, she said that no one had ever shown them the difference between right and what is wrong.

A lot of explorations that penetrated into Africa were designed for long-term accomplishments that are still affecting many operation systems in that continent. Consequently, the opening words in the above speech clearly indicated that the lady came to Africa on a mission to indoctrinate the continent with Christian theology and use it to further missions that could be invisible which is actually something related to what the Lord said in the Bible as "Not all who say Lord, Lord will enter the Lord's Kingdom". According to Emeagwali, the lady told them that they were a lost group of people because they didn't believe in the real God of all. She told them that they actually worshipped an inferior god and that they belonged to an inferior race among all the races of the world. While she did not offer any proof to support her claims or declarations, the lady worked extremely hard to dismantle what she described as "savagism" from the African indigenous culture and heritage so as to open the needed channels of expanding the European civilization to take root in Africa as planned over the centuries.

As mentioned earlier, most Africans who are currently very educated formally cannot actually find employment because of the basic racism outlined above and for which reason the current publication targets to explore and cultivate on the roots that can serve as the healing points of the inter-racial tensions in America and the whole world. However, as far as the current story confirms is that Emeagwali's country or continent ended up accepting the mission schools which were established to enlighten the society, without questioning the unforeseen costs of the so-called education and any attachment to the question of wisdom to determine the differences. It was quite amazing to learn that in those days the operating mission schools implanted something on the younger generations to the extent of believing that they could show them the real meaning of life which they assumed was absent among African groups. The intention or assumption was to boost their self-esteem by teaching them that, as Africans they were inherently stupid and bad people in general. Consequently, the underlying generation of young children grew up seeking for any available methods to turn white in skin complexion and not wanting to be citizens of the Africa continent. Instead, their education fostered the colonial ideal that they would be better off becoming citizens of the colonizing nations which is still the case we see today popular African singers like Lucky Dube could confirm.

In today's world a lot can be debated about education in relation to the inter-racial conflicts because an education that doesn't teach how the world can live together where we respect one another regardless of race, but by the content of character is worthless. That is because it will teach the old status quo where disasters are in a continuous motion and awaiting for a time to explode. Emeagwali spoke of the price Africans have paid and will probably keep paying for their education and "enlightenment" from his personal experience which he thinks will keep being seen unless stern measures are taken to change it in both theory and practice. It was kind of interesting that his issue on identity sounded somehow similar to my story that I clearly described while working at Kings county Hospital in New York City. Respectively, he stated that while he was born and named "Chukwurah," his missionary schoolteachers insisted that he had to drop his given name and be given an English name. The reasons given were amazing. As stated, the prefix "Chukwu" in his name represented the Igbo word for "God." However, as far as the case went the missionaries insisted that "Chukwurah" was a name befitting a godless pagan. The Catholic Church renamed Chukwurah as a "Philip," and Saint Philip became his patron and protector, replacing God, after whom he was named in order to proceed to the next level of education. The question that has not been answered till today is whether everybody who said education really meant education for enlightenment.

Part of the answer to the above question resides on the channel taken by emeagwali in his argument. Respectively, he had to argue that something more than a name or identity had been lost to fulfill other purposes. One major thing he thought is that something central to his heritage has been stripped away out of the African systems of operation and the consequences could be too damaging for many generations including the extinction of the related identities. Consequently, he concluded that the denial of the African past is the very antithesis of a good education as it is today and for which the proposed tribal-blind formula is being presented and for which Emeagwali may not be aware of as part of the main solution. Why is that considered a true fact by many professionals? Because our names represent not only our heritage, but connect us to our parents and past. As parents, the names we choose for our children reflect our dreams for their future and our perceptions of the treasures they represent to us.

As he continued to offer more explanation on colonialism and slavery defects that are still biting today, he reiterated that his indoctrination went far deeper than just a name. He was told to learn that the missionary school could teach about the saints making better role models than scientists in modern lives. Consequently, he had to learn and get lessons on how to write in a new language. The result was that he could be transformed because he became literate in English but remained illiterate in Igbo that was his native tongue. Emeagwali confirmed that he learned the Latin language which he would never use because he considered it a dead language. Even though he couldn't use it, he had to learn it because it was the official language of the Catholic Church and the Catholic Diocese is the one that owned all the schools that he attended from primary to secondary levels and even sponsorship to colleges and universities.

While Africa has been fighting to formulate their own official African language, some obstacles still exist that prevent that idea from full implementation on any proposal. Yet Lugha Ya Kiswahili was voted to become the official African language at around 2004 in the new millennium. However, today there are more French speakers in Africa than there are in France. There are more English speakers in Nigeria than there are in the United Kingdom. There are more Portuguese speakers in Mozambique than there are in Portugal. What is the meaning of all this if bright think tanks can pose the question with honesty? The Organization of African Unity never approved an African language as one of its official languages until the 2004 after a long time of reckless leadership.

In the given respect, we won the first battle of decolonizing our continent in the given political perspective in addition to the voted official African language, but we lost the war on decolonizing our minds if we let our mother tongue languages to become extinct. Many acknowledge that globalization shapes the future, but few acknowledge that it shaped history, or at least the world's perception of it which continues to evolve. Fewer acknowledge that globalization is a two-way street. Africa was a colony, but it is also a key contributor to many other cultures, and the cornerstone of today's society. The question is whether the current education for which we still dearly pay a lot of money will ever be collectively fruitful to heal the inter-racial tensions that are still quietly destroying Africans wherever they are because of discrimination and racism.

When people are totally colonized they really get despised in every situation because the suppressor believes that the slave is their right to own and for keeps in all aspects of life. Thus, the world's views tend to overshadow and dismiss the value and aspirations of colonized people from generation to generation until or unless the error is corrected as with the proposed tribal-blind formula. According to his narration, Emeagwali confirmed that he grew up serving as an altar boy to an Irish priest because he wanted to become a priest, but ended up becoming a scientist. Like Emeagwali, I onetime wanted to become a pastor and that is why I ended up preaching for 10 years as an assistant to my deceased Pastor even though not officially ordained in the traditional methods and capacity. Accordingly, he strongly agrees to the facts that religion is based on faith, while science is based on fact and reason. In the given regard as much as it is for human lives it is true that science is neutral to race by physical measurement and validation. However, it is unfortunate that many scientists are not neutral to race even though the biology of human beings is 99% similar. That is probably one disqualification mark on many and such like scientists wherever they may happen to be.

In consideration, let us take, for example, the origin of AIDS, an international disease that was greatly politicized in the early 1980s. According to scientific records, the first person to die from AIDS was a 25-year-old sailor named David Carr, of Manchester, England. The records revealed that Carr died on August 31, 1959, and because the disease that killed him was then unknown, his tissue samples were saved for future analysis. The "unknown disease" that killed David Carr was reported in *The Lancet* on October 29, 1960. On July 7, 1990, *The Lancet* then preceded on to retest those old tissue samples that were taken from David Carr and re-confirmed that he had died of the Human Immuno-Defieciency Virus. That was amazing and a blessing to the facts of science in the scientific field. Based upon scientific reason with respect to the given evidence, researchers should have concluded that the AIDS virus originated in England, and that David Carr sailed to Africa where he spread the AIDS virus with or without prior knowledge of the future consequences. That should have ended the debate as to how or when the virus was created and for what purpose. The future consequences confirmed that the virus was like a biological weapon for which anybody could be a launcher, but everybody was vulnerable or remained a target. Instead, some racist scientific community condemned the British authors because of those revealing articles for down-grading the great nation by proposing that an Englishman was the first known AIDS patient and not an African as they wanted it be known. While it is definitely not something that requires a lot of intelligence to envision we do reckon that it is something which needs to be corrected if the healing tensions on inter-racial factors are yet to be realized. The big question then is to question the global scientific community on safety and efficacy according to the federal regulations of the world or the International Center for Harmonization.

If these scientists were neutral to race and ready to answer the above question, their data should have led them to the conclusion that Patient Zero lived in England. If these scientists were neutral to race, they should have concluded that AIDS had spread from England to Africa, to Asia, and to America and not vice versa. Instead, they proposed the theory that AIDS originated in Africa and made sure all African Americans and the whole world race of Africans believed that propaganda education to downgrade the target as projected. That is why Africans need to develop their own theories and write them in their own languages whether they are recognized elsewhere outside or not.

It is a well-known fact that most historical books and textbooks are published by non-Africans and have actually taken the responsibility to degrade the African roots and civilization. That is why Universities like Capella could downgrade a student who tries to study anything to do with racist studies into re-inventing the wheel on the educational politics of establishment or focusing on exploring African culture and with extreme fury. It is one of the worst kind of institutionalized racism in the Hitler scale perspective and more or less the same way that the Zimbabwean President, Robert Mugabe displays it or will not want to hear such a thing as a reflection, but opposite in direction. For instance, many Africans go to Europe or to the United States and learn a history filtered through the eyes of non-African historians. More so they learn history filtered through the eyes of France, Belgium, England, German, or Hollywood movie producers. A few of the Africans concerned about such trajectories have complained that Hollywood is sending its distorted message around this globalized world to the extent that the raised complaints stood the base of confirming that Hollywood is a cultural propaganda machine used to advance racial supremacy. In contrast, former US president George Bush understood that Hollywood was a propaganda machine that could be used in his war against terrorism. Consequently and within a short time after the 9/11 bombing of New York City in 2001, Bush invited Hollywood moguls to the White House and solicited their support in his war against terrorism that eventually led to the propaganda war on weapons of mass destruction that were non-existent.

With the above example given about Capella propaganda on education, some have come to believe with a little argument that schools actually play a significant role as federal indoctrination centers used to convince children during their formative years that whites are superior to Africans or other races altogether. As a consequence, Fela Kuti, went on to detest indoctrination, and entitled one of his musical albums as the "Teacher Don't Teach Me Nonsense." Emeagwali confirms that while a lot of initiatives are being taken to correct the situation a lot is still desired and it scares him when he finds that an entire generation of African children is growing up brainwashed by Hollywood's interpretation and promotion of American heroes. The African children are continually getting lost because they are growing up idolizing American heroes with whom they cannot personally identify and will never do to enlighten them for the healing of the inter-racial tensions around the world and particularly in America.

Like many people have come to discover through discovery and deep gains in wisdom it has become true that we should tell our children our own stories from our own perspective for real education to start working for beneficial purposes. Thus, as mentioned earlier, we need to decolonize our identity on the basis of the proposed tribal-blind formula and hence our minds, and our thinking and examine the underlying truths in more than just movies. We need to apply the same principles to history and science, as depicted in textbooks for the betterment of African lives and from generation to generation.

Many Africans always ask the question as to why somebody else from a foreign country had to write our history and yet Africa was endowed with scientists and historians who are confirmed to be the fathers of modern civilization. For instance, we can look at the African science stories that were retold by European historians and begin asking ourselves even more questions such as why they say that John Rebman discovered Mount Kenya. Our African science was re-centered around Europe and manipulated to fit certain personal European interests. However, we do know that the earliest pioneers of science lived in Africa and then later European historians relocated them to Greece for the strategic manipulation. A plain fact is that science and technology are gifts ancient Africa gave to our modern world even though that fact is still being suppressed for selfish gains. Yet, the currently utilized history and science textbooks published by Europeans have ignored the contributions of such famous and popular people like Imhotep who is known as the father of medicine and designer of one of the ancient pyramids recognized all over the world as tourist attractions.

To attain an education that will contribute towards the healing of interracial tensions that are less likely to end, we must familiarize ourselves with certain important phrases. For instance, the word "science" is derived from the Latin word *"scientia"* or "possession of knowledge." That is besides the policy of talking and teaching wisdom. However, we are well aware that knowledge is not the exclusive property of one or a few races, but of all mankind as civilization started in very remote areas. By definition, knowledge is the sum of everything that every person can see and assess or more precisely all of what is known to humanity. Thus, it imperative to conclude that knowledge is a body of information and truth, and the set of principles acquired by mankind over the ages past or for years to come and in all generations in existence.

Public policy cannot be well developed with fairness unless most people are made aware of what education is important to their lives and what real knowledge calls for from elementary to university levels especially the one based on identity and co-existence. In essence, knowledge is like a quilt of feathers held together by a strong bond. It is like akin to a quilt where the latter consists of several layers held together by stitched designs and comprising patches of many colors like a rainbow which the Reverend Jesse Jackson utilized as name for his foundation of Rainbow Coalition. In that respect, it is revealed that the oldest patch on the quilt of science belongs to the African named Imhotep or more precisely the father of modern medicine in mankind civilization. Imhotep was the world's first recorded scientist, according to the prolific American science writer Isaac Asimov. Respectively, the oldest patch on the quilt of mathematics belongs to another African named Ahmes. Isaac Asimov also credited Ahmes as being the world's first author of a mathematics textbook that is being suppressed by tribalism and racism against Africans for selfish interests.

Therefore, the main and sole purpose of education is to understand the importance of history and science. In that respect, a study of history of science is an effort to stitch together a quilt that has life, texture and color just as history is itself the record keeping of world events. Consequently, African historians must insert the patches of information omitted from all the educational books written by European historians to accomplish the healing of inter-racial healing according to this publication. There are many examples of the mark Africans have made on world history, but there is just too much suppressed because of tribalism and racism and which should come into the light of the young and future generations for the respective healing of inter-racial hope.

According to many African scientists it is fascinating what kind of reactions we encounter when we try to tell the hidden side of the true stories of Africa. For instance Americans were very much surprised when Emeagwali told them that it was the Africans who built both Washington's White House and Capitol Hill as we see them today. From the written records and according to the US Treasury Department, 450 of the 650 workers who built the White House and the Capitol Hill were African slaves. That is something they should have been taught in elementary level of school work because the White House and the Capitol Hill are the two most visible symbols of American democracy. Thus, it is important to inform all schoolchildren in our globalized world that these institutions are the results of the sweat and toil of mostly African workers whose race is still being despised while America takes the pride it displays. This must also be an acknowledgement of the debt America owes Africa that should be utilized as the bargaining power for equality instead of qualifying slavery or employment discrimination as the suppressor's way forward. That is besides the reparation debate that some leaders try to talk about.

In view of the above information we do agree that the idea of reparations is still being encountered or debated to compensate those who were victimized because they were either too kind or were simply suppressed. Similarly, discussions of globalization should credit those Africans who left the continent and helped build other nations throughout the world as the Africans did to most nations on Earth.

Africans who have made contributions in Australia, in Russia, and in Europe must be acknowledged so our children can have heroes with African roots. In doing so the children could now understand what the real education is valid because they can know their own roots and be proud of them other than keep feeling like second class citizens.

As part of the solutions towards the healing of inter-racial tensions in America and many countries around the world, it is true that the enormous contributions of Africans to the development and progress of other nations has gone unacknowledged. That is because we have yet to acknowledge, for example, that St. Augustine, who wrote the greatest spiritual autobiography of all time, so called "Confessions of St. Augustine," was an African. It is very true that three Africans became pope and that Africans have lived in Europe since the time of the Roman Empire where a man by the name Septimus Severus, that was an Emperor of Rome, was in fact an African while it is also revealed that the reason Beethoven was called "The Black Spaniard" was because he was a mulatto of African descent. This sounds too much to accept by a modern racist, but it is the art of what it could take to begin resolving the inter-racial tensions of America to be part of the solution or remain part of the problem. We cannot stay as reluctant as we have been on acknowledging the contributions and legacies of our African ancestors because if you don't know where you are coming from you cannot know where to go. Consequently, we cannot inspire our children to look toward the future with pride and confidence unless they are taught and reminded about their ancestral backgrounds and the respective contributions in all matters that pertain to the current living conditions and global development.

When we remember Africa, we frequently focus on recent South Africa and former President Nelson Mandela because of the struggle of apartheid which many considered to be more torturous than slavery. However, when we look at the long struggle of African Australians, we find that they it was just recently that they became citizens with rights on their native continent. That is insane because how can that be the case in your own native land just like Mandela in South Africa when history confirms that Africans have been living in Australia for 50,000 years. Yet, African Australians were granted Australian citizenship just 42 years ago, in 1967 by the stranger to that land who actually self-ordained himself to be the new owner with authority to give citizenship.

In the given argument and with respect to the *CNN News*, African Australians were not recognized as human beings prior to 1967. They "were governed under flora and fauna laws." African Australians were, in essence, governed by plant and animal laws. For many years, African Australians were described as the "invisible people." In fact, the first whites to settle in Australia named it the "land empty of people." As much as Bernie Sanders could call for the establishment of more mental clinics in the 2016 United states presidential race it is definitely true that that was as insane as it could go.

We must expose all the African histories that are still hidden and suppressed. For instance, the contributions of Africans to Russia must be reclaimed with clear elaboration. In that perspective, it comes out that Russia's most celebrated author, A.S.(Aleksandr Sergeyevich) Pushkin, was actually of African descent and we should all be shocked as much as knowing that Pushkin's great-grandfather was brought to Russia as a slave. Russians proclaim Pushkin as their "national poet," the "patriarch of Russian literature" and the "Father of the Russian language." In essence, Pushkin is to Russia what Shakespeare is to Britain. Yet Africans who have read the complete works of Shakespeare are not likely to have read a single book by Pushkin because of colonialism and slavery in education suppression as mentioned earlier.

When we look at African scientists we acknowledge that racism is just a cruel ugly substance of containment that the oppressor utilizes in all phases of life to enhance it forever in greed and selfishness for wealth accumulation that will never be enough. Thus, according to Emeagwali, the journey of discovery to his supercomputer was a titanic, one-man struggle. He says that it was like climbing Mount Everest where on many occasions he felt like giving up because he was traumatized by the racism that he had encountered in science. However, he maintained a self-imposed silence on the supercomputer discovery that stands as the base for his claim to fame or the most intelligent scientist in history.

The superiority of African Scientists cannot be over-emphasized because Emeagwali reveals that he had was well equipped with a supercomputing insight that even the experts in his field did not know then and do not know now. According to his story, he reveals that in the 1980s, supercomputers could perform only millions of calculations per second and, therefore, their timers were designed to measure only millions of calculations per second. However, he was performing billions of calculations per second and unknowingly attempting to time it with a supercomputer timer, which was designed to measure millions of calculations per second. He did that because he assumed that his timer could measure one-billionth of a second. It took him two years to realize that his timer was off a thousand-fold but could not prove it to the world of racism and full of inter-racial tensions that kept knocking him down. However, he was operating beyond a supercomputer' s limitations, but he did not know it. The supercomputer designers did not expect their timers to be used to measure calculations at that rate. He almost gave up because he could not time and reproduce his calculations which, in turn, meant he could not share them, two years earlier, with the world. That happens with a lot of African scientists including myself and many others in various scientific fields of research.

Like many African scientists who are suppressed because of racism Emeagwali continued through several years of research, because the supercomputer' s timer was the only thing that stopped him from getting the recognition he had worked for and very well deserved. When he found that the timer was wrong, but without explanation, he spent two years mulling over why the timer was wrong and what it could probably take to fix it. It took two long and lonely years to discover why he could not time his calculations. His supercomputer's 3.1 billion calculations per second, which were then the world's fastest, were simply too fast for the supercomputer's timer. That was the beginning of the new invention that changed the world towards the development of internet as we know it today.

What do we learn from the above experience on racism and the healing of inter-racial tensions in America or the world at large? From the above story we do learn that when faced with racism the immediate priority is not to quit, but to persevere. In actuality, quitting is not an option when faced with an insurmountable obstacle as described and that believing in oneself makes all the difference in the world. Do the Africans believe in themselves as such? It is good to learn on how to take a step backward and evaluate the options that can transform oneself to a better destination in terms of whether to go through, above, under, or around the obstacle because quitting is the worst option. Many life experiences confirm that the old saying is correct as is states that when the going gets tough it is actually the tough get going and the prospects are always positive in eventuality. That is because in many a time we do learn that most limitations in life are imposed by some enemy like the devil or self-imposed at times. You have to make things happen, not just watch things happen. To succeed, you must constantly reject complacency. On the basis of the above story we do learn that we can actually set high objectives and goals and achieve them if we insist to do so.

From the age of ten years I have always had the same dream of achieving and contributing to the world as in the writing of this book, but racism and discrimination in general has presented the greatest hindrance. However, I have never been satisfied with my achievements especially in the subject of healthcare and medical sciences in general without publishing a book and one with all the contents herewith. The secret to my success is that I am constantly striving for continuous improvements in my life and that I am never satisfied with my achievements. The myth that a genius must have above-average intelligence is just that, a myth. Geniuses are people who learn to create their own positive reinforcements when their experiments yield negative results. Perseverance is the key and even freedom fighters never give up if they know they are fighting for justice and peace in and for the world.

While I have always believed that good health is the greatest blessing, I have also kept asking myself questions that cannot be answered by anybody in the world except God. That is why I still believe that any disease is treatable and even curable if scientists and politicians can put that goal first before the selfish gains of money and suppression based on race and tribe. My goal has always been to go beyond the known, to a territory no one has ever reached. I learned that if you want success badly enough and believe in yourself, then you can attain your goals and become anything you want in life. The greatest challenge in one's life is to look deep within him or her to see the greatness that is destined inside the person as well as those that relate to you in a given environment. So far the history books have depicted Africans of all or any greatness that might have existed in generations past, but even though the history books may deprive African children of the heroes with whom they can identify, they can still take a different course to attain their own goals and become that hero they dream about for themselves and other Africans.

As the old saying goes, experience is the best teacher, but I heard from the 1992 United States Presidential debate between Bill Clinton and George Bush when Clinton told former President Bush that even though that may be true, it is not everything. According to Emeagwali, he once believed that supercomputer discovery was more important than the journey or experience that got him there. However, like Bill Clinton he came to agree that he later understood that the journey to discovery is more important than the discovery itself and that the journey actually requires a belief in your own abilities. Just like me, he learned that no matter how often you fall down, or how hard you fall down, what is most important is your nature of absorbing the pain like the shock absorbers of a vehicle that can make you to rise up again and continue until you reach your final goal or destination. While it is important and good to be recognized, we have to remember as Emeagwali said that a racist person or institution like Capella University mentioned earlier will never do so for fear of losing their greed and selfish interests to a wrong hero or African based on tribe and inter-racial tensions that need to healed by reading this book. Thus, Emeagwali agreed that it is true, some heroes are never recognized, but what's important is that they recognize themselves and something Africans should start doing broadly to recover the destructive belief of slave mentality. That is part of the foundation solutions towards the healing of inter-racial tensions in America.

Nevertheless, the best message that can be extracted from this chapter is that inter-racial tensions in America are rooted in slavery, slave trade and colonialism that are institutionalized in the mindset of Africans. Consequently, the real healing has to start with the correction of the mindset through the proposed tribal-blind formula and implementation on the decolonization of the identity and the mind. While that may be costly, the costs are too minute in comparison to the price the Africans are paying for education in the world and yet not developing them in the right ways in terms of employment or infrastructure. It is that belief in thyself, that focus, and that inner conviction that Africans are on the right path, that will get them through life's obstacles. If they can give their children pride in their past and work on the above factors based on the proposed tribal-blind formula, then we can show them what they can be useful and hence give them the self-respect that will make them succeed for the betterment of future generations and the healing of inter-racial tensions.

CHAPTER XI

WORLD ORDER BY UNIVERSAL HEALTHCARE

Strategic Management of World Health Care Financial Systems.

When a politician talks about Universal health care in the United States of America, it scares a lot of greed people who may in turn go around to name such a person as a socialist. That happened on President Baraka Obama and currently is happening on the 2016 Presidential candidate Bernie Sanders. The truth is that a new world order may not be possible without a world health organization agreement on how it can be financed and afforded by everybody so as to heal the inter-racial tensions especially in America. If it has worked in next door Canada and some like Germany, it will work in the United States too if the leadership is truly working for its people without any fears of who will reimburse who on the final billing or where Bernie Sanders will get money to finance it with a debt-free education that he proposes for all Americans. Health care usually focuses on financial reimbursements as determined by money ownership and opportunity which have generated a lot of debates in the recent health reform policy developments than any other time in the United States history. It is a big factor in the new world order determination based on the roots of diversity and culture because all human beings respond well to a health security dictated by health insurance. This analysis is based on the principle of reimbursements as impacted by health literacy and cultural competency for organizational development within the minorities and the immigrants in the health policy reform processes. In terms of the past half of the last century of health reforms, no other study has superseded the financial impacts of policy developments as displayed by the cases with the health insurance reforms particularly in the developed countries. Most of those impacts studied have been experienced within the frequently emerging health care conditions within the chronically ill that require critical and immediate attention. While the impacts of many of those studies are felt in daily practices, not much has been done in terms of analyzing the effects of the disparity financial implications among certain groups of people and particularly the minorities. The impacts of trickle-down economics as the usual description goes and particularly within the minorities and immigrants display there is a tendency to serve as a special interest and a favorite example for comparative purposes and other healthcare analyses. Consequently, an evaluation of such impacts could be the prime objective of this analysis in both theory and the practical perspectives.

The most interesting feature in the underlying analysis is very much based on the recent health insurance arguments targeting those patients who cannot finance their healthcare services as they are delivered. For the past few years health insurance has been greatly impacted by health care reform policies in financial development that can deal with reimbursement issues for the related or the directly delivered services in the current health care administration. While the current politics are basically fueled by the debates on health insurance reform policies, health insurance is still a challenge or popular issue in health delivery and one of the most controversial and outstanding dilemmas in the much needed universal healthcare policy development in history. Even though many people may not be in agreement, it is true that it is motivated by the health literacy and cultural competency factors as highlighted by the quill of immigrants. The capacity of those two factors or related features along with the determination of how proper transparency on accountability and validation of the coverage issues in the medical care tend to be incorporated into the respective administrative services seem to be the most significant and ignored. Most health care providers who lack cultural competency may be putting several patients at risk of examination delays and appropriate treatment, inappropriate diagnoses, failure to abide by the compliance rules with health care prescriptions and appointments, and even death. I have encountered many cases including my own father who is my daily patient that support regular complaints from several community patients. Such experiences have shown that provider patient communication is linked to patient well-being or satisfaction, adherence to medical instructions, and health outcomes in all groups of people. On the same account poorer health outcomes may result when the ethnic or socio-cultural differences between patients and providers are not well dialogued for proper reconciliation in the common community and clinical interactions. In that perspective of ethnic differences, the impacts of health literacy and cultural competency have been the most challenging in patient satisfaction. It is the basis of the actual factor that surrounds the healing point of inter-racial tensions in the healthcare industrial development and particularly within the African immigrant context for which a resolution gap still sticks. Among the public health associations, the daily political communications have long supported principles of workplace diversity fairness, including equity, parity and non-discrimination without disparities in healthcare. However, it is found that only a few have actually walked the common talk that Bernie Sanders points to as a crucial factor in American democracy. It is also true that a few professionals in other health and mental health disciplines, including psychology and social work, have taken that one step further by declaring strong positions against racism and racial discrimination in all classes of life in support of the ideology of universal healthcare.

It is not well known and as to how deep cultural competency and health literacy factors or values affect immigrant health insurance and yet lack of specific structural components in those factors is still a healthcare systemic perception in controversy. That is part of the reason why immigration politics is a big factor in the 2016 presidential elections. The purpose of this analysis is to evaluate the severity and recovery extent among the minorities and immigrants within the reimbursement strategies in the medical paradigm and hence create room towards the possibility of a linear controversial settlement in issue. Previous research in health literacy and the role of culture include achievement values and socio-economic status which is the basis of the reimbursement programs or models in healthcare.

According to the American Medical Association, poor health literacy is a stronger predictor of a person's health than age, income, employment status, education level, and race. That seems to be a true scenario in cultural competency along several studies. Some of the relevant literacy reports are based on the Council of Scientific Affairs, Committee on Health Literacy for the Council on Scientific Affairs. In an initiative to a prescription to end confusion, the Institute of Medicine reports that ninety million people in the United States, nearly half the population, have difficulty understanding and using health information. As a result, patients often take medicines on erratic schedules, miss follow-up appointments, and do not understand instructions like "take on an empty stomach". The results of the 1992 Adult Literacy Survey (National Center for Education Statistics, US Department of Education) indicate that adults with low literacy were more likely than those with higher literacy levels to be poor and to have health conditions which limit their activities. There are both direct and indirect consequences of low health literacy. The direct effects include non-compliance or medication errors. The indirect effects are harder to measure, but may include reimbursement issues, accessibility to health care and poor health behavior choices. According to the Report on the Council of Scientific Affairs, Committee on Health Literacy for the Council on Scientific Affairs, American Medical Association, it is the minority groups with the highest prevalence of chronic disease and the greatest need for health care who have the least ability to read and comprehend information needed to function as patients.

As health care payers continue to search for ways to curtail health care costs, information on how reimbursement reductions affect quality of care will be exceedingly important. The current healthcare insurance debates are based on the inclusion or exclusion of minorities in terms of reimbursement strategies related to the recent bill of the Affordable Care Act of 2010. While there are several types of minorities in the current perspective, the main focus has been mainly directed on the African Americans who have the highest numbers of chronically related disorders like diabetes. The rationale of this reimbursement analysis is based on several studies in literature that assess the related health literacy factors as well as the cultural competency in that perspective.

According to various studies, African Americans are almost twice as likely to have diabetes as white Americans of similar age and approximately 14.7% of African Americans over age 20 years have diabetes compared to 9.8% of non-Hispanic American Whites. The prevalence of diabetes in African Americans has increased dramatically in recent times where Type 2 diabetes is the most prevalent type of diabetes in African Americans accounting for 90 to 95% of all cases. In the same notation, African Americans have higher incidence of and greater disability from diabetes complications than white Americans with death rates for people with diabetes being 20-40 percent higher in African Americans compared with white counterparts. Thus, evidence indicates that diabetes is a significant public health problem; and African Americans appear disproportionately burdened with the complications and disability that result from poorly treated diabetes due to lack of definitive reimbursement programs.

In a more recent study, national trends in processes of care and intermediate outcomes for diabetes between 1988-1994 and 1999-2002 were compared using national data in order to determine trend and offer proposals for the much needed solutions. The study showed that although diabetes processes of care and intermediate outcomes have improved nationally, 1 in 3 persons still have poor blood pressure control, and 1 in 5 persons still have poor glycemic control. Ethnic minority patients (including African Americans) had poorer improvements in glycemic and blood pressure control over the study period which are factorial in reimbursement activities.

While reimbursement factors are believed to be first hand features in chronic diseases, several reasons contribute to poor chronic or diabetes outcomes in African Americans. These include actors at the patient, provider, and health systemic levels. Patient level factors include poor diabetes-specific knowledge, negative belief and attitudes about diabetes, lack of self-management skills, and non-adherence to lifestyle behaviors. Other factors include mismatch of patient and physician expectations, differential socioeconomic levels that impede physician-patient communication, and distrust of physicians that may decrease adherence. Language barriers and low literacy rates also impede physician-patient communication. Other important patient level factors include lack of a locus of control and fatalism. Provider level factors include negative beliefs and attitudes about diabetes, perceived complexity and difficulty of treating diabetes, lack of adequate time and resources for diabetes treatment and clinical inertia. Health systems factors include accessibility, availability and convenience of appointments, organization of care, and availability of interpreters, health insurance coverage, reimbursement levels, and formulary restrictions.

While provider and health system level factors are important for improved glycemic control, they explain less than 10% of variance in diabetes outcomes including glycemic control, lipid control, and resource use or cost. Most of the variation in diabetes outcomes is due to patient level factors. Of the patient level factors, consistent differences between African Americans and American Whites with Type 2 Diabetes Mellitus (T2DB) have been found in diabetes knowledge, self-management skills, empowerment, and perceived control among most disorders.

One aim of this type of analysis is to achieve economic gains by taking advantage of economies of scale and scope (especially with regard to management costs) and as a result of rationalizing the provision of services. It is also argued that trusts with a single focus can provide higher quality services. Other publicly stated reasons include the investment of savings into services for patients, safeguarding specialist units, and ensuring that quality and amount of services provided were maintained.

It is not absolutely clear as to how extensive the analysis of the impacts of health literacy and cultural competency can contribute towards the future of the reimbursement programs on insurance policy reforms, but the proposed Universal healthcare ideology of Bernie Sanders in 2016 presidential race seems to hint on how to deal with the problem. At the peak of the health care debates of Affordable Care Act, the impacts are better pronounced within the minorities and the immigrants in America. The suspected burden that undocumented immigrants may place on the U.S. health care system has been a flashpoint in health care and immigration reform debates. That is why many Americans believe on the idea of creating a path towards citizenship for all undocumented aliens. An examination of health care spending during 1999–2006 for adult naturalized citizens and immigrant noncitizens which included some undocumented immigrants found that the cost of providing health care to immigrants was lower than that of providing care to U.S. natives and that immigrants are not contributing disproportionately to high health care costs in public programs such as Medicaid. However, noncitizen immigrants were found to be more likely than U.S. natives to have a health care visit classified as uncompensated care. Thus, to deepen such an understanding and fill any prevailing gap, the impact of such classifications and their consequences on health insurance policy reforms is highly recommended for analysis. In that respect, the approach to analyze the recommended idea and other related studies is quite imperative for further understanding of reimbursement or insurance issues and hence universal healthcare development.

One of the most outstanding dilemmas in the universal healthcare policy development on the reimbursement programs is the determination of the fair financial accountability and validation of the coverage issues in the medical care as well as their incorporations into the related administrative services. Previous research has shown that provider patient communication is linked to patient satisfaction, adherence to medical instructions, and health outcomes. On the same account financially poorer related health outcomes may result when socio-cultural differences between patients and providers are not reconciled in the clinical encounter. In that perspective, the impacts of health literacy and cultural competency have been the most challenging in the healthcare reimbursement analyses in industrial development and particularly within the minority context. Among the public health associations, the American Psychiatric Association has long supported principles of fairness, including equity, parity and non-discrimination.

While healthcare organizational development has not been well unified, the developed nations keep displaying a lack of competence and strategically effective concepts on the reimbursement issues in the healthcare industry. Competence can broadly be defined as a concept that incorporates a variety of domains including knowledge, skills and attitudes. Health professionals may demonstrate overall competence in their relevant discipline via a four step process including; (1) knowledge, (2) competence (specific to the task), (3) performance, and (4) action. Apart from knowledge, skills and attitudes, competence also incorporates a health professional's problem solving skills such as the ability to critically think and apply clinical reasoning and ability to work as a team member and communicate effectively, both in a written and verbal format. Assessing competences can focus on any one of these domains. Consequently, many countries like the European countries, Australia, and Canada use cost-effectiveness analysis to decide which health technologies to provide, but the United States policy makers do not routinely use cost-effectiveness analysis to set health care priorities. That is why it is still struggling to determine the way forward and as to how universal healthcare can be accomplished in development and hence the healing of inter-racial tensions of hope. One concern is that many studies in healthcare still use the cost-consequence approach and report costs and effectiveness separately. Those partial evaluations do not provide decision makers with information on any trade-offs between costs and outcomes. Methods are available that provide cost-effectiveness estimates appropriate for use in policy making. Some reports illustrate how appropriate cost-effectiveness analysis techniques can be applied to evaluate a health service intervention using a case study comparing reimbursement models for mental health care. A new technique called genetic matching is used to adjust for baseline differences in patient mix across the intervention groups. Genetic matching is more appropriate than alternatives such as model-based adjustment, as it does not rely on parametric assumptions that are implausible in this context. Some of these studies recently reported that reimbursement by capitation was associated with lower costs compared with fee for service. Other studies found that capitation was associated with worse quality of care. None of these studies combined costs and effectiveness in a formal cost-effectiveness analysis version.

In retrospect, the cost-effectiveness analysis found that the capitation model with the for-profit component was the most cost-effective at all levels of willingness to pay for a what is gained. Respectively, the cost-effectiveness analysis incorporated any differences in both costs and outcomes across the reimbursement models, and therefore extended previous cost minimization analyses that have focused on the relative costs of managed care compared with the terms fee for service. The cost-effectiveness analysis used appropriate techniques to measure and value outcomes, to deal with baseline imbalances across the groups and to allow for the skewed distribution of the cost data. The techniques presented could be used more generally for evaluating different ways of financing and providing health services where there may be differential impacts on costs and outcomes and where the needed data are unavailable. A previous study revealed that cost results from the project found that both the not-for-profit capitation model and the capitation model with a for-profit element were associated with cost reductions compared with Fee for Service methods. In that report the study illustrated that cost-effectiveness analysis can provide clear information on the relative cost-effectiveness of alternative reimbursement methods. Methodological guidance for economic evaluation requires that authors place appropriate limits on the generalizability of their results. It is therefore important to recognize that the finding that a capitation model with a for-profit element was more cost-effective than a not-for-profit capitation model may not be transferable to other health care contexts. When capitation was introduced for Colorado Medicaid mental health services, the state took steps to try and maintain service quality.

Determinant turning point of hope still reside in more studies including some which found that the only difference in pharmaceutical costs was that the Capitation Model group uses more antipsychotic dedication compared with Fee for Service methods. Hence, including these costs would further substantiate the conclusion that the model would not cost-effective. Of greater concern is the relatively short time frame adopted. While a follow-up study found that the Capitation models and other reports had similar costs after 6 years, further research is required to evaluate the long- term cost-effectiveness of different reimbursement mechanisms using the techniques outlined. The cost-effectiveness analysis offers highlights on trade-offs between costs and outcomes, allowing policy makers with differing views on the relative importance of costs versus outcomes to use the same analysis. Accordingly, it seems that a capitation model with a for-profit element may be more cost-effective than either a not-for-profit capitation or an fee for service model for Medicaid patients with severe mental illness. These techniques can be applied to a wide range of contexts in health services research, to help policy makers identify which health care programs to prioritize for better reimbursement processes.

For the past several decades the delivery of health care has been mainly implicated on the account of the effectiveness of cost control and public policy reimbursement procedures. Due to the dilemma that is currently encountered in the Affordable Care Act reform of 2010, it is imperative to consider other successful delivery systems around the world as lessons or working ethical examples on the basis of culture and health literacy skills. Thus, the French delivery system offers a precise analytical comparison in the current evaluation that seems to be highly cultured with comprehensive literacy in perspective. The French health care system seems to be a good example of the given scenario. Over the past 3 decades, successive governments have tinkered with health care reform; the most comprehensive plan was Prime Minister Juppé's in 1996 and beyond. Since then, whether governments were on the political left or right, they have pursued cost control policies without reforming the overall management and organization of the health system.

Respective analysis reveals that even though the French ideal is now subject to more critical scrutiny by politicians, the system functions well and remains an important model for the United States. After more than a half century of struggle, at around the year 2000, France covered the remaining 1% of its population that was and offered supplementary coverage to 8% of its population below an income ceiling. This extension of health insurance makes France an interesting case on how to ensure universal coverage through incremental reform while maintaining a sustainable system that limits perceptions of health care rationing and restrictions on patient choice. Following an overview of the system and an assessment of its achievements, problems, and reform, this article explores lessons for the United States out of the French experience with NHI for the development of universal health insurance.

The French National Health Insurance evolved from a 19th-century tradition of mutual aid societies to a post-World War II system of local democratic management by "social partners" trade unions and employer representatives, but it is increasingly controlled by the French state. In that respect, National Health Insurance consists of different plans for different occupational groups all of which operate within a common statutory framework. Health insurance is compulsory; no one may opt out. Health insurance funds are not permitted to compete by lowering health insurance premiums or attempting to micromanage health care. For ambulatory care, all health insurance plans operate on the traditional indemnity model reimbursement for services rendered. For inpatient hospital services, there are budgetary allocations as well as per diem reimbursements. The French indemnity model allows for direct payment by patients to physicians, coinsurance, and balance billing by roughly one third of physicians.

Like Medicare in the United States, French National Health Insurance provides a great degree of patient choice. Unlike Medicare, however, French National Health Insurance coverage increases as individual costs rise, there are no deductibles, and pharmaceutical benefits are extensive. In contrast to Medicaid, French National Health Insurance carries no stigma and provides better access. In summary, French National Health Insurance is more generous than what a "Medicare for all" system would be like in the United States, and it shares a range of characteristics with which Americans are well acquainted fee-for-service practice, a public–private mix in the financing and organization of health care services, cost sharing, and supplementary private insurance.

The health literacy and cultural competency has been part of the delivery system in the given policy. Thus, the French tolerance for organizational diversity, whether it be complementary, competitive, or both, is typically justified on grounds of pluralism. Although ambulatory care is dominated by office-based solo practice, there are also private group practices, health centers, occupational health services in large enterprises and a strong public sector program for maternal and child health care. Likewise, although hospital care is dominated by public hospitals, including teaching institutions with a quasi-monopoly on medical education and research, there are, nevertheless, opportunities for physicians in private practice who wish to have part-time hospital staff privileges in public hospital*s*.

The foremost theoretical considerations in reimbursement analysis include those pertaining to the policy process in health promotion with respect to research which can be extended to the universal insurance developments within the looming minority disparities. Likewise, the literal use of 'critical theory' as an intention to describe any theory founded upon health needs, it explains why injustice and disparities in healthcare are based on economic status quo structural features in the underlying applicable spectrum. According to the critical theory, the issues of power and justice with respect to minorities are applicable in the imbalances experienced in policy developments on the basis of the prevailing reimbursement insurance system. In that respect, the knowledge that best reveals the context of the phenomenon is called or based on the critical theory. As with positivism its ontology is a critical realist where truth is still expected to be really there, but hidden by more superficial or transient truths in the reimbursement system. In such a sense the researcher considers different perspectives and meanings that are not immediately obvious. Its epistemology is simply subjectivist in that critical theory values what people know from experience as in this financial analysis that has contributed to the development of the new banking institutions like BRICS that were mentioned earlier. Its methodology is dialogically negotiable where people of different cultures and skills debate the rights and wrongs of different versions of the truth to remove false consciousness and arrive at a better version of the financial or general truth as on universal health insurance. This approach uses research methods, such as case studies that focus on a contemporary phenomenon within some real-life contexts. Validity requires harmonic agreement between different perceptions that pinpoints the so-called real truth. The origins of critical theory are attributed to the German philosopher, Jurgen Habermas, who maintained that our understandings of the world are distorted because we are blinded too much on the basis of what is relevant. Contemporary application of critical theory is "concerned in particular with issues of power and justice and the ways that the economy, matters of race, class and gender, ideologies, discourses, education, religion and other social institutions, and cultural dynamics interact to construct a social system.

The next base is the immigration theory which hints a lot on the reimbursement analytical impact on the bases of healthcare when it talks about the importance of immigrants in research and development as well as other desirable areas. Yet immigrants and minorities are the first victims of reimbursement meltdown processes.

According to social disorganization theory, instability makes it difficult for residents to establish strong social ties, which undermines informal social control. The social disorganization theory identifies neighborhood disadvantage on analytical insurance functional disparities as one of the strongest predictors of community violence and policy reform development. Yet the evidence suggests that the link between disadvantage and violence may be less pernicious for Latinos than for Africans. Recently, it found that neighborhood disadvantage is a stronger predictor of African than Latino homicide victimization. Such a disparity can be a victim of downsizing within the financial mergers under the previous descriptive terms and processes.

Organization theory is a tool that can be applied to analyze and understand the impacts that lead to inter-racial conflicts as we see them today in the development of universal health insurance or more precisely universal healthcare. It can be utilized for an examination of the associations between physician reimbursement incentives and such diseases as disorder processes and explore potential confounding strategies with the physician organizational models. In that order, the transaction cost theory could be used to explain, in a unifying fashion, the myriad changes being undertaken by different groups of constituencies in health care. The agency theory could them be applied into the aligning of economic incentives needed to ensure Integrated Delivery System success. By using tools such as Organization theory, a clearer understanding of organizational reimbursement changes is possible. Others in low quotation include the critical theory, immigration theory, disorganization theory and the policy governance approach all of which could substantially matter in terms of the development of the Universal health insurance for all Americans.

According to the current analysis it is quite reasonable to evaluate the application of the reimbursement impacts of healthcare changes due to health literacy and cultural competency among minorities and immigrants in America. The purpose is to provide an in-depth analysis of the chosen issue. The analysis is supported by the underlying reimbursement theories, approaches, and methods, as well as relevant examples taken from the literature, and professional experience in the health care environment. Practical applications such as ethical leadership are quite significant.

A major cultural and health literacy impact on healthcare reimbursement is compliance and affordability. One application method for analyzing the impacts as described above is to evaluate how costs and prices change following an adoption of a healthcare compliance skill as well as the incorporation of culturally diversified principles so as to compare the results of such changes with those lacking similar characteristics. In a respective study, the effects of cuts in Medicare reimbursements on hospital mortality were analyzed. To expedite that study, an analysis was undertaken to determine if patients treated at hospitals under different levels of financial strain from the Balanced Budget Act of 1997 had differential changes in a 30-day mortality period, and whether vulnerable diverse patient populations such as the uninsured minorities and immigrants were disproportionately affected during that process. According to the findings, it was demonstrated that there is a possibility of some differences among the unadjusted mortality rates to be encountered. Operating margins decreased significantly over the time period for all hospitals that participated in that study report.

Within the above impacts, health literacy and cultural competency has had specific implications in healthcare reimbursement especially when health insurance is a factor. Thus, for the past few years it has been suspected that the burden that undocumented immigrants place on the U.S. health care system is a flashpoint in health care and immigration reform debates. An examination of health care spending during 1999-2006 for adult naturalized citizens and immigrant non-citizens which included some undocumented immigrants found that the cost of providing health care to immigrants is lower than that of providing care to U.S. natives and those immigrants are not contributing disproportionately to high health care costs in public programs such as Medicaid. However, non-citizen immigrants were found to be more likely than U.S. natives to have a health care visit classified as uncompensated care.

On the given perspective criteria, studies have indicated that medication adherence is one of the factors related to reimbursement benefits and other consequences. In that respect, reports examined persistently low-cost Medicare beneficiaries and determined the extent to which health behavior, preventive services, race, and socioeconomic status are related to low spending. The objective of the project was to identify which disease states and beneficiary segments show the greatest promise for improved compliance and persistency in use of preventive therapies. In the process, Stuart and colleagues' analyses explored the role of health behaviors in combination with medication adherence to control costs. They concluded that higher medication adherence among diabetic Medicare beneficiaries resulted in lower medical spending. At the margin, Medicare savings exceed the cost of the drugs.

In reference to the healthcare reimbursements disparities related to such disorders as diabetes, the issue of health literacy and cultural competency effects indicate preference in terms of susceptibility among the minorities and to a good incidence in percentage of the second to third generation immigrants in the United States and other developed countries. Related studies have been conducted with the objective of examining the various associations between physician reimbursement incentives and processes and hence explore the potential confounding with the physician organizational models. According to a particular examination, it was observed that without controlling for physician organizational model, care processes were better when physician compensation was based primarily on direct salary rather than the Fee-For-Service reimbursement and when quality or satisfaction scores influenced physician compensation then three were better, with relative risks from 1.17 to 1.26 under the same categories of analysis.

Inter-racial or basically an inter-cultural health care provider who lacks cultural competency may be putting patients at risk for delays in treatment, inappropriate diagnoses, noncompliance with health care regimens, and even death. In order to justify the underlying analysis the evaluation of the standards of the financial, qualitative, and ethical balances is quite pertinent in any healthcare operational environment. Consequently, a study of the impact of health literacy and cultural competency was explored to accomplish such a goal. The project was achieved by a descriptive search criterion which was performed for an ongoing four-year randomized clinical trial. That was a study which would test the efficacy of separate and combined telephone-delivered, diabetes knowledge/information and motivation or behavioral skills training interventions in high risk African Americans with poorly controlled Type-2-Diabetes-Mellitus. The results from that study could provide important insight into how best to deliver diabetes education and skills training in ethnic minorities and whether combined knowledge, information and motivation or behavioral skills training are superior to the usual method of delivering diabetes education for African Americans with poorly controlled Type-2-Diabetes-Mellitus.

In another study, it is revealed that a group of physicians in South Los Angeles after the closure of Martin L. King (MLK) Hospital provided important insights into how the roles and practices of primary care physicians change after a local safety-net hospital closes. A majority of the physicians from both underserved and non-underserved practice settings acknowledged an effect in the year after hospital closure. More than half of the physicians that were interviewed reported widespread and noteworthy effects of the hospital's closure on their practices. Although health care reform may extend insurance coverage, it may still leave out certain populations such as the African immigrants, particularly in states with large numbers of them that are undocumented. Safety-net hospitals will thus continue to serve a vital stop-gap role for those who do not meet coverage criteria for Medicaid, Medicare, and other targeted programs without invalidating the development of universal health in that perspective.

The establishment of a universal health insurance is a debate which continues to focus on how all people can be accommodated into a workable policy system regardless of the culture or literacy status. However, the 2016 Presidential candidate, Bernie Sanders thinks it is a birth right thing which should not be debated if well planned with the proposed taxation that is fair to all Americans. In a particular example, it is stated that Taiwan established a system of universal National Health Insurance in 1995. The study assessed changes in amenable mortality before and after implementation of universal health insurance coverage in Taiwan. The introduction of was found to be associated with a significant acceleration in the rate of decline of causes of death considered amenable to health care. In contrast, there was no clear change in the trend of mortality from conditions not considered amenable to health care that could be associated with the introduction of the National Health Insurance. These findings are in general consistent with the reimbursement hypothesis and with studies reviewed by reporters such as Levy and Meltzer which, while noting methodological limitations, found that improved health insurance coverage was associated with improved reimbursement systems in healthcare. Hence, there should be no fear on the Bernie Sanders universal health insurance.

According to the underlying analysis, the debates on reimbursement policy reforms in universal healthcare seem to be the central basis that would determine the future of health in America. While there are new and renewable models that are currently reliable and productive, the accompanying analyses confirm that many are not well understood by all parties involved to generate popular and long term affordable healthcare programs or more precisely universal health care insurance. Thus, research has done a great deal of work and more to do to achieve the final determination of the route towards such an achievement. If that is done, there is no doubt that the current healthcare debates will cease for the betterment of social and medical sciences in healthcare administration and universal health care.

CHAPTER XII

WORLD ORDER BY POLICY DEVELOPMENTS BY INEQUALITY FACTORS

When Donald Trump talks about making America great again, many Americans don't find it easy to digest that idea because he seems not to attach the factor of equality into that equation. The question is whether he intends to make it great for just a few people or simply forming a new particular type of political establishment. World Health Organization can influence the new world order if it insists on equality on everything that dictates fair opportunity and healthcare and stands as the base of inter-racial tensions in America. The launching of various health care proposals in recent years has generated a lot of debates in health reform policy developments than any other time in history. This analysis is based on the principle of proposal formulations on policy reforms as impacted by health literacy and cultural competency for organizational development in America, the land of opportunities and home of immigrants. In terms of the past half of the last century of health reforms, no other study has superseded the financial impacts of policy reform proposal developments as displayed by the cases with the health insurance reforms particularly in the developed countries. Most of those impacts studied have been experienced within the frequently emerging health care conditions within the chronically ill that require critical and immediate attention. While the impacts of many of those studies are felt in daily practices, not much has been done in terms of analyzing the effects of the health literacy and cultural competency implications among the greater diversity of people within the United States and the rest of the world. The impacts within the minorities and immigrants tend to serve as the favorite example for comparative purposes and other analyses. Consequently, an evaluation of such impacts of proposal formulations would be the prime objective of this chapter and analysis in both theory and the practical perspectives.

For the past few years the financial and economic impacts of most governments on healthcare has continued to escalate while some like the United States keep debating on the feasibility of the Affordable Care Act bill of 2010 in various proportions. While there are many causes to such consequences, there's no doubt that pharmaceutical economics under the wave of cultural incompetency and health literacy represents one of the major obstacles to the availability of new medicines or their affordability and hence the healthcare dilemma. That is motivated by many factors including health literacy and cultural competency where various interventions as in children's healthcare prevention and welfare can be applied for the possibility of a better change in health insurance costs for the future improvement of universal healthcare. An example of such an interventional analysis was a recent study of the effect of a pharmacy-based health literacy intervention and patient characteristics on medication refill adherence in an urban health system. The question as to how such impacts can be evaluated and analyzed to realize the desired effects is a subject that has attracted a lot of interest to many professionals around the world including the United States 2016 presidential race.

While conceding that the above statements are politically timely and quite imperative, it is relevant to point out that one of the hardest tasks to deal with in health care administration is the invention or generational development of a policy reform that can address a blanket community problem whether acute or chronic in nature and pass it into an implementable law respectively. Various modern communities have experienced different types of health care problems including the pre-existing conditions as demonstrated in many adults, but children's welfare is usually given priority over most other needs. In that respect, a children's health policy that can address clinical or community prevention under the given proposal is highly considerable in the future of health care development in the required advocacy for universal health insurance. Such a policy has been addressed in recent developments and described as follows:

- The Patient Protection and Affordable Care Act of 2010 affect children's basic coverage in a number of ways. Beginning in 2014, it makes Medicaid coverage mandatory for children ages 6-19 in families between 100 percent and 133 percent of the federal poverty level.
- The reform law maintains the Children's Health Insurance Program through 2019. In 2015, states will receive a 23 percentage point increase in the given match rate, up to 100 percent of costs. Current match rates range from 65 to 85 percent.
- Effective in September 2010, private insurers must provide coverage for children with pre-existing conditions. This means both providing coverage for preexisting conditions for currently insured children and not excluding children with preexisting conditions from future coverage.

On the basis of what we have learned in the past few years and before the address of the described policy above, the following facts were analyzed and found to be important for the expected debates that could come up and shape up the future of cultural competency and health literacy of the children's welfare and in the order listed:

- There were approximately 7.3 million children in this country uninsured for all of 2008, according to the Census Bureau equal to 9.9 percent of the nation's children.
- Uninsured rates for children vary dramatically by state, from a low of 3.4 percent in Massachusetts to a high of 19.1 percent in Nevada in 2008.
- Hispanic children are almost three times as likely to be uninsured as non-Hispanic white children – 17.2 percent vs. 6.7 percent in 2008. Black children (10.7 percent) and Asian children (10.9 percent) were also more likely to be uninsured than whites, but significantly less so than Hispanic children.
- More than half of children (58.9 percent) had health insurance coverage through their parent's employer in 2008. Some 33.2 percent had public coverage and 5.1 percent had individually purchased private insurance.

- Almost two out of every three uninsured children in 2007 were eligible for Medicaid or the Children's Health Insurance Program.
- The Patient Protection and Affordable Care Act of 2010 affect children's coverage in a number of ways. Beginning in 2014, it makes Medicaid coverage mandatory for children ages 6-19 in families between 100 percent and 133 percent of the federal poverty level.
- The reform law maintains the Children's Health Insurance Program through 2019. In 2015, states will receive a 23 percentage point increase in the Children's Health Insurance Program match rate, up to 100 percent of costs. Current match rates range from 65 to 85 percent.

A healthcare policy reform proposal which can address and focus on a conceptual framework that can relate to inter-racial culture, health literacy, and health insurance is currently acute and the matter is gaining a lot of interest and attention by several politicians, healthcare professionals and other researchers around the world. That is motivated by the financial instability that is experienced all around the world even though there are still many other underlying causes that are complex in various perspectives. However, on the basis of the growing immigration movements and diversity in healthcare and other areas in general, a composite bill that can address cultural competency, health literacy and education may be a question of policy reform initiative in an establishment that could be worth considering for advocacy in order to balance the health insurance issues and implicative answers in the underlying economics. That is quite in consistent with many reports where in various perspectives, several public health and health promotion researchers are calling for better training and a stronger research culture in health policy in organizational development for inter-racial healing.

Part of the answer to the above proposal in question resides on the exploration of the underlying theories of transformation towards innovative leadership needs as well as the current dilemma in its diversified structural context. To address such needs, key principles of complex adaptive systems theory could be prospectively applied to healthcare planning and research so that new transformations can be adopted to streamline health literacy and cultural health beliefs. Consequently, the aim of the underlying policy proposal is to provide a prospective approach on leadership transformations in healthcare organizations through the utilization of the complex adaptive systems principles as well as the transformation theories. By so doing an innovative new type of policy reform inheritance might be generated and hence illustrate its relevance to policy reform professionals focusing on the effective transformations for the future healthcare service delivery. An incorporation of policy integrity is fitted into the theory in description to study its applicability in health care reform advocacy for universal healthcare. Respectively, the field of complex adaptive systems theory that is also known as "complexity" theory, seeks to understand how order emerges in complex, non-linear systems such as social systems and neural networks just as what it would take in the formulation and implementation of a health care reform policy under the current consideration on inter-racial tensions. Complexity scientists suggest that living systems tend to migrate to a state of dynamic stability which they call the "edge of chaos. The balance point often called the edge of chaos is where the components of a system never quite lock into place, and yet never quite dissolve into turbulence either. Along the same line the theory of social cognition models addresses the individual level which focuses on the individual's readiness to change and the person understands of the threat of a health problem and the recommended behaviors to deal with a challenge such as policy debates and advocacy as emphasized by the 2016 United States Presidential candidate Bernie Sanders.

While it is true that any type of change as in healthcare policy reforms is difficult and complex, the theory of social cognition models addresses the individual level which focuses on the individual's readiness to formulate or change and the person's understanding of the threat of a health problem as well as the recommended behaviors to deal with the problem. While social marketing that is popular on policy advocacy uses the communication theory that encompasses (behavioral, persuasion, and exposure models) to target changes in health risk behavior, social cognitive theory is based on response consequences of individual behavior, observational learning, and behavioral modeling and is widely used. Persuasion models indicate that people must engage in message "elaboration" which means developing favorable thoughts about a message's arguments especially on the inter-racial healing dilemma for long term persuasion to occur. Exposure models do study how the intensity and length of exposure to a message affects behavior as in the spirit or inspiration of policy advocacy as in the 2016 Bernie Sanders communication strategies for the presidential race in America. Respectively, some professionals describe social cognition theories as those that examine the connection between personal and environmental factors on human behavior. They add that these theories focus on individuals as they relate to influence in groups and organizations as it may be expected in the formulation of a new policy proposal and advocacy as in the current undertaking. They emphasize that social cognition theories of health promotion are the most frequently used theories of health behavior. These models tend not to consider the social world or material or social factors. The cons are that it is difficult to measure the impact of these models over time, keep them going, and reduce all barriers to participation. The theory addresses self-empowerment and focuses on empowerment of groups and individuals through participatory learning in order to control one's social and internal environments. There is a focus on examination of social structure and resources. This theory does not take into consideration inequalities in power distribution which influences healthcare insurance quite frequently. It assumes that power can be mobilized by individuals. The advantages of this type of model are that it can enable sustainable change and create greater community capacity when used with other methods. Some negatives are due to the fact that it may be dominated by professionals and not favored by government funders who prefer an individual approach. The theory that relates to community development or collective action seeks to address the socio-economic and environmental factors that cause ill health. Communities that have shared interests and assets come together to collectively address these issues rather than changing individual behavior. The self-empowerment approach may be a first step in the community development approach or self-empowerment may be a consequence of the community development approach. This approach is influenced by the concept of critical consciousness. Participatory action research is seen as a vehicle for community development and quite consistent with the underlying question in the proposed health care idea of universal health insurance.

On the basis of the above analytical facts, it is quite conceivable to note that for any related health policy and especially in the given case, it is not only a big task to tackle or confront, but a long process to debate and reach a plausible agreement. Even after enacting initiatives, the implementation process could still stand a chance of experiencing stiff and conflicting debates on the basis of competition that may call for several amendment propositions towards repealing.

In view of the above statement, it was found reasonable to seek some health care policy advocacy that is related to the above proposal for the human welfare with intensified dialogues in health care reforms. In contrast, children's advocates often cite the phrase "children are not little adults" in order to make the case that children have special health care needs related to their development that are unique and special in the given proposal. That is in consistent with other studies in literature which are expected to shape the underlying advocacy. In common experience, health policymakers have long recognized and highlighted the unique needs of children as the backbone of human welfare and of which cultural competency and health literacy policy should be the first hand in that perspective. In the given perspective, the Children's Health Insurance Program was enacted to help children who don't qualify for Medicaid but whose families can't easily afford private coverage. In Medicaid, broad pediatric coverage and benefits are provided through what is known as early and periodic screening, diagnosis, and treatment. This benefit, specific to children, was added to Medicaid in 1967 in response to high levels of preventable physical, dental, and mental health conditions among low-income children at that time, from pre-school children enrolled in the Head Start program to young working populations.

Nonetheless, it is quite conceivable that the development of any policy reform proposal as indicated above is a challenge that takes time to create and debate before a justified consensus can be attained. According to the above given health reform statement in proposal, it is quite conceivable that it can serve as a workable devise for the current dilemma on the issues of universal health insurance. If that is well taken and enacted, it might give a breakthrough in the future development of universal health in administration.

According to the modern practical operations, concepts and strategies of healthcare organization evaluation and analysis play a big role on policy formulation and development. That includes the influence of cultural competency and educational health literacy features on the development and policy advocacy of a healthcare reform proposal that can address pure vision on a conceptual framework of universal health insurance. Such an operation can also provide a practical question or theoretical approach to analyze, critique, or apply the justification methods; or provide background information such as the current related issues or concerns that health care administrations face around the world. Part of the answer to such a developmental question resides on the feasible methods that can be utilized for analyzing the relationship between cultural diversity and health literacy on health insurance developments. That could in turn enhance the overall understanding of the processes as to how quality improvements have changed qualitatively and quantitatively over time. It is important to evaluate how such changes vary by characteristics of individuals, institutions and markets for better quality improvements and hence for the policy reform proposal developments and advocacy in the given context. In that respect, various world report studies indicate several of such evaluations for the current development which are useful in this development.

A major evaluation step towards the development of the proposal in question is revealed in the reports where studies support the integration of literacy, culture, and language to attain improved health care quality for diverse populations. Thus, according to an evaluation attempt to try to understand the interrelationship of literacy, culture, and language as well as the importance of addressing their intersection in health care policy developments and advocacy is strongly supported and well cited in various revelations. Respectively, the health literacy, cultural competence, and linguistic competence strategies to quality improvement were analyzed to determine the effects of a composite development for a bold boost in universal healthcare advocacy. According to their findings, strategies to improve health literacy for low-literate individuals are distinct from strategies for culturally diverse people and individuals with limited English proficiency. The lack of integration is indicated to result in health care that is unresponsive to some vulnerable groups' needs. Thus, the study presented a vision for integrated care as part of the validation that may be needed for policy advocacy in universal health care development in the given proposal.

On a mission to determine the value of diversity responses during health care emergencies a report supported a study that was performed to assess the cultural diversity preparedness in such circumstances as the current inter-racial conflicts. Racism costs the United States a good amount of trillions of dollars. Depending on the value which could be translated into the benefit-cost analysis, an evidence-based structural feature would be extracted that could become useful in the advocacy of the underlying proposal on the inter-racial conflicts. In a related report, a description was illustrated to identify and determine the status of cultural diversity preparedness for emergency health care situations. It was noted out that during an emergency situation, material and physical resources are stretched thin and, often, the needs of those who at the greatest need for help, namely the vulnerable populations, are actually left unmet. It states that vulnerable populations can be defined broadly to include those who are not able to access and use the standard resources offered in disaster preparedness and planning, response, and recovery. Hence, it is considered that age, class, race, poverty, language, and a host of other social, cultural, economic, and psychological factors may be relevant in terms of policy reform advocacy and development depending on the nature of the emergency in that perspective.

An interesting policy advocacy study whose objective was aimed at determining how well or health literate the Spanish-speaking Latino parents were with Limited English Proficiency, written instructions accompanying a routinely prescribed medication was performed. Inter-racial illiteracy is the worst form of any ignorance in the current world and for which a lot to do with health or mental health literacy is based. Health literacy measures the degree to which individuals understand health information. It has not been studied among parents with Limited English proficiency. On that project, a cross-sectional survey of parents of young children was conducted. On the basis of the findings obtained, it was concluded that only a few parents with Limited English proficiency were able to understand routinely dispensed written medication instructions. In that respect, pediatricians should not assume that Spanish-speaking Latino parents who are comfortable speaking English will understand a prescription label written in English, or that Latino parents who speak Spanish will understand drug information written in Spanish. Thus, the study seems to support the advocacy of the underlying proposal in the indicated composite terms with respect to such situations.

Along the same line on the above issue on the defects of emergency preparedness among diverse groups of people, a study was conducted whose objective was to make an evaluation review of the effective implementations of diverse public health preparedness programs and policies that past experience confirms to be a requirement of compliance from all racial and ethnic populations in diversity. The project focused on the current resources and limitations so as to suggest future policy advocacy directions for integrating diverse communities into related strategies in policy reform developments as indicated. It documented research and interventions, including promising models and practices that address preparedness for minorities. However, findings revealed a general lack of focus on diversity and suggested that future preparedness efforts need to fully integrate factors related to race, culture, and language into risk communication, public health training, measurement, coordination, and policy at all levels for better inter-racial healing of hope in development.

Other related reports as in the above evaluation have based their policy advocacy assessments on traditional factors for any possible formulations. Consequently, in the related report it is stated that most cultural competence programs are based on traditional models of cross-cultural education that were motivated primarily by the desire to alleviate barriers to effective health care for immigrants, refugees, and others on the socio-cultural margin. The main driver of renewed interest in cultural competence in the health professions has been the call to eliminate racial and ethnic disparities in the quality of health care. This mismatch between the motivation behind the design of cross-cultural education programs and the motivation behind their current application creates significant problems. First, in trying to define cultural boundaries or norms, programs may inadvertently reinforce racial and ethnic biases and stereotypes while doing little to clarify the actual complex sociocultural contexts in which patients live. Second, in attempting to address racial and ethnic disparities through cultural competence training, educators too often conflate these distinct concepts. To make this argument, the authors first discussed the relevance of culture to health and health care generally, and to disparities in particular. They then examined the concept of culture, paying particular attention to the structure as to how it has been used and misused in cultural competence training. Finally, they discussed the implications of these ideas for health professions education and the consistent support for the underlying policy reform proposal in advocacy which was very positive for the development of universal healthcare.

One of the major calls for the underlying proposal is based on crisis communication during natural disasters that extend to health care emergency situations with respect to the ethnic groups in various communities as revealed in a few reports. In those reports the project compared differences in crisis preparation, information-seeking patterns, and media use on the basis of race in the aftermath of Hurricane Katrina. Surveys were collected from 935 Katrina evacuees relocated in different areas of the United States. The results obtained indicated differences in crisis preparation and information seeking on the basis of race. Results also demonstrated a continued need to create messages encouraging crisis preparation, especially among at-risk sub-populations. On the basis of that project, the advocacy of the current project proposal cannot be overemphasized on the issues related to communication disparities as in health care which strongly approves the implementation case of universal health and the healing of inter-racial tensions in the United States of America.

Further reports on the question of emergency preparedness mentioned above for the underlying proposal advocacy in policy reform formulation for universal health development were performed by cultural scientists. Respectively, the researchers in question described cultural competency in terms of the level of public emergency knowledge and perceptions of risks among Latin American immigrants, and their preferred and actual sources of emergency preparedness information including warning signals. In that project, a research involving five Latino community member focus groups, and one focus group of community health workers, was conducted in a suburban county of Washington D.C. Participants came from thirteen Latin American countries, and 64.7% immigrated during the previous five years. Participants had difficulty in defining emergency health care and reported a wide range of perceived personal emergency risks that included: immigration problems; crime, personal insecurity, gangs; home or traffic accidents; home fires; environmental problems; and snipers. As in previous studies, few participants had received information on emergency preparedness, and most did not have an emergency plan. It was concluded that findings regarding key messages and motivating factors can be used to develop clear, prioritized messages for communication regarding emergencies and emergency preparedness for Latin American immigrant communities in the U.S. That can become a factor in the call for universal health development

In another project, an examination of the historical evolution of both cultural competence and patient centeredness was explored to determine its possible applications in proposal formulation and advocacy in the current undertaking. In doing so, it was demonstrated that early conceptual models of cultural competence and patient centeredness focused on how healthcare providers and patients might interact at the interpersonal level and that later conceptual models can be expanded to consider how patients might be treated by the healthcare system as a whole with respect to the proposed universal health concept. It was then compared to conceptual models for both cultural competence and patient centeredness at both the interpersonal and healthcare system levels to demonstrate similarities and differences. The project concluded that, although the concepts have had different histories and foci, many of the core features of cultural competence and patient centeredness are the same. Each approach holds promise for improving the quality of healthcare for individual patients, communities and populations and hence its applicability in policy formulation.

On the issue of the validity of a composite integration of the proposed formulation policy in advocacy, a study was conducted which described the culture and health literacy integration approach in terms of how public health preparedness is transforming public health agencies. In that study, it was noted that the key signs of change include new partnerships, changes in the workforce, new technologies, and evolving organizational structures in diversity. It was determined that each of those elements has had some positive impact on public health whenever such an integrative program was initiated. However, integration of preparedness with other public health functions remains challenging. The preparedness mission has also raised challenges in the areas of leadership, governance, quality, and accountability as far as the policy formulation in development is concerned.

When the question arises as to whether states can effectively address the above issue without waiting for solutions from the national government, a different type of strategy becomes inevitable that pinpoints on the defects of racial health care disparities. The purpose of such a movement in the related study was to propose ways of reframing the disparities issue that might give state policy makers more leverage and might strengthen political will to address the issue. It is suggested that there exists a moral frame based on a concept of distributive justice in which medical care must be distributed according to need. It is explained that the rationales for such a frame and consideration of its strategic advantages and disadvantages are instrumental in health policy reform advocacy in development. Some policies based on this framing are within the power of state legislatures.

Another study related to interracial challenges on the issue of disparities was performed to determine the mitigating effects of disasters for the medically underserved populations. The study was conducted with an initiative aimed at enhancing the provision of health care by installing Electronic Health Records and Tele-psychiatry systems throughout the Gulf Coast. Through the program Centers, the provisional plans to perform screening and surveillance projects within the communities and develop research projects focused on eliminating health disparities affecting underserved populations in the region. Another goal is to establish partnerships with program Centers, Community Health Centers, and other essential primary care practices in hurricane-ravaged communities. Through these partnerships, the overarching goal is to create a balanced health care system model that academic institutions can integrate into preventive care for emergency planning and research.

Further evidence that supports the formulation development of the proposed policy reform for advocacy is based on a particular study whose objective was to develop cultural competence in disaster mental programs among various ethnic groups. In that study the nature of culture and disaster was explored. The study was accomplished by defining culturally related terms, discussing diversity within racial and ethnic minority groups, and describing cultural competence. The study discussed cultural competence in the context of disaster mental health services. Initially, it presented the Cultural Competence Continuum and a list of questions to address in a disaster mental health plan. The study also set forth nine guiding principles for culturally competent disaster mental health services and related recommendations for developing these services through a formulated reform policy as indicated in the underlying composite proposal. It also presented the key concepts of disaster mental health; important considerations when working with people of other cultures; staff attributes, knowledge, and skills essential to the development of cultural competence; and a cultural competence self-assessment for disaster crisis counseling programs. In addition, the study provided suggestions for working with refugees and guidelines for using interpreters.

The impact of the health care policy analysis is the most instrumental tool for any new policy reform development and advocacy. While the economic strength still holds the major force in such a perspective, the effect of politics and policies on health and on social inequalities in health has only been slightly studied for proposals such as the underlying project. According to literature, some studies have previously proposed a multidimensional conceptual framework that has been used to understand the relationship between politics and health outcomes. The welfare state and labor market policies have had an effect on income and social inequalities in the population.

For a strong policy reform proposal advocacy to take effect as in the underlying project, cultural diversity has to take root with full employment policies and a higher percentage of women in the labor force as indicated support in other chapters could confirm. In so doing, there could be less social and income inequalities, better health outcomes and less inequalities in health as exemplified by reduced infant mortalities in various studies. The specific mechanisms of how social democratic countries influence health and health inequalities as in the current policy proposal have been revealed in similar studies. Those mechanisms could be as follows:

(I) Cultural diversity is about public benefits; Public benefits are high and are for everyone as much as universal health care can be defined: Furthermore, those benefits are offered for the whole life of a person. Benefits directed to the whole population enable investments to be directed to everybody, facilitating access to all public goods in education, healthcare, social care, maternity leave, home care and so forth. The benefits of welfare state imply being protected in the face of adverse situations as in unemployment, sickness and so forth, which are related to worse health outcomes.

With respect to healthcare, it is worth mentioning that health services financed through taxes are important to permit healthcare for everyone and coverage of the costs of illness. The absence of health coverage has been related to poor health and less utilization of preventive and curative healthcare services. With such ideas in place, the proposal of cultural competency and health literacy is highly likely to pass.

(II) Low socioeconomic and income inequalities: Although there has been a debate in recent years, there are many studies showing that income inequalities are related to worse health outcomes. Two main explanations have been offered for how income inequalities affect health: First, psychosocial pathways such as perceptions of place in the social hierarchy, social cohesion and interpersonal trust or psychosocial conditions at work (stress, social support, lack of control) can provide an explanation for the health effects of income inequality. Second, neo-material pathways: this explanation is based on the importance of material factors such as income, living conditions, lack of resources and investments, these factors being the pathways to poor health.

(III) Strong labor movements: If labor movements are strong, working conditions will probably be more favorable and better chances of policy advocacy. It has been shown previously that working conditions are related to health outcomes: traditional occupational diseases, illness related to physical and chemical exposures, accidents at work, and also lifestyles and psychosocial factors at work have a role in health and diseases and hence health policy advocacy.

(IV) Full employment policies and a high percentage of women in the labor force are related to health and well-being, especially women's health: Studies that have compared self-perceived health of women, both in paid work and otherwise, show the protective effect of employment. Income provides women with economic independence and increases their power in the household. Moreover, the job environment can offer opportunities to build self-esteem and confidence in one's decision making, social support and experiences that enhance life satisfaction and hence recognize the advocacy sense of the underlying proposal.

As stated above, few studies have analyzed the effect of the outlined influences in advocating for possible proposals in health policy developments. However, with the given facts as outlined, it is quite optimistic for a cultural diversity proposal to pass with health literacy where a highly supportive reform inspiration would be witnessed.

In the past few centuries, social politics around the world have monopolized health care policy reform developments and advocacy with the lobbyists' collaborations even when medical casualties are highly encountered. While such monopoly dialogues have reduced tremendously, the vestigial challenges of such interactions can still be visualized in modern health care as indicated in the recent debates in the Affordable Care Act of 2010 in the United States of America health care reform proceedings. However, as technology advanced with new tools of instrumentation in science and mathematics, theories were formulated that could analyze various data for better interpretations and usefulness for quality improvement and development despite the prevailing social political contexts. Thus, in the 1920s, Walter A Shewhart, a physicist, was charged with improving the quality of telephones in Bell Laboratories, USA. According to his work, he won the accolade of the "father of modern quality control". Consequently, Shewhart developed a theory of variation which forms the basis of Statistical Process Control for quality improvement evaluation and analysis. His theory is easily illustrated as there is evidence that SPC is being increasingly applied in health care. For instance, very good examples include a keyword literature search by using the term "statistical process control" of the Medline database found zero hits for 1951–88, two for 1989–91, 26 for 1992–5, and 71 for 1996–2004. In addition, a number of recent publications have reported the use of SPC in high profile cases such as the Bristol Inquiry and that of Shipman. This can form part of the contributive procedures in the process of policy reform and formulation developments in the advocacy of inter-racial healing tensions in America and around the world.

Nevertheless, policy development initiatives require cumulative data for better analysis and interpretation, but for progressive measurements to occur in healthcare quality improvements and other sectors, straight forward statistical analysis is quite imperative. Thus, to be more successful at continuous improvement in health care professionals must recognize that it embodies a science encompassing a range of disciplines from SPC to human psychology in order to face the political challenges in the given environment. However, due to the fact that the majority of many healthcare leaders and professionals have not been exposed to this science, an initiative program must be developed to address that deficiency through widespread education and training for the betterment of medical practice and administration as in the current proposal.

According to the proposed policy reform in advocacy, it is quite conceivable that the past world immigration movements and cultural diversity experiences would justify the necessary enactment of the cultural competency and health literacy composite policy bill in the given proposal for the foreseeable future in inter-racial healing and health care development. To say that there are ethical universals or in other words that there are norms and values having cross cultural validity is to make an understatement in such an underlying proposal that requires diverse advocacy before passing. It would be more accurate to say that all ethical norms or rules are cultural universals, because a rule or norm cannot properly be described as "ethical" unless it is understood as having cross cultural validity, in the sense of being perceived as applying in all similar circumstances, irrespective of place and time. In a more precise terminology, it would be to say that accepting the possibility of a justifiable exception to the applicability of a moral rule in no way implies moral relativity, let alone the absurd idea of "geographical morality" or ethics which change at territorial boundaries and which is as consistent with a few studies as positive researchers can reveal.

In view of the underlying proposal, it would be accurate to focus on the potential strength of the results that are likely to be validly ethical from a local and international perspective on inter-racial healing. International ethical guidelines need to be formulated, not only in general as opposed to particularistic terms, but in such general terms as would make sense and meaning to variously and differently situated and circumstanced human communities, groups, and assemblages. In that respect, it is not a task that is likely to be adequately accomplished by one conceptually or ideologically homogenous group of human beings, no matter how altruistically minded or how well intentioned and well equipped it may be, for and on behalf of the heterogeneous all. What a good international ethical guideline requires in its formulation and expression is a balancing of different but not necessarily conflicting points of view and perspectives as demonstrated in this proposal.

On the basis of the above evaluation under the proposed health care proposal for the formulation of inter-racial policy reform and the related advocacy for enactment, it is quite conceivable that the current analysis and the research studies are strongly in support of such a development. Research findings are increasingly being recognized as an important input in the formulation or formation of the inter-racial healing care policy. There is concern that research findings are not being utilized by health policy-makers to the extent that they could be useful to support such an enactment. In recent years and even currently, the factors influencing the utilization of various types of research by health policy-makers are beginning to emerge in the literature studies. However, there is still little known about these factors in many countries including the developed and developing ones. The objective of this policy proposal in the project study was to explore those factors by examining the policy-making process for a health care policy common in both developed as well as the developing countries for the future of health care administration and development.

Like most publications in this field, this and related reports would continue to use qualitative methods with the majority of the data coming from in-depth interviews on diverse participants in any given arena. It is expected that for such an accomplishment to occur and successfully, qualitative methods are chosen as they are ideal for questions that require an answer about understanding the participants' views. In using such methods, concerns about the validity of the results can arise, but would become creditable in the long run. It is important to recognize that this evaluation project did not evaluate policy-makers' actual behavior, nor did it measure objective factors that influence their utilization of research findings. Instead, the gathered findings representing policy-makers' perceptions of those factors that is much the same way politicians like Bernie Sanders could do on his 2016 presidential bid.

Within the above collective reports and the results evaluated, it is indicated that by using three or more separate data methods, the validity of the relative findings tend to be improved and accepted by various politicians and other professionals as in the 2016 presidential contenders. In addition to supplementing the information from the in-depth interviews, the classical analytical discussion provides an opportunity to give feedback to the respective peers or participants and hence allowing for respondent validation. The selection and number of reviewer members is important for effective evaluations, but it may be a limitation in this proposal survey project. The results of the given report document in analysis may help to validate the above statements regarding sources and records that would be utilized. This analysis is limited however because it is not known how much consideration, if any, such documents would take in effect to produce an implementable reform policy. However, the reliability of the results would be improved through the use of independent investigators in several stages of the policy proposal data analysis. There are limitations in the extent to which the study can generalize the findings of this composite policy proposal to other policy-makers and other countries, due to the exploratory nature of the project and the fact that it would examine only two aspects of policy-making equation in one particular setting. However, on the basis of the compiled facts in the given chapter, it is strongly presumable that it could be well advocated and passed as a new health care bill for the betterment of health care organizational development in the new world order policy reforms that can implement the cure of inter-racial healing. It is my guess that if Republican presidential candidate and front-runner reads this book then he will gather more than enough information on how to make America great again as he claims without telling us how exactly he hopes to do that other than just beating the democrats like Hillary Clinton or Bernie Sanders in the 2016 general elections. At the same time or once that is done, then Bernie Sanders would have the opportunity to celebrate on the implementation of Universal Health Care bill that he proposes through fair taxation and debt-free education for all Americans for the betterment of national prosperity like other great countries do for the current and the future generations.